Insurgent Communities

Insurgent Communities

How Protests Create a Filipino Diaspora

SHARON M. QUINSAAT

The University of Chicago Press
Chicago and London

The University of Chicago Press, Chicago 60637
The University of Chicago Press, Ltd., London
© 2024 by The University of Chicago
All rights reserved. No part of this book may be used or reproduced in any manner whatsoever without written permission, except in the case of brief quotations in critical articles and reviews. For more information, contact the University of Chicago Press, 1427 E. 60th St., Chicago, IL 60637.
Published 2024
Printed and bound by CPI Group (UK) Ltd, Croydon, CR0 4YY

33 32 31 30 29 28 27 26 25 24   1 2 3 4 5

ISBN-13: 978-0-226-83166-4 (cloth)
ISBN-13: 978-0-226-83168-8 (paper)
ISBN-13: 978-0-226-83167-1 (e-book)
DOI: https://doi.org/10.7208/chicago/9780226831671.001.0001

Funding for the publication of this book was provided by an award from the Association for Asian Studies First Book Subvention Program.

Library of Congress Cataloging-in-Publication Data

Names: Quinsaat, Sharon M., author.
Title: Insurgent communities : how protests create a Filipino diaspora / Sharon M. Quinsaat.
Description: Chicago : The University of Chicago Press, 2024. | Includes bibliographical references and index.
Identifiers: LCCN 2023027048 | ISBN 9780226831664 (cloth) | ISBN 9780226831688 (paperback) | ISBN 9780226831671 (ebook)
Subjects: LCSH: Filipino diaspora—Political aspects. | Social movements—Philippines. | Filipinos—Political activity—Foreign countries. | Filipinos—Political activity—United States. | Filipinos—Political activity—Netherlands. | Transnationalism—Political aspects. | National characteristics, Philippine. | Philippines—Emigration and immigration—Political aspects. | Philippines—Politics and government—1986–
Classification: LCC DS665 .Q85 2024 | DDC 305.899/21—dc23/eng/20230614
LC record available at https://lccn.loc.gov/2023027048

♾ This paper meets the requirements of ANSI/NISO Z39.48-1992 (Permanence of Paper).

For my mother

Contents

List of Abbreviations ix
Preface xi

Introduction 1

1 Movement(s) and Identities: Toward a Theory of
Diaspora Construction through Contention 13

2 Roots and Routes: Global Migration of Filipinos 27

3 Patriots and Revolutionaries: Anti-Dictatorship Movement
and Loyalty to the Homeland 50

4 Workers and Minorities: Mobilizations for Migrants'
Rights and Ethnic/National Solidarity 83

5 Storytellers and Interlocutors: Collective Memory
Activism and Shared History 117

Conclusion 152

Acknowledgments 161
Appendix: Methodology 167
Notes 173
References 195
Index 217

Abbreviations

ALAB	Alay sa Bayan (Gift to the People)
AMLC	Anti–Martial Law Coalition
BAYAN	Bagong Alyansang Makabayan (New Patriotic Alliance)
CAMD	Coalition against the Marcos Dictatorship
CFMW	Commission on Filipino Migrant Workers
CFO	Commission on Filipinos Overseas
CID	Chinatown–International District
CPP	Communist Party of the Philippines
CWFLU	Cannery Workers' and Farm Laborers' Union
DDS	Diehard Duterte Supporters
EDSA	Epifanio delos Santos Avenue
EO	Executive Order
EVP	Exchange Visitor Program
FACLA	Filipino American Community of Los Angeles
FACT	Filipinos against Corruption and Tyranny
FFP	Friends of the Filipino People
FGN	Filippijnengroep Nederland (Philippine Group Netherlands)
FLAME	Filipinos in the Netherlands against the Marcoses and Their Return to Power
IAFP	International Association of Filipino Patriots
ILWU	International Longshoremen's and Warehousemen's Union
IMF	International Monetary Fund
JFAV	Justice for Filipino American Veterans
KDP	Katipunan ng Demokratikong Pilipino (Union of Democratic Filipinos)
KM	Kabataang Makabayan (Nationalist Youth)
MFP	Movement for a Free Philippines
MNLF	Moro National Liberation Front
NCRCLP	National Committee for the Restoration of Civil Liberties in the Philippines
NDF	National Democratic Front
NGO	Nongovernmental organization
NPA	New People's Army

NYU	New York University
OFW	Overseas Filipino worker
PACE	Pilipino American Collegiate Endeavor
POEA	Philippine Overseas Employment Agency
PSAP	Philippine Seafarers' Assistance Program
SANA	Salvadoran American National Association
SEIU	Service Employees International Union
SMO	Social movement organization
SNV	Stichting Nederlandse Vrijwilligers (Foundation of Netherlands Volunteers)
TAN	Transnational advocacy network
TWLF	Third World Liberation Front
UN	United Nations
WB	World Bank

Preface

In the midst of writing this book, Ferdinand "Bongbong" Marcos Jr., the son of the former dictator who ruled the Philippines for almost two decades, became the seventeenth president of the country in May 2022. Based on official results from the Commission on Elections, Marcos Jr.—or more popularly referred to as BBM during the elections—won by a landslide, obtaining 58.77 percent of votes, while his main contender, Maria Leonor "Leni" Gerona Robredo, received only 27.94 percent. Among Filipinos overseas, Marcos Jr. clinched a runaway victory, with Australia and the Vatican City as the only places where he lost to Robredo.[1] Many of those who did not support him were nonplussed, demoralized, and felt hopeless about the future of Filipinos. How could this have happened?

The popular take was that massive disinformation through social media orchestrated by Marcos Jr. essentially changed not only the interpretation of what happened during his father's regime but the events and facts themselves.[2] It was not a period of economic and political plunder, poverty, human rights abuse, and social unrest; it was a "golden age" in Philippine history—a time of massive growth and progress, high quality of life, and peace and prosperity that made the country the envy of its neighbors. But some scholars and activists on the Left believe that historical revisionism is only the tip of the iceberg. In their piece published in *New Left Review* just after the Philippine Congress declared Marcos Jr. as the new president, Maria Khristina Alvarez and Herbert Docena argue that two contiguous failures after 1986 led to his victory: one, the liberals were unsuccessful in forcing significant concessions from the oligarchy, and, two, the Philippine Left could not advance a compelling alternative to elite rule.[3] This analysis is echoed by others who see the return to power of the Marcos dynasty and the election of Rodrigo Duterte in

2016 as outcomes of the 1986 People Power Revolution not really delivering its purported promise of stripping power from the ruling class and transferring it to the masses.[4]

Still, why was Marcos Jr. the overwhelming choice among the overseas population, most of them living in liberal democratic societies where socialist parties have had significant influence? I was living in Amsterdam from September 2021 to May 2022, and I was able to observe the dynamics in the migrant community during the height of the campaign period. To some degree, the arguments about disinformation and failures of liberal democracy and the Left do explain Marcos's immense support from Filipinos abroad. But like most structural explanations, these analyses downplay the agency of migrants. How did they make sense of the disinformation they received on Facebook? How did they bridge their experiences in a foreign land to transformations in democracy at home?

Nelia[5] gave me some answers to these questions. I met her through a friend who employed Nelia as a house cleaner, and she opened up to me immediately. Like most Filipinos who provide domestic services, she is undocumented. She went to the Netherlands in early 2000s as an au pair[6] and did not go back to the Philippines when her resident permit expired. Nelia has a child with a Filipino man, Nestor, who also does not have papers. They live in a two-bedroom apartment that they share with another Filipino couple south of Amsterdam. Already in her fifties, Nelia is yearning to return home, complaining that her body is "giving up" from cleaning two houses a week regularly and additional ones by demand. She also cannot see a future in the Netherlands, especially since she and her family have not been able to legalize their status, not even her teenage daughter who was born and raised in the country. With the remittances Nelia sent for twenty years, her siblings in the Philippines were able to finish their schooling. They also helped her and Nestor build a house and start a rice-milling business in preparation for their eventual homecoming. Despite protestations from her daughter who wants to finish high school in the Netherlands, Nelia was adamant about going home. "It's just time," she told me. "We will have more freedom in the Philippines." When I asked what she meant by that, she responded, "Well, first, we will not be illegals in our own country. And also, we can have our own house. My daughter has always wanted to bake, but she cannot do it where we live because we share the house with another family, and we must keep the electricity down. *Ganoon, malaya* [Like that, free]."

Nelia claims that she has no social or political life. When she became undocumented, migrants' rights groups reached out to her, and she attended several of their meetings and activities. But after a while, she lost interest. "I

PREFACE   xiii

appreciate what they do, but after work, I was just too tired to participate in discussions. I could not follow the conversations." In contrast, at church where she spends most of her time outside of work, she felt relaxed, because she did not have to talk about issues that are *"mabibigat sa loob* [emotionally heavy]."

One rainy November day, over a cup of coffee and *oliebollen* (Dutch beignets), Nelia shared with me her thoughts about the Philippine elections. I was surprised. Without prompting, she recounted how many of our *kababayan* (compatriots) in her church have started bickering in person and in social media over who should be the next president—BBM or Leni Robredo. The Leni faction apparently accused the BBM supporters of being duped into believing all the lies that the Marcoses have fabricated. The BBM camp responded, mocking the other party's elitism. Vile attacks were exchanged. "It was very un-Christian," Nelia said. A leader intervened and, as a group, members of her church came up with a resolution: absolutely no discussion of Philippine politics. "We are all Christians and Filipinos here. Our community is so small. We cannot let the election divide us." Thus, within the religious space, the reality of the outside world was suspended, as political differences were subdued in exchange for peace and unity. "But that's okay, I have my family in the Philippines, my close friends here, and Facebook to turn to if I want to talk about why I am voting for BBM," she remarked nonchalantly. It was the first time I learned about her electoral choice.

Nelia follows news on the Philippine elections through Facebook, and unfortunately, many of them were from dubious sources. She showed me YouTube videos of obscure and self-proclaimed political experts and historians analyzing the Marcos dictatorship. The takeaway was the same: it was a period of boom, and his son will continue what the former president started. I asked Nelia her thoughts after we watched two videos together. She replied, "Well, I want to make sure that it's true, so I talk to my brother about it, who I call regularly. '*Ano na nangyayari diyan sa atin?* [What's happening there in our country?]' He is older than me, you know, and he was already an adult during martial law. I was just in high school. And he said, it's really what happened back then. But I also remember that period. *Tahimik, walang krimen. Malinis. Disiplinado mga tao, sumusunod sa batas* [Peaceful, no crimes. Clean. The people are disciplined, they follow the rules]. I want to go home to a Philippines where my daughter will not be raped."

As I talked to Filipinos I encountered at Amsterdam Centraal Station, Albert Cuyp Market, and KFC (which, I was told, many Filipinos frequented); attended events organized by cultural, political, and religious organizations; and followed the Facebook group BBM-Sara Netherlands, I found out the centrality of *disiplina* (discipline) in their narratives, like Nelia's, when talking about the presidency of Marcos. This was not surprising to me. I have heard this from my mother and relatives in Italy who are overseas Filipino workers (OFWs). But since my family is Ilocano, I dismissed their assessment of the authoritarian regime as purely ethnolinguistic attachment to *Apo* Marcos like all the other loyalists. In my interviews and field observations, I discovered a persistent feeling of exasperation and resentment among Filipinos living in the Netherlands that stems from being confronted everyday by what they believe the Philippines can achieve with discipline. Moreover, for Filipinos who work in "unfamiliar, precarious, and often risky conditions in foreign countries with strict criminal justice systems," they attribute their ability to make it against all odds to their self-discipline.[7] A Filipino who works at an international organization in The Hague and as an active organizer in the Robredo campaign observed, "I notice here in the Netherlands, Filipinos follow the pedestrian lane. They park their bikes where they should be, even follow the quiet sign in trains. But when they go home to the Philippines, it's frustrating to see they don't obey the rules. I know because I do that too. I don't follow the traffic signs. Why? Because no one cares. So, I think that we are not the problem. But the culture that does not hold the concept of discipline important. We are encouraged in our country to be *pasaway*."[8] Somehow, order in traffic epitomizes the society that can be attained with proper leadership.[9] And that's when I realized that Filipinos in both the BBM and Leni camps are not as polarized as they appear to be on issues that matter to them such as transportation, inflation, criminality, and corruption.[10]

The story of Nelia does validate the arguments about disinformation and disappointment with liberal democracy that facilitated the election of Marcos Jr. It also renders more visible the local contexts of meaning making—the small-scale domains—where we see the intersection of agency of migrants and structural forces. Through the intimate groups to which Nelia belongs (transnational family, friends, church, and to some extent, BBM-Sara Netherlands on Facebook), she was able to construct her perception of reality in the Philippines that weaves together the (dis)information she acquired, her personal experiences, her imagined future for her daughter, and the discourses in which she seriously engaged. In other words, it is through the groups where she was embedded—the interactions, relationships, routines, and rules in these arenas—that Nelia was able to make sense of the messy world of politics. We therefore need to account for this interpersonal influence over attitudes and beliefs, not just the structural and historical environment that shapes them. As sociologist and ethnographer of small groups Gary A. Fine argues, "we organize our lives by relying on known others to create meaning and then reacting to these proffered meanings."[11]

PREFACE   XV

What does the victory of Marcos Jr. mean for diaspora formation? In this book, I argue that migrants become a diaspora in times of conflict, when norms, routines, and understandings that constitute everyday life and undergird our identities are disrupted. Social movements then emerge as a key site, means, and actor for mobilization. In the process, through interaction with allies and opponents, they develop collective identities derived from loyalty and continued belonging to the homeland, solidarity with co-nationals/co-ethnics, and shared history. I investigate the activism of Filipino migrants in three social movements—anti-Marcos dictatorship, migrants' rights, and collective memory. Through the first one, migrants challenged the state as a natural reference point for their homeland loyalty. By protesting the Marcos regime, they opened the arena for different imaginations of national membership to flourish—one that disentangles the state from the nation. Just like his father's presidency, Marcos Jr.'s rule has created divisions among Filipinos. And just like in the past, a movement against Marcos Jr. has emerged. But as the 2022 electoral results show, a staggering majority of Filipinos supports his vision for the Philippines—that is, unlike his father, his mass base in the homeland and in other countries is real. We can therefore expect pro-BBM organizations in migrant communities to play a dominant role in the formation of a collective identity whereby allegiance to the homeland means loyalty to Marcos Jr.—or a shared history based on a revisionist reading of the dictatorship. In any case, conflict remains central to the construction of the Filipino diaspora.

When I asked Nelia if she approved of Marcos Jr.'s proposed policies and programs for OFWs like her, she said laughing, "I don't even know. I guess now that I'm going home, it doesn't matter." I can only hope that Nelia and her family find the freedom they have been longing for when they return to the Philippines.

Introduction

Maria, a fifty-four-year-old Filipina, cleans the house of two Dutch families three times a week in a scenic neighborhood in the city of Utrecht, with the Rijn en Zon Windmill at the end of the street and quaint cafés and restaurants dotting the narrow roads. She came to the Netherlands as an au pair in the early 1990s with the help of her aunt, who is married to a Dutch man. When Maria's residence permit expired, she decided to stay. She did not have any job prospects in the Philippines, and as the oldest child, she felt it was her obligation to help her parents with her siblings' educations. "It's true what they say, it's *gezellig* here,"[1] she said, as we drank coffee and admired the flowers in the late spring of 2019. But it is not just the income or the picturesque landscape that prompted her to risk undocumented status. Since 2002, she has been organizing for the movement on migrants' rights, where she met other Filipinas who, like her, overstayed their visas and are currently making a living out of irregular domestic work. Through her activism, Maria found a purpose. She is more than a responsible daughter and sibling to her family in the Philippines or a diligent cleaner to her Dutch employers; she is an agent of social change. In her frequent interactions with Filipino migrant workers, she developed affective ties with them, and together, they built "communities of care"[2] based on fictive kinship. They forged a collective identity based on their common experience of displacement from the homeland as overseas Filipino workers (OFWs), marginalization in their country of destination as undocumented and racialized migrants, and alienation in their jobs that entail *kuskos at kudkod* (scrub and scrape), a colloquial reference to washing a soiled toilet.

Despite her strong involvement on migrant issues, which have broadened through the years to encompass the problems of second-generation Dutch

Filipinos such as discrimination and racism in education, Maria was never drawn to politics in the Philippines. Her feelings of attachment to her home country were limited to family—until the election of Rodrigo Duterte in 2016. The War on Drugs immediately caught her attention, conjuring up memories of martial law, even though she was still young when it happened. When she learned that the son of Ferdinand Marcos was going to run for president in 2022, with Duterte's daughter as his running mate, she took it upon herself to remind her *kababayan* (compatriots) in the Netherlands, through online platforms, not to forget the atrocities of the authoritarian regime. But upon realizing that this might cause estrangement from Filipinos who support the Marcoses and thus affect her ability to organize them on their concerns as migrants, she deleted her social media posts. "What can you do? They're from Ilocos and Mindanao," she said in exasperation, pointing to the strength of regional and ethnolinguistic identification despite their shared nationality as Filipinos and social position as *allochtoon* (foreigners) in the Netherlands. She recognized that activism is filled with contradictions, where mobilizing participants entails carefully navigating the intricacies of identity.

The state-authorized extrajudicial killings under the administration of Duterte also stirred emotions and evoked memories in Elena, propelling her back into activism after having "retired" from it and simply enjoying a quiet and slow life raising vegetables in her small garden in California. Elena is the daughter of upper-middle-class Filipino immigrants to the US. As a second-generation Filipino American who came of age during the historical turmoil of the Vietnam War in the 1960s, she was involved in a range of revolutionary movements that sought to dismantle global capitalism and US imperialism. Combined with her desire to discover and understand her Filipino heritage, the era paved the way to her participation in the movement against the Marcos dictatorship, where she and her fellow activists discredited the regime in the international community as an illegitimate representative of the Filipino people. Elena came out of her retirement to join the coordinated worldwide mobilizations against the burial of Marcos in Libingan ng mga Bayani (National Heroes Cemetery) on September 8, 2016. Duterte authorized the interment, an act that essentially honors Marcos for his patriotism and valor and institutionalizes historical revisionism. The protests in front of the Philippine consulates served not only as a space for resistance but also for community-building and intergenerational dialogue, as former anti-dictatorship activists reunited with each other, brought their families with them, and shared stories about the regime and the movement.

Although Brandon did not go to the demonstrations, he identified with the protesters' moral indignation toward Marcos's burial and other actions by

INTRODUCTION 3

Duterte to reverse the outcomes of the People Power uprising, of which his family played a huge part. He is a third-generation Filipino American, who comes from a lineage of community and union organizers. Despite this personal history, he is not actively involved in any social movement and does not consider himself an activist. "It's not that I don't take interest in politics or problems in society. I read and talk to my friends about them. My path has just been different from my parents and relatives," he explained, as he enthusiastically shared with me his passion for film photography and T-shirt design. But he admits that growing up around Filipino activism has equipped him with the language and lens to understand his everyday racialized experiences. He expresses pride that Filipinos in the US mobilized from afar and contributed to the overthrow of the Marcos dictatorship, the same way that they have struggled against systemic racism locally and nationally since the first wave of migration. Knowledge of this history—and seeing Filipinos in his city organize and protest around domestic issues such as gentrification, police brutality, and job insecurity as well as developments in the Philippines such as the War on Drugs and the continued US military presence in the country—has made Brandon conscious of how his personal life intersects with others and thus feels connected to Filipinos other than his biological kin.

When people move and settle in other countries, do they automatically form a diaspora? Based on the use of the term "diaspora" in current popular and scholarly literature, yes, leaving the homeland is sufficient to explain its constitution.[3] The stories of Maria, Elena, and Brandon suggest, however, that migration is only one piece of the puzzle. The other pieces have to do with recognizing group fate and developing community. These processes appear automatic and natural. After all, as Filipinos, they all have roots in one culture, nation, and territory; thus, they possess the same values derived from this genealogical tree. But diasporas do not emerge simply from primordial impulses based on attachment to ancestry and land. They arise when migrants create a collective identity that springs from the shared meanings they ascribe to and the actions they take because of these attachments. In other words, diasporas materialize when a common discourse to make sense of migrants' personal lives is forged—when actors interpret their individual biographies to a collective experience within a critical juncture. In a way, its formation results from what C. Wright Mills calls "the sociological imagination."[4]

My goal in this book is to demonstrate how a group of migrants evolve—or not—into a diaspora, focusing on the mechanisms and processes that turn them from individual to collective actors. This allows us to comprehend the construction of diasporas more methodically than conventional approaches that take their existence as a given—that is, migrants have already constituted themselves as a unified entity by virtue of their shared experience of leaving their home and being dispersed to foreign lands. Rather than assume that networks of migrants cluster together due to their culture and nationality, the task is to empirically demonstrate why and how they do so. In some respects, I approach the process of diaspora formation akin to that of ethnic groups in that they both engage in social boundary making. Andreas Wimmer, in his book *Ethnic Boundary Making: Institutions, Power, Networks,* argues that "a boundary displays both a categorical and a social or behavioral dimension. The former refers to acts of social classification and collective representation, the latter to everyday networks of relationships that result from individual acts of connecting and distancing. . . . Only when the two schemes coincide, when ways of seeing the world correspond to ways of acting in the world, shall we speak of a social boundary."[5] In explaining the making of a diaspora, we therefore need to look at the formation and articulation of collective identities and the interpretations, choices, and actions of migrants and subsequent generations that result from and shape these identities. The boundedness of a diaspora then is a function of collective identity formation.

Using the case of Filipinos in the US and the Netherlands, I show that diasporas must be created, and one way of doing this is through transnational activism. Migrants become a diaspora when they develop collective identities in times of political and social conflicts—when they reflect on and discuss what gave rise to their grievances, how to frame and where to lodge their demands, what kinds of tactics to pursue, and why some circumstances are favorable for certain strategies over others. During conflicts in the homeland and in their countries of settlement, cleavages in the social order become visible. Since migrants are not homogeneous, the communities become arenas for deliberation and negotiation. When they then make claims and stage demands in public, they deliberately form and articulate collective identities derived from loyalty and continued belonging to the homeland, solidarity with co-ethnics/co-nationals, and shared history. In these dialogues and debates among migrants and public performances for various targets, a diaspora is formed. This book thus responds to the invitation by sociologist Stéphane Dufoix "to take the illusions of essence, community, and continuity in the static analytical framework . . . and transform them into dynamic dimensions of active processes"[6] in the study of diasporas. I show how social movements can be these "active processes" that produce collective identities that often draw on "essence, community, and continuity" in the course of political contention. In other words, I am deploying a meso-level analysis of diaspora construction.

Understanding the formation of diasporas also necessitates looking at the actions and identities of migrants in more than one country of destination.

INTRODUCTION

5

After all, as Africana studies scholar Kim Butler argues, the term "diaspora" implies dispersal, not a transfer from the homeland to a single place.[7] But the intellectual discourse on Filipino diaspora has been predominantly shaped by studies of permanent immigrants in the US, who have limited or no ties with and whose experiences greatly differ from the vast majority of Filipino migrants with temporary employment contracts in Asia, the Middle East, and Europe.[8] In this book, I remedy this research gap by looking at the activism of Filipinos in the US and the Netherlands, two countries that are similar in terms of liberal democratic principles, which permit migrants to organize and publicly express their grievances, but different in terms of Filipino migration history. American colonization of the archipelago in the nineteenth century and a preference system in immigration policy have resulted in Filipinos being one of the biggest and oldest immigrant groups in the US, concentrated mostly in large metropolitan areas. In contrast, the community in the Netherlands is small, diffuse, and largely invisible, because the country became a destination for Filipinos only in the mid-1960s. Yet both communities became deeply entwined through transnational social movements focused on both homeland and hostland[9] issues. Because my goal is to explain the construction of a transnational collectivity, I refrain from conducting a systematic comparison of the two communities or treating them as two separate cases, especially given their disproportionate differences in size, number of migrant generations, and diversity of legal status, among others. Rather, I investigate the Filipino mobilizations in the US and the Netherlands in different periods as a "transnational social field."[10] In essence, my book allows us to see the operation of crossing and transcending borders and boundaries in political mobilization and collective identity formation.

In showing the processes and mechanisms by which social movements create a diaspora, I do not claim that contention is the only way migrants become a diaspora. I recognize the numerous contributions of scholars in literature, language, and the arts who have theorized about the development of diaspora culture marked by hybridity and heterogeneity through the examination of works by writers, visual artists, filmmakers, performers, and translators, often deploying a postcolonial or post-structuralist reading.[11] I build on the work of social scientists who have theorized that diasporas are political projects by elite actors, not organic outcomes of mass migration. Diasporas form when symbols, ideologies, and relations that undergird identities are destabilized and questioned during conflicts and, through discursive and strategic mobilization, political entrepreneurs influence not only their targets, allies, and bystanders but the wider culture. I argue that social movements are a site, a means, and an actor in the making of diasporas, because at the heart of mobilization is the formation of collective identities through debate, dialogue, negotiation, and public performance. The task of this book, therefore, is to show the necessity and centrality of conflict—of antagonistic relations and contests for power—in the formation of collectivities. In doing so, the factors, mechanisms, and processes laid out in *Insurgent Communities* can be relevant in understanding the experiences of contemporary migrants and refugees such as the Oromo people in Europe protesting the Ethiopian government and calling for an independent nation, the Indonesian domestic workers across East and Southeast Asia organizing for increased rights and protection from their host states, and US-born children of Korean immigrants using arts and music to memorialize and preserve the stories of "comfort women" and initiate intergenerational dialogues.

Conflict and Group Boundaries

Social theorists have long argued that group formation, while often associated with unity and harmony, also results from discord and dissension. The often-quoted statement from Karl Marx and Friedrich Engels's *The German Ideology* emphasizes the role of conflict in making individuals aware of their interests, thus instigating the constitution of classes based on relations of production: "The separate individuals form a class only insofar as they have to carry on a common battle against another class; in other respects they are on hostile terms with each other as competitors."[12] Group consciousness, in this regard, results from the realization of a shared social location as actors interact with each other vis-à-vis a mutual adversary. Like Marx and Engels, Georg Simmel saw conflict as a pervasive feature of social systems and as performing a group-building task, arguing that it may "not only heighten the concentration of an existing unit, radically eliminating all elements which might blur the distinctness of its boundaries against the enemy; it may also bring persons and groups which have otherwise nothing to do with each other."[13] Distilling the central theses in Simmel's essays, American sociologist Lewis A. Coser further developed a theory on the positive functions of conflict in group relations.[14] Rather than fracturing relationships that leads to the dissolution of the group, conflict regulates social interactions, facilitates the establishment and reaffirmation of group identity, and maintenance of boundaries.

The works of contemporary scholars who focus on the dynamics of social life at the meso- and microlevels help us grasp the premise that a certain degree of conflict is necessary for a collective to emerge and persist. For instance, the concept of "quotidian disruption" by David Snow and his colleagues unpacks the mechanisms that explain why people are likely to turn

INTRODUCTION   7

to group response rather than resort to individual coping strategies when social order breaks down.[15] They contend that when disruptions occur in the
taken-for-granted routines and understandings that constitute everyday life,
uncertainties about the social world crystallize. Since these routinized pat-
terns are relational, the disruption does not occur at a purely individual level
but is felt collectively, thus heightening the prospect for group action. This
argument—that groups are loci of interpretation and action in periods of dramatic dislocations and change—corresponds with Gary A. Fine's postulation
about the centrality of "tiny publics" in civic engagement. These small groups
serve as interactional and cultural fields where individuals develop and negotiate meanings, norms, and identities and "directly confront the power structure of the social order."[16] In short, we make sense of and take part in conflicts
in the small groups in which we are embedded.

It is therefore not surprising that in times of political and social strife, especially those that involve the state and other institutions that structure our
daily routines and habits, we start to question and reflect on our beliefs, loyalties, and values—elements that make up our identities. Who do I support?
Why do I feel this way? What does it say about me? We are often forced to
think in "us vs. them" terms and take sides. We turn to our "tiny publics" to
understand the situation because these arenas are where we spend most of
our time and live our lives. But one small group arises from quotidian disruptions and can influence the discourses of other groups. Sustained action
against opponents, bolstered by well-structured social ties and networks and
catalyzed by collectively shared beliefs, ideologies, and values lead to social
movements, which are typically represented by more than one organization.[17]
As they rally constituents and adherents and appeal to bystander publics con-
tra target authorities, they deliberate on a common interpretation of what is
at stake, who they are, and how their action alters the status quo. In essence,
what we have is a conflict-mobilization-collective identity nexus: conflict exposes contradictions and cleavages in the material and symbolic structures
that underpin our daily lives, and mobilization to understand and confront
these paradoxes and fissures occurs through social movements, where actors
discursively and strategically construct and negotiate a collective identity.

Political Contention and Cultural Change

But how can a diaspora be constructed from social movements, whose actors
constitute a minority in the migrant population? To put it simply, can we create a diaspora from activism when not everyone can be an activist? According
to sociologist Ann Swidler, during unsettled periods, culture "makes possible

new strategies of action-constructing entities that can act (selves, families, corporations), shaping the styles and skills with which they act, and modeling forms of authority and cooperation."[18] In these times, when politics polarize, separating allies from adversaries, meaning making processes become more articulated and explicit compared to settled periods when a competition on ways of organizing experience is closed or absent.[19] In short, unsettled periods provide opportunities for actors to openly challenge and transform the culture that people use to guide them and make sense of their lives. Because movements are embedded in social fields, when they mobilize openly to achieve their strategic goals, they are not merely engaging in direct confrontation with target authorities but also changing the shared understandings and practices that uphold the structures of domination. As Swidler asserts, based on the impact of punk subculture, the Black Panthers, and the New Left, "even without conscious efforts at publicity, one of the most important effects social movements have is publicly enacting images that confound existing cultural codings."[20] In turn, the collective identities they construct can become public goods that everyone can consume and perform, especially if these movements are successful.[21] In essence, social movements transform the culture that influences action, giving people—even those not involved in movements—"the vocabulary of meanings, the expressive symbols, and the emotional repertoire with which they can seek anything at all."[22] Thus, even if only a few participate in social movements, their impact on the wider culture is far-reaching.

Given these arguments, diaspora construction through contention occurs because conflicts in the homeland and hostlands—unsettled periods—expose fissures and paradoxes in the myths, norms, and traditions that undergird migrants' identities. As mentioned in the previous section, during political turmoil, people may start to doubt their prevailing beliefs or ideas about who they are as people. Migrants are not always conscious of these in their day-to-day routines and decisions, especially in settled periods, where culture has become the "undisputed authority of habit, normality, and common sense."[23] But, as stated earlier, ruptures in existing power relations during conflict destabilize culture and challenge migrants' identities. In these unsettled high-ideology periods, the purported unity of migrants based on their shared ancestry and nationality can fracture, and divisions within the community that are less visible during settled times are exposed. Social movements among migrants emerge from these conflicts, especially if the issues directly or indirectly affect them materially or symbolically and if the state as the primary source of people's grievances and target of their demands is a key player. Activists, in interaction with the state and other actors in a dynamic

INTRODUCTION   9

field of relations, debate, elaborate on, and apply new strategies of action, simultaneously shaped by and shaping culture. Through contention, social movements disrupt, question, and transform the congealed narratives, practices, rituals, and symbols that migrants pull from in the formation of collective identities vis-à-vis the state and the imagined community of the nation— identities that stem from and build on loyalty to the homeland, ethnic and/ or national solidarity, and shared history, or, put another way, identities that construct a diaspora.

The Case of Overseas Filipinos

Filipino migrants offer an interesting case for looking at the political and social processes of diaspora construction for three reasons. First, the Filipino population abroad is one of the largest of any nation. Second, labor migration is a key component of the Philippine state's official development agenda. Several state agencies have been established for the sole purpose of exporting migrants and for promoting overseas work as a patriotic deed. To normalize and nurture out-migration in the Filipino psyche, these agencies construct OFWs as "modern-day heroes" willing to sacrifice proximity to their families to serve the nation. Finally, the movement of Filipinos abroad is not the result of ethnic or religious persecution and banishment with collective trauma as a foundation for group identity, as was true for the cases of Jews and Armenians that were used for early theorizing of diasporas. Put simply, there is no master narrative that ties together the experiences of dispersed Filipinos. In addition, due to Jews' and Armenians' expulsion and loss, their involvement in homeland politics does not appear unusual. It is, in fact, expected since they regard their ancestral homeland as their true and ideal home, to which they or their descendants would eventually return when conditions were suitable.[24] But overseas Filipinos are comprised mostly of state-brokered temporary economic workers and permanent immigrants who relocate in search of better opportunities for themselves and their families.

For Filipino historian Filomeno V. Aguilar Jr., labor migrants are "amenable to the construction of diaspora" since they share a collective experience of marginalization and hardship in both the Philippines and their host societies, retain their Philippine citizenship, and maintain links to the homeland, where they will eventually return—a goal they idealize, nurture, and invest in throughout their stay in their countries of destination.[25] But despite the plethora of studies that point to Filipino Americans' diasporic consciousness and practices,[26] Aguilar is doubtful of largely middle-class permanent immigrants in the US as being part of the diaspora, for he argues that they do not share a narrative of privation that pressured them to leave the Philippines and no dream of return is cultivated and passed on to future generations. My perspective departs from Aguilar's. The perpetual racialization of Filipinos based on white supremacist ideology in the US and continuous flow of immigrants from the Philippines due to neoliberal policies have made their cultural distinctiveness salient and their race a master status. Thus, they cannot "do away" with ethnic attachment and search for their roots in the development of their selves. The experiences of racialization and encounters with recent migrants *may* encourage them to be involved in political activism or other avenues that lead them to develop collective identities oriented toward the homeland, solidarity with co-ethnics/co-nationals, and shared history.

In this book, I analyze the creation of diaspora through three overlapping and linked transnational social movements: the movement against the dictatorship of Marcos, the movement for migrants' rights, and the movement to (re)construct collective memory of the authoritarian period. These movements tackled issues that created conflicts within Filipino communities and drove the formation and negotiation of collective identities through debate and dialogue. This book thus reveals the elements that work together to form a diaspora—elements that migrants and the succeeding generations confront, challenge, and reconstitute in times of unrest: loyalty, solidarity, and history.

Organization of the Book

In the first chapter, I explain how I apply theories of collective identity from the social movements field in diaspora studies. Past scholarship presumes a diaspora constituted prior to activism. This a priori assumption misses both the structural and cultural dynamics of collective identity formation, dynamics that are often fraught with incongruities and tensions. The chapter lays out the theoretical road map to the book argument: migrants become a diaspora when they develop collective identities through activism—when they deliberate on how to frame their claims and demands, what kinds of tactics to pursue, or why certain circumstances are favorable for particular strategies. I clarify why the study of diasporas must depart from previous approaches that treated migrant and refugee groups as homogeneous units. Instead, research must consider conflicts and negotiations in which individuals make sense of their social and political environments as well as their lived experiences.

Chapter 2 shows how migration has long shaped Filipinos' way of life and aspirations, from the circular movement of Filipinos between the Philippines and the US in the early twentieth century due to colonization to the contemporary mass exodus of contract-based workers to Asia, Europe, and the

INTRODUCTION

Middle East that started in the 1960s. If collective identities and diaspora are simultaneously created through mobilization, we need to understand who is migrating and why and how they migrate. The political and social contexts in which they leave their countries, the resources they bring, and their experiences in the countries of settlement shape the kinds of discourses that inform their collective identities. In this chapter, I examine the heterogeneity of the transnational Filipino community. This allows me to examine how competing discourses based on individual or group experiences are negotiated during mobilization to form collective identities and the diaspora. I also show the power and strategies of the state to construct a Filipino diaspora and the agency of migrants in building their own communities, which both shape the processes of identity formation.

The development of a collective identity in relation to the homeland is crucial in the construction of diasporas. In chapter 3, I argue that through the anti-dictatorship movement, migrants challenged the state as a natural reference point for this identity. By protesting the Marcos regime, they opened the arena for different imaginations of national membership to flourish—one that disentangles the state from the nation. In the US, where activists pursued foreign-policy lobbying, they drew on symbols and activated narratives that alluded to the Marcos dictatorship as an outcome of US colonization of the Philippines—thus being loyal to the regime did not mean being devoted to the homeland. In contrast, through an international tribunal, activists in the Netherlands combined nationalism and a commitment to universal values such as human rights to strip the Philippine state of its authority as a representative of the Filipino people. Thus, in both countries, identities based on opposition to and collective action against the homeland regime-state were central to diaspora formation.

Chapter 4 shows how, through the migrants' rights movement, Filipinos in different countries of temporary and permanent settlement developed affective bonds with each other and created these "decentered, lateral connections."[27] As they participated in activism, they built relationships, networks, and communities rooted in their country of settlement. In the process, they reconfigured symbolic boundaries and developed intersectional identities. I demonstrate how narratives that reflected the violence of dislocation, alienation from the homeland, marginalization in the host countries, and empowerment through organized resistance became the ties that bound Filipino migrants together. Filipino activists' stories demonstrate that as they began to understand how the social structures in the US and the Netherlands shaped the life chances of their co-ethnics and other marginalized groups, they began to question their multiple identities. They recognized the experiences, grievances, and goals they had in common with other Filipinos living in their host countries. Regardless of migration cohort, class, gender, or religious differences, overseas Filipinos created a collective identity rooted in discourses of empowerment, of displacement by the homeland state, and of marginalization in their countries of residence.

Diasporas are not only invented; they must also endure. Thus, homeland orientation and kinship with dispersed co-ethnics in other countries must be continuously nurtured. Narratives of the past—the way a history is told—is important in constituting and sustaining a community, especially one that is transnationally imagined. In chapter 5, I argue that collective memory of the Marcos dictatorship and its overthrow in 1986 in the context of populist support for Rodrigo Duterte facilitates a continuous reimagining of the homeland that sustains a diaspora. The May 2016 Philippine presidential election saw overwhelming support for the eventual victory of Duterte, who had no qualms calling himself a dictator. He expressed admiration for the achievements of the Marcos dictatorship in terms of economic development and crime prevention. The election had the highest turnout in overseas ballots since the passage of the Philippine dual citizenship law in 2003. In this chapter, I show how Filipino migrants strategically used the collective memory of the authoritarian regime and the collective resistance against it in the campaign to prevent the burial of the dictator in the National Heroes Cemetery—an act of historical revisionism—and to hold Duterte accountable as he ruled through illiberal democracy, especially in the first two years of his administration. I explain how former anti-dictatorship activists in the US and the Netherlands have become "memory entrepreneurs" who mobilize memories of the past to galvanize subsequent generations of Filipinos abroad, especially the descendants of migrants who have fully assimilated in their countries of settlement, to support the people's movement in the homeland.

I conclude the book by summarizing and tying together the arguments and discussing the applicability and limitations of diaspora formation through contention in other cases and situations. I also discuss how the changing global economic landscape and challenges to democracy both in the Philippines and in the migrants' countries of settlement have influenced the project of Filipino diaspora formation. The elections of Rodrigo Duterte and Donald Trump have strained bonds among overseas Filipinos. Families, social networks, and communities have become divided in their political affiliations. These developments have implications for the construction of the Filipino diaspora through activism.

1

Movement(s) and Identities

*Toward a Theory of Diaspora
Construction through Contention*

To escape repression during the regime of Augusto Pinochet in the 1970s, thousands of political exiles fled Chile and settled in every continent, predominantly in Western Europe. Upon arrival, they immediately established an "external front," rallied the exile community, and appealed to sympathetic citizens in their host countries to destabilize and eventually overthrow the dictatorship from afar.[1] On the same continent in 1999, the arrest of Partiya Karkerên Kurdistan (Kurdistan Workers' Party) leader Abdullah Öcalan by Turkish authorities sparked coordinated demonstrations among Kurdish immigrants and their descendants from Greece to Russia. Strategies of protest ranged from hunger strike to self-immolation outside the Greek embassies and consulates of major cities around Europe.[2] And in the US, on October 31 to November 1, 2020, thousands of Armenian Americans gathered on Hollywood Boulevard in Los Angeles to call attention to and draw support for Armenia in its conflict with Azerbaijan over the disputed border region of Nagorno-Karabakh.[3] Southern California is home to the largest Armenian population in the United States, with a neighborhood in East Hollywood designated Little Armenia in 2000. The protesters waved the Armenian flag and carried signs that said, "End the Cycle of Genocide," "Artsakh is Armenia," and "Defend Armenia." These examples demonstrate the persistence of homeland ties among migrants, especially those who experienced suppression and displacement by the government in their countries of origin. They also illustrate migrants' membership in different yet overlapping transnational networks and communities and the articulation of their identities during periods of heightened political contention in their home countries. Because of the widespread perception that migrants eventually become or are already diasporas simply by moving across borders, we often overlook that

14   CHAPTER ONE

these episodes of protests and sustained campaigns are fundamental to diaspora construction.

The mobilization of migrants on homeland issues is one of the oldest and most familiar forms of transnational activism, but the use of a social movement framework in unpacking its complexities remains a recently developed practice.[4] In this book, I enrich and refine the idea that diasporas are constructions by applying theories on collective identity from the field of social movement studies to show how diasporas are created in and through protest—they do not precede protest. I employ an actor-oriented approach to elaborate on how activists, as political entrepreneurs, strategically mobilize discourses, narratives, and symbols, and ascribe meaning to their actions and relationships. I reveal how individual migrants with their own personal interests, goals, and motivations for leaving their countries of origin come together and constitute themselves as a group with collective identities oriented toward loyalty to the homeland, ethnic or national solidarity, and shared history. In a way, through social movements, I show how migrants do not simply wait for the state—in either the homeland and/or hostland—to turn them into political subjects based on its goals; they are active agents of their own political incorporation.

Insurgent Communities lies at the intersection of the fields of migration, social movements, and global/transnational sociology. It advances the understanding of structures and processes that transcend or go beyond the national level by importing social movement theory into migration studies in ways that benefit both fields. In this chapter, I discuss some of the key concepts and theories that inform the conflict-mobilization-collective identity nexus in my inquiry of diaspora construction through contention.

Constructivist and Processual View of Diasporas

Early conceptualizations of diaspora center on forced dislocation and dispersal and the imagination of community around the idea of a homeland.[5] Dislocation occurs not only by being "out of place" when one leaves one's home and lives elsewhere; rather, the uprooting takes place due to coercion and thus emphasizes unintended action or limited agency.[6] Certainly, this raises the question of what constitutes coercion, an important issue for contemporary application of the term. Colonization, famine, repression, slavery, and war may drive groups of people to flee their homelands. In these unforeseen circumstances, migrants are viewed as bereft of alternative choices for their survival. But regardless of the reason and the manner in which they left, they remain members of the political community of their home nation.[7] Robin Cohen claims that the idea of a diaspora varies greatly but stresses the power of the natal (or imagined natal) territory on migrants' loyalty and emotions and the "acceptance of an inescapable link with their past migration history and a sense of co-ethnicity with others of a similar background."[8] Thus, the belief that they cannot or should not intend to be fully assimilated in their host societies informs their actions to preserve their culture and retain a separate identity.[9]

While the definition of diaspora has evolved, scholars agree on the following characteristics: migration to at least two destinations due largely to coercion; maintenance of relationship with an actual or imagined homeland, a place of origin from which migrants were dispersed and with which they feel a strong sense of belonging; creation of institutional links and affective solidarity among the scattered migrant communities; and cultivation of a shared history to distinguish themselves from others and to ensure its existence across generations.[10] These elements suggest that the interrelated processes of dispersion, homeland orientation, and boundary maintenance in early conceptualizations of diaspora are not just objective circumstances but also subjective interpretations that lead to the formation of a collective identity. This collective identity is not arbitrary but deliberate; it is "created for specific purposes, not to guide an entire life; it is a necessary fiction . . . largely a claim to unity and relevance, whether of a nation-state, a social movement, or some demographic category."[11] The Jewish case has thus remained as an "ideal type"—with the Armenian, Maghrebi, Turkish, Palestinian, Cuban, Greek, and perhaps Chinese also fitting the definition—to which other migrant groups are to be compared and evaluated as to whether and to what extent they are considered a diaspora.[12]

But James Clifford cautions against the recourse to an ideal type in the study of diasporas and suggests that "Jewish (and Greek and Armenian) diasporas can be taken as nonnormative starting points for a discourse that is traveling or hybridizing in new global conditions."[13] While recognition of the inextricable link between Jewish history and the language of diaspora is important,[14] the concept is heuristically fertile only if it is extended to all dispersed populations that refer to and maintain a collective identity and solidarity—"a matter to be analyzed in its complexity."[15] Further, Kim D. Butler discourages the use of a facile "checklist" approach, a useful but inadequate point of departure due to its tendency to reify.[16] Rather, the analysis of diasporas needs to incorporate a framework that explains the "structuring of the collective experience abroad based on the link maintained with the referent-origin and the community stance this creates,"[17] by "bring[ing] the struggles themselves into focus without presupposing that they will eventuate into bounded groups."[18]

From the constructivist tradition, political scientist Fiona Adamson, sociologist Rainier Bauböck, and anthropologist Martin Sökefeld argue that diasporas are not pre-political objects in a natural state of existence and instead point to the role of discourses, elite actors, and strategic mobilization in their construction.[19] They view diasporas as the products of transnational mobilization, whereby political actors interpret and frame events, grievances, and interests in ways that bring a community together around a collective identity. Sentiments of belonging and attachment to a homeland do not turn migrants into a diaspora since they only provide the symbols for which a diaspora is imagined.[20] Central to this imagination are discourses on shared identity and transnational membership to a political community that catalyze or hinder mobilization and, at the same time, are also products of the mobilization process. But these discourses can only be understood with reference to their historical context and the experiences of individuals. This is where key agents are needed to articulate and amplify these discourses in ways that make sense—that is, they capture the personal everyday struggles of migrants—but also encourage the recognition of commonality leading to collective action. Thus, diaspora construction can be undertaken either "by governmental actors from above or by non-governmental actors from below."[21]

In his study of the Taglit-Birthright, a free educational trip to Israel offered to young Jewish adults, Yehonatan Abramson illustrates that "the reproduction of diasporic identity across generations does not happen naturally or automatically, but involves political actors (state-based or not) who are trying to imbue the identity of younger generations with new meaning."[22] In other words, diaspora formation relies on political entrepreneurs who deliberately mobilize, cultivate, and transform identities. If we consider diaspora as a political project, a crucial task of these actors is "to construct or deploy ideologies and categories that can be used to create new political groups out of existing social networks . . . and frame the experiences of those who subjectively experienced dislocation and marginalization."[23] This is because migration does not entail the mere transfer of identities from the country of origin to that of settlement, but rather a recreation in a new context. To foster mobilization, political entrepreneurs may resort to essentialist beliefs and parochial or particularistic ideas, articulated in the language of ancestry, national loyalty, and attachment to a territorial homeland.[24] They may also use universalist frameworks such as liberalism to advance the goals related to their homeland.[25] For example, both Jewish and Arab Americans have portrayed their commitment to Israel and Palestine, respectively, as an extension of their allegiance to American democratic values and strategic interests.[26]

But diasporas must not only be invented; they must also be sustained through intergenerational continuity and lateral links.[27] This means that identities are continuously being made and remade, as fresh cohorts of migrants arrive, subsequent generations are born, and new countries of destination or settlement emerge, resulting in either the contraction or expansion of the boundaries of membership. To understand this dynamic, geographer Elizabeth Mavroudi deploys a processual view to diaspora construction, where migrants themselves are involved in boundary maintenance as varied groups compete for dominance in defining the parameters of belonging. She argues that while diaspora is not a fixed grouping, "displaced people may manipulate and create visions of identity, community and the nation-state that are static, essentialised and fixed for political, socio-economic and cultural reasons."[28] In her study of second-generation Palestinians in Athens, she shows that notions of homeland and belonging must be actively learned, as migrants and the new generations may feel ambivalence toward constructions of the nation. Events such as the Nakba in 1948 trigger and cement feelings of a shared identity based on trauma and dispossession.[29] She further contends that by looking at the changing relationships between people and places through time and space, we can understand how they negotiate their multiple identities as they are "subject to power relations, tensions, disconnections and the specific, situated processes that enable (or force) the constructions of shared (and often politicised) notions of belonging, identity and community."[30]

In a way, Mavroudi's argument dovetails Paul Gilroy's critique of racial essentialism in his opus *The Black Atlantic* and Stuart Hall's perspective on identities as constantly producing and reproducing themselves through the dialectic of sameness and difference. Both cultural theorists find discomfort in the assumption of a primordial essence that lies at the heart of diaspora—that a natural and undifferentiated community organically emerges from a group of migrants due to their perceived sameness based on their common roots. Gilroy advances an understanding of diaspora that rejects the overlapping of ethnicity, culture, and nation; rather, he emphasizes agency, fluidity, and hybridity in the formation of identities in the context of evolving political and social conditions.[31] Similarly, Hall recognizes that while "our cultural identities reflect the common historical experiences and shared cultural codes which provide us, as 'one people,' with stable, unchanging and continuous frames of reference and meaning, beneath the shifting divisions and vicissitudes of our actual history . . . there are also critical points of deep and significant difference which constitute 'what we really are'; or rather—since history has intervened—'what have we become.' "[32] In other words, a diaspora is formed not only through unity but also through conflict, as migrants discover and navigate the fault lines and chasms in the ongoing formation of their identities.

A constructivist and processual view, therefore, recasts the analysis of diaspora by treating it as a dependent variable or an outcome. We cannot assume groupness to simply materialize among migrants of the same ethnic, national, or religious origin; it must be explained. Diasporas are discursively and strategically invented at certain historical junctures. This means that for diasporas to come into existence, categories, symbols, and practices—whether based on trauma from war, political persecution, or economic hardship—need to be created or appropriated by political entrepreneurs to tie together dispersed networks and mobilize them under a collective identity. Migrants themselves are active agents, and they work out their identities and belonging in accordance with their own experiences and their perceived difference from and similarity to others. But under what conditions is this dynamic process of diaspora construction that includes mobilization and negotiation best observed? It is when the homeland, hostland, or both are going through upheavals, and migrants engage in contentious politics through social movements.[33]

Social Movements and Collective Identity

At the core of contentious politics are the antagonistic relations between dominant and subordinated groups. To be sure, not all political activities that migrants engage in fall under this domain—be they on issues related to their countries of origin or settlement. The participation of Salvadoran immigrants in the presidential elections in El Salvador, the solicitation and donation to the lobby group American Israel Public Affairs Committee among Jews in the US, and the peace-building initiatives of Irish Americans in Northern Ireland through petitioning officials in Washington, DC, do not challenge the existing structures of authority such as the state; therefore, the status quo is often maintained. In electoral politics and lobbying, migrants do not confront elites, authorities, and opponents; rather, they validate their position in society.

As in any group process, in making claims and demands to target authorities, whether to institute or change a policy or overthrow a regime in power, actors in social movements engage in what Michael L. Schwalbe and Douglas Mason-Schrock refer to as identity work, "which is anything people do, individually or collectively, to give meaning to themselves or others . . . [that] includes the creation of the codes that enable self-signifying and the interpretation of other's signifying behavior."[34] Certainly, each individual has different identities. Social psychologists have theorized that people possess internalized meanings of what is expected of them based on the structural position they occupy in society (role identity). These definitions exist alongside their membership in certain groups (social identity) and their view of themselves as unique entities (personal identity).[35] Because a person is constantly interacting with others, "one is always and simultaneously in a role and in a group, so that role identities and social identities are frequently and at the same time relevant and influential in individuals' perceptions and actions."[36]

Within social movements, collective identity does not arise simply from aggregating these individual-level identities. After all, a person who joins a protest or sympathizes with a cause may share only a few interests, experiences, or goals related to their role or social identities with other movement constituents or adherents. Italian sociologist Alberto Melucci defines collective identity as "an interactive and shared definition produced by several individuals (or groups at a more complex level) and concerned with the orientations of action and the field of opportunities and constraints in which the action takes place."[37] He stresses three interrelated elements—cognitive, interactive and communicative, and emotive. Essentially, through repeated interactions in a network of active relationships, individuals forge a common interpretive framework for them to make sense of their grievances, define their interests, and make decisions, and in the process develop a degree of emotional investment and feel one with others. In essence, it is both a process and an outcome that is in constant reconfiguration as social movements evolve and confront external and internal challenges.[38]

Social psychologist Bert Klandermans adds that this collective identity is politicized, which implies "a cognitive restructuring of the social environment into opponent and (potential) allies."[39] In social conflicts, identification inevitably means choosing and aligning with a group wrestling for power and distancing from the rest.[40] As collective identity is constituted through and oriented toward shared action that occurs within contentious politics, boundary work is also accomplished, setting the parameters for group membership and difference with opposing—often dominant—groups.[41] Actors construct a collective identity not only to maintain group boundaries vis-à-vis an "other," but also to solidify "against *thems* inside, as particular subgroups battle to gain or retain legitimate *us* standing."[42]

While collective identity is produced through group interaction, it cannot exist unless it is within an individual's perception of who they are—their sense of self,[43] for "to partake of a collective identity is to reconstitute the individual self around a new and valued identity."[44] For instance, in 1977, a small group of women that would later comprise the human rights organization Madres de Plaza de Mayo (Mothers of Plaza de Mayo) initially mobilized based on their role identity as mothers demanding the return of their disappeared sons and daughters because of state-sponsored terrorism in Argentina. They also possessed social identities based on their gender, social class, religion, and hometown. As their activism expanded and their protest repertoire[45] of silent walks and marches in plazas became a site for regular interactions, they developed strong emotional bonds with each other and created a collective identity based on the shared definition of "mothers of the disappeared" that incorporated ideas about motherhood and sisterhood, mainstream human rights discourse, and analysis of women's position in Argentinian society. This collective identity transformed their self-conceptions, in particular their understanding of their role and social identities, especially as they became further embedded in the language, practices, and rituals of the organization.[46]

Thus, as Klandermans cogently puts it, collective identity is a group characteristic in a Durkheimian sense,[47] wherein in the process of political contestation, individuals create a social movement culture that enables them to express their common interests and solidarity by developing codes, narratives, rituals, and symbols[48] and "transform cultural representations, social norms—how groups see themselves and are seen by others."[49] We see this dynamic in the strategies that social movements use to achieve their goals. While strategies are often considered as rational decisions selected based on probability of success, they are in fact also statements about identity.[50] Strategy lies between structure and agency, wherein activists make choices based on an assessment of the political environment, cultural climate, available resources, and their own perceptions of effectiveness.[51]

The type of grievances and the ways that activists choose to air them communicate what a group's identity is publicly. Those choices make up the activity of framing, which involves "conscious strategic efforts by groups of people to fashion shared understandings of the world and of themselves that legitimate and motivate collective action."[52] Collective action frames provide individuals and organizations a way to identify an unjust condition or event, specify blame or cause, offer prescriptions for change, motivate action, and articulate a collective identity.[53] Thus, in framing, culture can be strategic, and any strategy is inherently cultural.[54] Activists may frame collective identities—including those rooted in structural inequalities—in different ways.[55] Among migrants and exiles, nationalism can easily mobilize emotions such as love, loyalty, and pride, especially during high points of contention.[56] But migrants involved in homeland activism may simultaneously create new, hybrid identities and solidify primordial bonds.[57] An interesting question is,

When, why, and how do migrant activists frame their identities in particularistic or universal ways?

Activists deliberate on appropriate strategies based on interaction with other players in the arena of political contention, which include state targets and other forms of authority; bystanders and potential allies; mass media; movement adherents and supporters; and opponents.[58] These other players are themselves agents engaged in cultural performance, interpretation of outcomes, and strategic decisions based on the institutional context.[59] As all players act and react to each other's maneuvers in a shifting environment, they become more embedded in the norms and conventions that govern their interaction within a particular setting.[60] Thus, David Meyer and Suzanne Staggenborg suggest that to understand movement strategy as a dynamic process, we need to look at "how a changing web of relations in a multiorganizational field of actors constrains and enlarges strategic options over time."[61]

Moreover, collective identity formation does not occur only when activists are confronting their targets and appealing to allies in the public sphere—at rallies, strikes, congressional hearings, occupation of buildings, and so on. It also transpires in the everyday politics of social movements, especially during periods of abeyance, which "depicts a holding process by which movements sustain themselves in nonreceptive political environments and provide continuity from one stage of mobilization to another."[62] During these times when large-scale mobilization and mass-based challenges are unlikely, activists nurture affective bonds and a commitment to ideological beliefs as well as sustain oppositional culture through quotidian activities such as celebration of members' birthdays or anniversaries and tea gatherings.[63] These usually take place in small settings that are structurally isolated from control by power holders—referred to as free spaces, sequestered sites, or submerged networks[64]—thereby allowing activists to engage in prefigurative politics, that is, the practices and relationships that model the society a movement seeks to build.[65] Through mundane daily pursuits, they "reduce[s] the distance between daily life and . . . activism which, in turn, helps 'normalize' these practices and the beliefs they articulate."[66]

In sum, in contentious forms of politics, social movements confront dominant power structures where they develop a politicized collective identity to unify constituents and adherents and distinguish themselves from their targets and opponents. This collective identity is embedded in and constitutive of the movement culture, shaping the decision making on strategies for public claims making, the day-to-day workings of organizations, and the ways of life of activists. Incorporating collective identity formation in the analysis of diaspora construction prompts us to regard the migrant community as a discursive field for the conflict-riven process of meaning making by various, often opposed, actors. In this field, migrants question ethnicity and nationality as the core foundation for establishing group boundaries. Discourses pivot not only on their common culture but also on interpretations of national history, especially the social and political forces that have shaped their homeland, and their shared experiences in their host societies.

From Protests to Diasporas

But how does collective identity formation within social movements give rise to diasporas, when not all migrants engage in activism? In fact, transnational political practices even among migrant cohorts is the exception rather than the rule and may fade over subsequent generations.[67] As Peggy Levitt and Robert Smith have vividly illustrated in their research on Dominicans in Boston and Mexicans in New York, respectively, migrants engage in such activities selectively on a periodic basis.[68] Often, these are through electoral participation and other conventional forms of political engagement. They are also more translocal than transnational, aimed at improving the situations in their hometowns, since their emotional affiliations are usually with specific localities, not with nations.[69]

Mobilizing on homeland issues also depends not simply on affective bonds. Material conditions such as economic, legal, and social statuses shape even the perception of political efficacy.[70] When people leave their homelands, most often they do so primarily as mothers, siblings, and spouses who want to provide for their loved ones and secondarily as workers—that is, they migrate based on their role identities. Studies have shown that their decisions to take their chances overseas are made within and through the family unit, especially among women,[71] and their sense of identity is tied up with the expectations of a dutiful member of the household such that their contributions become "central and integral to affirming their personal identities."[72] Participation in activism may therefore threaten the fulfillment of these obligations and responsibilities based on their social roles.

If we recognize identity making as part of a broad process of cultural struggle, then the contentious mobilization of this small number of individuals forming and sharing a collective identity is not insignificant. Ann Swidler (1986) argues that culture serves as a tool kit that we rely on to make everyday decisions and solve problems; it can be understood only in relation to the strategies of action they sustain.[73] Culture consists of "symbolic vehicles of meaning, including beliefs, ritual practices, art forms, and ceremonies, as well as informal cultural practices such as language, gossip, stories, and rituals of daily life."[74] As a dialectic of system and practice, cultures are contradictory, loosely integrated, contested, constantly changing, and weakly bounded.[75] In every society, a dominant culture exists, which is imposed by the ruling class and accepted either consciously or unconsciously by subordinated groups, as Antonio Gramsci has elaborated in the concept of hegemony.[76] This culture appears to be largely stable. But in reality, it is riddled with gaps, inconsistences, and paradoxes that permit alternative codes and symbols to take root and thrive, facilitating the rise of social movements that in turn become a source of cultural change.[77]

I show that through social movements, conflict offers an opening for migrants to change the tool kit that undergirds definitions of loyalty, solidarity, and history. Dominant understandings of these are monopolized by the state, as it possesses the "legitimate use of physical and *symbolic* violence over a definite territory and over the totality of the corresponding population . . . incarnat[ing] itself simultaneously in objectivity, in the form of specific organizational structures and mechanisms, and in subjectivity in the form of mental structures and categories of perception and thought."[78] As a powerful actor that inscribes categorizations into the social order, it is actively engaged in identity making. In her book *Courting Migrants: How States Make Diasporas and Diasporas Make States*, political scientist Katrina Burgess shows how states construct, cultivate, and make exclusive claims on migrants' loyalty and national identity, thereby turning them into diasporas.[79] She conceptualizes loyalty based on affective and strategic considerations, arguing that "affective loyalty is guided by emotion and often linked to identity construction, whereas strategic loyalty is based on an iterative exchange of benefits that builds trust while remaining contingent."[80] Burgess further contends that state-led diaspora-making hinges on loyalty to the homeland—where migrants feel and perceive that they have a stake in the place they left behind— and loyalty to the state's political project. The state works hard to ensure that migrants recognize the link between these two loyalties—that is, that migrants are emotionally and materially invested in the regime in power because it is good for the homeland—and in the process, they "self-identify as loyal, self-disciplining subjects."[81] The state thus appropriates some and suppresses other identity discourses.

But sociologist James Jasper asserts that we do not always think about our loyalty to anyone—whether to our families, an organization to which we belong, or the nation.[82] As an affective commitment, it is mostly stable and therefore we only feel it when we ruminate about who are we loyal to. It does not mean that it recedes or disappears in our unconscious state; rather, "our loyalties remain in the background, ready to be reactivated when we again pay attention to them."[83] Moreover, they are often intensified over time through "preexisting building blocks of trust" within social groups, and while they can change, they offer the foundation for collective identities and goals of action, influencing our moral principles and responsibilities.[84] Loyalty, therefore, is interactive, relational, and dynamic, and we reflect on and sense it in situations where our identities are challenged. These occur during periods of conflict when schisms materialize and taking sides is unavoidable.

Like loyalty, solidarity is built through existing relationships that are suffused with emotional attachments, thus binding individuals to the group and giving them a sense of identity. For instance, in his study of the development of class consciousness among American workers in different types of union action, Rick Fantasia shows how "cultures of solidarity" are created and expressed through the processes of mutual association.[85] In their struggle against the dominant structure, workers embodied practices and meanings, further embedding them in the social spaces where class consciousness emerges and grows via interactions with collectivities in opposition with one another. But solidary obligations may be present even in the absence of dense ties like those in a labor union. In *Inventing the Ties That Bind: Imagined Relationships in Moral and Political Life*, sociologist Francesca Polletta argues that people creatively imagine and invent relationships using cultural schemas that guide how we interact with each other based on reciprocity, respect, and equality.[86] In fact, she adds that we can forge new schemas of belonging when we deem familiar ones insufficient, and social movements have been instrumental in producing schemas of solidary relationship that have diffused more widely than conventional ones. One way of doing so is enacting a mode of talk that attaches importance to "sharing experiences, values, and beliefs at least as preliminary to expressing opinions, and sometimes as an alternative to doing so; striving to empathize with experiences different from one's own; and speaking as an individual rather than as a representative of a group."[87] Through talk that create bonds of trust and affection, relationships based on empathy are forged, creating actionable solidarity.

Finally, loyalty and solidarity to a given community cannot endure without a collective understanding of a common past. In his noted essay "Cultural Identity and Diaspora," Stuart Hall argues that "far from being grounded in a mere 'recovery' of the past, which is waiting to be found, and which when found, will secure our sense of ourselves into eternity, identities are the names we give to the different ways we are positioned by, and position ourselves within, the narratives of the past."[88] This contention agrees with the claim by Jeffrey K. Olick that identities are not possessions but projects and practices, and that collective memory constitutes the elements that stimulate and galvanize the often-inchoate activities related to identity formation.[89] Memory offers individuals with a cognitive map—a narrative frame—to make sense of who they are and lays out a cultural program to shape and guide motivations, emotions, and actions.[90] Memory narratives then serve as "vehicles of communication that reveal the attachments and anxieties of the narrators in negotiating their self-identity."[91] But while it is individuals who remember, memory itself is an intersubjective act, and collective memory is a contested and dynamic social process.[92] French philosopher and sociologist Maurice Halbwachs contends, "individuals, being located in a specific group context, draw on that context to remember or recreate the past."[93] Therefore, collective memory is constitutive of collective identity: acts of remembering—and forgetting—strengthen social bonds and group solidarity by marking the boundaries of membership,[94] providing a shared history to make decisions that impact the group in the present and shape its future,[95] and delineating "the 'when,' the 'who' and the 'where of the group as it is consolidated and reproduced over time and space."[96] Thus, in the sociology of memory, we are not only interested in what people remember but also how they remember.[97]

In this book, I show that even if only a few participate, social movements among migrants that focus on "Politics with a capital P," such as regime change and national policy reforms, create a diaspora by engaging in cultural struggles through "politics with a small p"—that is, the politics of everyday life—where ideas, habits, scripts, and practices that inform identities vis-à-vis the state and community are questioned and transformed. Certainly, measuring whether all migrants subscribe to the collective identities that social movements have constructed to constitute a diaspora is beyond the task of this book, as the focus is on how the actions, discourses, and strategies of political entrepreneurs invent a transnational community based on loyalty to the homeland, solidarity with co-ethnics/co-nationals, and shared history. Scholars have recognized the dearth of research on cultural results of social movements, stemming from the difficulty of studying them due to the wide range of actors and contextual factors in their production.[98] Nella van Dyke and Verta Taylor acknowledge that changes in culture are often the most significant and lasting effects of activism, since "movement's cultural content is both created and diffused to the larger society through its collective performances, social networks, and other forms of interaction and communication, including new social media."[99] But as Thomas R. Rochon notes, while the cultural arena is where activists achieve success, it is also where they easily lose their place, as the wider society adopts their understanding of an issue: "As the culture takes hold of a new idea, adaptation occurs to make the concept fit with existing cultural beliefs. . . . In effect, the critical community loses exclusive ownership of the issue—precisely because the new concepts are now part of the wider culture."[100]

To conclude, the use of social movement theory allows us to parse the mechanisms and processes at play in the factors that scholars from the constructivist and processual view of diaspora have identified—discourses, political entrepreneurs, and strategic mobilization. By making collective identity formation during public contestations with state targets as well as in the everyday activities of movement organizations central to the analysis, we can account for how key actors recognize, negotiate, and articulate group interests and ideals based on loyalty and continued belonging to the homeland, solidarity with co-nationals and co-ethnics, and shared history. But does this mean that diaspora construction through contention privileges the role of elite actors? Yes and no. Social movements are dynamic and involve complex interactions. While the political entrepreneurs who initially mobilize, establish organizations, articulate claims and demands to authorities, and influence public discourse possess the economic resources and/or cultural and symbolic capital to engage in transnational activism for regime change, migrants' rights, and memory work, the evolution and diffusion of contention from state engagement to prefigurative politics, from geographic centers to the peripheries, from closed spaces to open hubs, allow for the participation and leadership of multiple actors in the migrant community.

2

Roots and Routes

Global Migration of Filipinos

When Typhoon Haiyan[1] swept across the Philippines on November 8, 2013, an estimated 6,300 people were killed, 94 percent of whom were from the agricultural region of Eastern Visayas. The most powerful tropical cyclone in the country's modern history caused US$1.7 billion of damage in infrastructure and left 1.8 million Filipinos homeless and more than six million displaced.[2] International and supranational bodies, governments, nonprofit organizations, corporations, and celebrities immediately sent messages of sympathy and support and donated a total of US$866 million and in addition provided humanitarian aid and supplies for post-disaster recovery and relief.[3] But according to the report by the Inter-Agency Standing Committee, a forum of the United Nations (UN) and non-UN philanthropic partners, "the diaspora played possibly the most direct and important role for many affected communities. In a year-on-year comparison, remittances to the Philippines rose by US$600 million in the first three months following Haiyan."[4] Indeed, cash transfers from countries where a significant number of Filipinos reside—the US, Saudi Arabia, the United Arab Emirates, the United Kingdom, Singapore, Japan, and Canada—increased by 10 percent to a total of US$2.17 billion at the end of December 2013.[5] The mobilization of the Filipino diaspora in the aftermath of the catastrophe shows not only the size and scale of the overseas population but also its level of transnational social infrastructure, economic resources, and political influence as well as its degree of loyalty to the homeland.

With 10.2 million in more than two hundred countries and territories, according to the Commission on Filipinos Overseas (CFO), the Filipino diaspora is one of the biggest in the world.[6] This figure constitutes about 11 percent of the total population of the Philippines, supplying US$30.1 billion in remittances, which account for 9.3 percent of the gross domestic product.[7] Thus, the contemporary overseas Filipino population is predominantly an economic actor that functions "as an outlet, particularly as a social safety valve."[8] It is vast and heterogeneous, exhibiting not only cross-national differences but also diversity within each country of destination. Like other migrants, Filipinos distinguish themselves from each other based on their ethnolinguistic group, immigration status, region of origin, religion, and socioeconomic position (in both homelands and hostlands). But unique to the Filipino case is the role of the Philippine state in stimulating and managing the migration of its citizens, recognized by the World Bank for "its highly developed support system for migrant workers that is a model for other sending countries."[9] In addition, together with civil society, the state has developed discourses and narratives to transform its development weakness as a sign of national strength, thus "grounding—and legitimizing—the place of the Filipino diaspora in cultural terms."[10]

While diasporas are not natural products of cross-border movements but rather discursive and strategic constructions by political actors, we need to understand the macrohistorical structures and conditions that have stimulated migration to account for the discourses, networks, and practices in the community that are mobilized during conflicts. The demographic characteristics of the migrant population after all determine the sort of cultural, economic, and political means available for transnational activism. Using the framework of contexts of exit and reception,[11] this chapter provides a historical overview of the movement of Filipinos to the US and the Netherlands. I argue that both colonialism and neoliberalism as ideologies, modes of governance, and policies created the conditions for migration, shaped the contours of the overseas community, and as will be illustrated in the subsequent chapters, provided the material and symbolic resources that helped advance the transnational anti-dictatorship struggle, campaigns for migrants' rights, and memory activism. I show that colonialism and neoliberalism spurred the movement of political entrepreneurs to these countries, built the state and civil society linkages that facilitated transnational mobilization, and equipped activists with the language, signs, and meanings to frame their claims, demands, and identities. However, the effect of these factors on cohort or individual experiences, in particular assimilation or integration into the host societies, is beyond the scope of this book.

Since the state is a central institutional actor in migration and a target of social movements in this book, I also elaborate on the approach of its agencies organizationally and discursively to construct a Filipino nation beyond its territorial borders, drawing on the work of Katrina Burgess that frames "diaspora-making as a political project that is increasingly embraced by states while at the same time transforming them."[12] But because migrants are active agents, they themselves are engaged in practices in various sites and spaces—within or outside the purview of the state—that contribute to the formation of a diaspora. From religious rituals to linguistic codes, Filipino migrants in key countries of destination build transnational communities that may subvert or validate the hegemonic constructions of their subjectivities by the state. Thus, although the Philippine state actively encourages its citizens to migrate and contribute to and identify with the nation, as Burgess argues, past studies and my research on transnational social movements show that the actions of migrants themselves determine the extent to which they participate in and accept the state's project of diaspora formation.

Colonialism and the Creation of a Mobile Workforce

Sri Lankan–born British writer and theorist of state racism and Black liberation politics A. Sivanandan astutely commented on the relationship between colonialism and immigration: "We are here because you were there."[13] Colonialism not only established the ties and avenues for Filipinos to leave their homes and go back, but it also gave them the lived experiences encapsulated and passed on to their families, friends, and neighbors as stories to nurture the idea of a world beyond their hometowns—the rich metropole. In essence, through colonialism, the Philippines was predisposed to become a migrant-sending nation. While the annexation of the Philippines by the US on December 10, 1898, marked the "real beginnings of Filipino emigration,"[14] cross-border movement of Filipinos started during the Spanish colonization of the archipelago. In 1587, laborers in the Spanish galleon trade that sailed every year between Manila and Acapulco were aboard a vessel that landed in Morro Bay, California.[15] Due to harsh treatment from the Spaniards, they eventually abandoned their ship and set up communities in Barataria Bay south of New Orleans in 1763, a year after Spain gained possession of what later became the state of Louisiana.[16] The bayous inhabited by these "Manilamen" in Louisiana are believed to be the oldest continuously settled Filipino community in the US.[17]

But Spain, being *La Madre Patria* (The mother country), was the destination of Filipinos who would play a pivotal role in the establishment of an independent Philippine nation. In the late nineteenth century, reforms within the colonial system prompted the migration of three groups to Spain:

suspected *filibusteros*[18] who had been expelled to the Marianas because of their involvement in the Cavite mutiny of 1872, an uprising of about two hundred soldiers, laborers, and residents at the Spanish arsenal in Fort San Felipe, Cavite; young men who voluntarily banished themselves to escape persecution; and students who traveled to Europe to further the education that they had begun at universities in the colony.[19] All three groups belonged to either the *principalía* nobility that ruled the towns and municipalities or *ilustrados* (erudite or enlightened ones) from the educated middle class and comprised mostly of Spanish Filipinos and mestizos.[20] In Spain, they banded together to form associations and to establish a mouthpiece to project their demands for reforms, *La Solidaridad* (The Solidarity) and the Propaganda Movement, whose historical imprint will find expression in the anti-dictatorship movement discussed in chapter 3.

After its defeat in the Spanish-American War, the Spanish Empire ceded the Philippines to the US in the Treaty of Paris, ushering in the American colonization of the country. To develop an American-style democracy in the archipelago, the colonial government gave priority to education and established the public school system, with English as the medium of instruction.[21] Through this structure, Americans pursued the policy of "benevolent assimilation"—to train Filipinos in democratic governance until they were "ready" to govern themselves.[22] This enabled young Filipinos to possess a sense of familiarity with American life and an imagination of the US as a home to which they had never been.[23] Political and economic developments connected to US expansionism opened the doors to the arrival of Filipinos in the US. Although they arrived with American passports because of the Philippines' status as a colony, they were ineligible for citizenship and were legally barred from voting, establishing a business, holding private and public office, and owning land and other property.[24]

In 1903, Governor General of the Philippines William H. Taft passed the Pensionado Act, allowing qualified Filipino students—mostly from the elite in Philippine society—to obtain their college, graduate, and professional degrees in the US at the expense of the colonial government, so they could later govern the Philippines in American fashion. Between 1903 and 1907, about two hundred students—nearly all men—were studying law, medicine, and politics. Upon graduation, most returned to the Philippines and became legislators and ministers under the administration of Manuel Luis Quezon, the first president of the Commonwealth of the Philippines.[25] News of their success spread and fueled immigration by many self-supporting students. However, a lot of them were unable to complete their studies, forcing them to join the ranks of agricultural laborers and low-skilled workers.[26]

ROOTS AND ROUTES

In 1906, the US government also began formal recruitment of Filipinos as stewards of naval installations of the US armed forces and as agricultural laborers to work on plantations in Hawai'i and the mainland's West Coast. The Hawai'i Sugar Planters Association facilitated intensive labor recruitment in the Philippines, following the enactment of the Gentlemen's Agreement of 1908, which curtailed Japanese immigration and created a labor shortage. Most of the Filipinos hired—called *sakadas*—were unmarried young men from rural villages in the Ilocos region,[27] with little to no formal education. Between 1907 and 1919, over twenty-four thousand Filipinos went to Hawai'i, and by 1922, they constituted the largest ethnic group (41 percent) in the plantation workforce.[28] The US military bases in the Philippines also served as recruiting stations for the navy and, thus, became another gateway to the US for many young men. Since Filipinos were the only foreigners who were allowed in the US Armed Forces, the navy enlisted them primarily as stewards and mess boys—positions previously assigned to African Americans.[29] Starting with nine Filipinos in the navy in 1903, the number grew to around six thousand by World War I and approximately twenty-five thousand by 1930.[30]

American colonial policy granted the status of "US national" to Filipinos, which allowed them freedom of movement within the territorial jurisdiction of the US.[31] In 1924, demand for Filipino labor in Hawai'i decreased. After the passage of the Immigration Act in the same year, which excluded entry of certain Asian and other groups into the US, Filipinos, who initially worked at the plantations in Hawai'i, began to arrive in significant numbers on the West Coast. Unlike the *sakadas* in Hawai'i who were rooted in one plantation, the Filipinos on the mainland were seasonal workers. They traveled the West Coast for most of the year—in the spring and summer, some worked in the salmon canneries of Alaska and Puget Sound in Washington, while others harvested asparagus and lettuce in Salinas Valley in Northern California; in the fall, they picked apples in Yakima Valley, also in Washington; and during the winter, they moved to Los Angeles, Portland, San Francisco, and Seattle to work at hotels and restaurants as bellmen, cooks, dishwashers, and janitors.[32] During World War I, shipbuilders in San Francisco and Philadelphia also hired Filipino carpenters, machinists, and coppersmiths.[33] But in 1934, the US Congress passed the Tydings-McDuffie Act, which initiated a ten-year transition period toward full Philippine independence.[34] The legislation reduced the quota of Filipino immigrants to fifty persons per year, ending the large-scale migration of Filipinos to the US.

Despite formal independence from American rule in 1946, Filipinos continued to arrive in the US. By 1946, the US government had extended the rights of naturalization and full immigration to Filipinos, as a reward for their "good behavior" during the war and the delayed independence given to the Philippines.[35] Congress also passed the Luce-Celler Bill, which increased the annual Philippine quota from fifty to one hundred.[36] Post–World War II ushered in the "second wave," which included war veterans, who were conscripted to provide workers for the US mobilization efforts against the Axis Powers. The US government promised automatic citizenship to Filipino war veterans, and between 1946 and 1965, about thirty-four thousand Filipinos entered the US.[37] With the War Brides Act of 1946 in effect, almost half comprised the wives of American servicemen, including Filipino Americans, who had served in the Philippines during the war. The postwar immigration, thus, reduced the skewed gender ratios of the first half of the century. In 1940, the census only counted 5,327 married Filipinos; this figure increased to 17,616 in 1950.[38]

The granting of independence to the Philippines officially ended the active recruitment of Filipino nationals to the US Navy. However, a provision in the 1947 Military Bases Agreement allowed the navy to continue with the practice. The onset of the Korean War in the early 1950s facilitated the enrollment of up to two thousand Filipinos per calendar year for four to six years in the US Navy.[39] These recruits eventually gained American citizenship after continuous service and, along with their wives and children, would join the Filipino World War II veterans in the US. Home to the largest base of the navy, San Diego has been a prominent area of settlement for many Filipino men and their families. The dominance of the navy influenced the formation of ethnic infrastructures—the first Filipino organization in San Diego was the Fleet Reserve Association, and the first community center was the Filipino American Veterans Hall.[40]

The Filipinos who arrived after World War II did not settle in the rural areas and Chinatowns where the early Filipino migrants established their community. Instead, as better housing became available, they set up home in suburban neighborhoods where other minority families already lived.[41] Due to favorable structural and institutional conditions, this group of Filipino immigrants lived modestly but comfortably compared to the Filipino workers of the previous wave. They possessed US citizenship, families, government jobs, and military benefits that assured stability as they assimilated into American society. Like the early Filipino migrants, they also forged national consciousness. The war effort facilitated the emergence of a pro-US and pro-Philippine nationalism that transcended the ethnolinguistic solidarity and regionalism of the first wave, a nationalism that incorporated loyalty and gratitude to the American "liberators."[42]

American colonization laid the foundation for the development of the Philippines as the world's main suppliers of peripatetic workers, as it built the infrastructure of training and professional development that equipped them with the skills to be readily employed in the US and in other parts of the world. In 1899, the colonial government created the Philippine Nautical School, which developed a maritime education with full English instruction and in line with international standards.[43] In 1948, the US Congress passed the Information and Exchange Act, authorizing the State Department to establish the Exchange Visitor Program (EVP). In the context of the brewing Cold War, the EVP intended to educate professionals from other countries about American democracy and then to return them to their homelands.[44] Through the EVP, the US government authorized Filipino nursing graduates to combine postgraduate study with practical experience in American hospitals, with the condition that they go back to the Philippines to improve the health-care system.[45] Although the Philippines was not the sole participant in the EVP, Filipino nurses dominated the program with over eleven thousand of them between 1956 and 1969, and because of a post–World War II nursing shortage in the US, especially in public hospitals, they were able to obtain permanent residency and remain in the country as employees.[46]

The training of Filipino nurses based on American standards made them desirable workers to other countries. After World War II, the Netherlands had a shortage of hospital staff. When Princess Beatrix visited the Philippines in 1962, she noted the large number of English-speaking nurses. With the princess's recommendation, the Netherlands pursued an agreement with the Philippines to import Filipino nurses and employ them in Dutch hospitals for three years, with the condition that they return to their country after fulfillment of their contracts. Facilitated by Wilhelmina Gasthuis in Amsterdam, small groups arrived in 1964 to work in Leiden, Rotterdam, and Utrecht. From 1968 to 1969, sixty nurses—thirty arriving each year—were in Amsterdam, Eindhoven, Bussum, and Heerenveen, while one hundred were in Apeldoorn in 1976.[47] Most of the nurses, however, regarded their entrance in the Dutch labor market as a first step toward permanent immigration to Canada, the United Kingdom, and the US, especially since the tasks they performed in Dutch hospitals were confined to housekeeping.[48] Eventually, they asked to be released from their contracts and left for other countries. To replace the nurses, the hospitals changed their recruitment targets to midwives.

Proficiency in English also facilitated the recruitment of Filipino factory workers to the Netherlands through the Dutch Catholic organization in Manila, the Social Communication Center. Coming in batches of ten in 1966, sixty-two women were assigned to work as seamstresses for three years at the Berghaus textile factories in Amsterdam, Gendringen, Ulft, and Wehl. Each arriving group had a designated social worker, who was also Filipino.

Berghaus provided food and lodging, the cost of which was subtracted from their salary. After these deductions and forced savings, they received twenty-five Dutch guilders a week.[49] Many of the workers—referred to as "Berghaus girls"—were young college graduates from different parts of the Philippines. Until the mid-1970s, Berghaus employed more than seven hundred Filipinas in groups of sixty to work in the factories in Ulft and Amsterdam, where a few Filipinas were given office jobs in the latter location.[50] While working at the factories, they were not obliged to learn Dutch; rather, they gave English language lessons to their Dutch colleagues.

In sum, American colonization of the Philippines produced four conditions that would shape the process of creating a diaspora through contention. One is the creation of an elite class of politicians and bureaucrats that would eventually rule the archipelago through patrimonialism, clientelism, and US sponsorship, of which Marcos would take advantage in his pursuit of power. Another is the migration of workers whose collective experience of exclusion based on legal status and race would lead to the formation of movements demanding rights as minorities in the US, as will be discussed in chapter 4. The third is the crystallization of Filipino patriotism and nationalism that incorporates gratitude and loyalty to Americans. And finally, the American Empire, through education, positioned the Philippines to be a country that could produce a global and mobile labor force, with the advantage of English language training and American-accredited technical skills that would allow them to seek employment anywhere and compete with other nationalities. In short, colonialism laid the foundations for diaspora construction by setting up the means and routes for political entrepreneurs to cross borders, mobilize, and forge collective identities.

Neoliberalism and the Global Dispersion of Filipinos

While colonization initially stimulated Filipino migration in large numbers, it was only to one destination—the United States. The scattering of Filipinos that characterize diasporas occurred only after Philippine president Ferdinand Marcos issued Presidential Decree 442, creating the Labor Code of 1974 and officially instituting the overseas employment program to address the country's rising unemployment and to take advantage of the opportunities created by the oil boom in the Middle East in the 1970s.[51] The executive order shifted the locus of international migration from the US to new destinations around the world, such as Asia, Europe, and the Middle East. It also changed the sociodemographic composition of overseas Filipinos, with male, semi-skilled, contract-based workers—bound for the Arabian Peninsula to look for employment in infrastructure and development projects—dominating the early stream of temporary migrants. After Marcos was overthrown through the People Power Revolution of 1986, Corazon Aquino not only continued but intensified the dictator's labor export policy as part of her espousal of neoliberalism, which during her government, gained ideological ascendancy.[52]

Neoliberalism, as an ideology and mode of governance that favors free markets and a limited state role in the economy, is implemented by governments through a policy package that includes deregulation, privatization of public enterprises, promotion of foreign direct investments, trade liberalization, and a reduction in social welfare.[53] In short, maximum economic growth is achieved when the market is not constrained by state protections. In the Philippines, neoliberalism first came in the 1980s in the form of a structural adjustment program imposed by the International Monetary Fund/World Bank (IMF/WB) to strengthen the economy's capacity to service its massive external debt.[54] Since then and with each administration's doctrinaire neoliberal approach, the Philippines has experienced worsening economic crises, due to its underdeveloped agriculture and manufacturing industries being unable to compete in the global market, resulting in massive growth in unemployment in both rural and urban areas.[55] Combined with a reduction in public services and welfare, poverty became widespread. For instance, in the capital, Manila, where people in the countryside often end up searching for their livelihoods in the informal economy, the commodification of socialized housing for real estate profits has further displaced the marginalized population.[56]

Thus, migration not only became an official policy solution to temper the impact of the crises through remittance inflows but also a coping strategy—an accepted way of life—for ordinary Filipinos to overcome day-to-day hardships brought by state failure, with family members abroad serving as social safety nets that the government is unable to provide. In 2017, the Philippine Overseas Employment Agency (POEA) estimated about 2.2. million Filipinos have increasingly taken up short-term, contract-based employment in the Middle East and Asia, with the largest share in Saudi Arabia, the United Arab Emirates, Singapore, and Hong Kong.[57] The Philippines is also the world's largest source of seafarers, with an estimated seven hundred thousand deployed to domestic and foreign-flagged vessels and contributing US$6.5 billion in remittances.[58] Known as OFWs, this group of temporary migrants differs from their counterparts in North America, Western Europe, and Oceania in that they are rarely permitted to bring their families and have limited to no prospects of becoming permanent residents or naturalizing even if they have spent years in these countries.

Paradoxically, while neoliberalism reduces the role of the state to the minimum in the provision of goods and services, income redistribution, and active stabilization of the economy, it assumes an ascendant position in the administration of its citizens' cross-border movement to address the problems created by the implementation of neoliberal orthodoxy. Fiona B. Adamson and Gerasimos Tsourapas consider the Philippines as "the emblematic country that has used emigration as an explicit developmental strategy."[59] The state pursues this through labor brokerage, wherein it marshals a transnational bureaucracy to promote Filipino workers abroad, negotiate with labor-importing countries, and equip migrants with the necessary training and official documents for their overseas employment.[60] The Philippine state has rationalized the export of migrants to ensure efficiency, predictability, and control throughout the process. A network of agencies is engaged in identifying global labor market trends; establishing education infrastructure to respond to labor shortages abroad; marketing Philippine workers based on gendered and racialized qualities; negotiating agreements with host-country governments; training laborers to comply with specific skill requirements attached to different visa categories; and processing documents to legally authorize Filipinos' overseas employment and departure from the country.[61] By performing these functions, state bodies not only sanction and hasten the process of migration; they also serve as a mechanism for disciplining workers.[62] In her study of Filipino domestic workers in the Arab states, migration and gender scholar Rhacel Salazar Parreñas explains that the Philippine state, through its transnational bureaucracy, exercises Foucauldian biopower and pastoral power simultaneously, enacting nonpunitive disciplinary governance "to create a migrant population that is docile and subservient but also equipped with knowledge about labor rights and thus, in essence, empowered."[63]

Neoliberalism as a hegemonic paradigm has not only affected developing and migrant-sending countries like the Philippines. It has also transformed developed and migrant-receiving countries such as the US and the Netherlands. For instance, welfare state restructuring has led to a decline in social spending to help families—especially women—with social reproduction, opening the way for market-based solutions such as privatized care for children and the elderly and low-wage household services.[64] The result is reliance on women immigrant caregivers and domestic workers from the developing world, resulting in an international division of care work.[65] In addition, transnational corporations that dominate deregulated industries often outsource jobs to countries with cheaper labor or bring in lower-paid foreign workers. The state establishes guest worker programs and visa regimes that allow employers to hire migrants at substandard wages and living conditions compared to the native-born population. Examples in the US are the H-2A and H-2B programs, for temporary agricultural and nonagricultural work, respectively.

The interaction of the effects of neoliberal policies in migrant-receiving and migrant-sending countries can be seen in the movement of Filipinos to the Netherlands from the 1970s and to some extent to the US after the enactment of the Immigration and Nationality Act of 1965. But even though Philippine migration to the Netherlands started with contractual labor arrangements, the country never became a prominent site for deployment of Filipino workers compared to Asia and the Middle East. When an economic recession hit the Netherlands in the 1970s, prompting the government to discontinue the recruitment of foreign medical and factory workers and to tighten migration policies, migrants were left without protection. For example, in early 1973, approximately three hundred Filipino women were working at Berghaus.[66] When their employers ended their contracts in February 1974, most of them stayed in the Netherlands through marriage with a Dutch citizen, while around sixty acquired work permits to Canada and the US. Only a few returned to the Philippines due to the absence of job opportunities.[67]

Since the 1980s, the au pair arrangement then became a popular way for Filipinas to enter and work in the Netherlands legally. Middle- and upper-class Dutch families began to turn to the au pair program as solution to the poor institutional development of child care, in light of the increased participation of Dutch women in the labor force.[68] Unlike the midwives, nurses, and seamstresses of the previous waves whose tasks were clearly stated in their contracts, Filipino au pairs were "employed" by families through a vague cultural exchange program and, thus, were vulnerable to abuse and exploitation.[69] In 1994, the Dutch newspaper *NRC Handelsblad* reported that Filipina au pairs worked fifty to sixty hours a week, with an allowance of 600 guilders a month, and received no social security contributions from their employers. A Dutch domestic worker who works forty hours a week, on average, would cost 4,000 guilders per month, with high social premiums.[70]

Filipinos also entered the Netherlands as seafarers. The country is one of the major commercial shipping flag states in the world and home to the largest port in Europe, located in Rotterdam. When industry crises hit foreign shipping firms in the 1970s, they were forced to seek cheaper workers and were attracted to Filipinos due to their English language training and American certifications.[71] To further take advantage of the labor market, the Philippine state and recruitment agencies differentiated Filipinos from their competitors by depicting the former as possessing "natural" qualities that make them ideal docile workers.[72] In the 1980s, an estimated three thousand Filipino seamen and three hundred officers worked on board ships owned by Dutch companies or on Norwegian, German, and other European ships that pass through Rotterdam each day.[73] To guarantee a regular supply of crew for the Dutch fleet, some employers have supported nautical schools in the Philippines.[74] Filipinos were also employed by companies involved in the development of the North Sea oil and gas deposits. The first batch of Filipino offshore labor, recruited directly from the Philippines, obtained jobs in the mining industry as oil rig workers. Both Filipino seafarers and oil rig workers lived in run-down areas in Rotterdam occupied by a mixture of ethnic minority groups, including Moroccans, Turks, and Cape Verdeans. Unable to speak Dutch, they relied only on other Filipinos for social support and friendship.[75]

Dutch development aid to the Philippines also stimulated migration flows through educational and cultural exchanges. Every year since the late 1970s, through the Netherlands Fellowship Program, an average of one hundred Filipino students and early career bureaucrats have pursued postgraduate study and professional training in the Netherlands. Dutch-Filipino pen pal clubs, conceived to learn about each other's customs and lifestyles, also gave rise to marriage migration, which intensified in the 1990s with the dawn of the internet. The same decade also saw a rise in the number of undocumented Filipino domestic workers and victims of sex trafficking.[76] By 2020, an estimated thirty thousand undocumented Filipino migrants were in the Netherlands, working informally for multiple households as cleaners and nannies and earning between ten and fifteen euros per hour.[77] Marisha Maas characterizes the present-day Filipino population in the Netherlands as "the product of demand-driven and regulated migration, changing migration regimes, and the creativity of established immigrants to get around the entrance regulations."[78]

Unfortunately, complete and reliable figures on Filipinos in the country do not exist. Until the mid-1990s, the Dutch census subsumed Filipinos under the "Asian nationalities" category due to their small number.[79] As a result, the Dutch government did not afford them minority status. Filipinos were not considered a specific target of the Dutch *allochtonenbeleid* (policy on the entrance and integration of foreigners) and were subject only to general policies toward immigrants. When the census finally counted them as a separate category in 1996, there were 7,736 Filipino nationals, most of them women, concentrated in three Randstad provinces—Amsterdam, The Hague, and Rotterdam.[80]

Across the Atlantic, US president Lyndon Johnson signed the Hart-Celler Act into law in 1965, which abolished the national origins quota system and gave rise to two distinct chains of migration: one based on family reunification and the other on meeting the labor needs of the US economy. Foreign professionals and skilled workers filled the labor shortages that accompanied the postwar economic boom in the US, as global capitalist restructuring shifted production and manufacturing to developing countries and concentrated financial and service industries in the developed world. The immigration of Filipinos to the US after 1965 was due to "a combination of factors stemming from family obligations, colonial history, economic conditions, images fostered by the media, and an overall quest for prosperity."[81] Five years after the immigration law took effect in 1968, the US granted entry to more than 7,300 Filipino accountants, doctors, engineers, nurses, scientists, and teachers under the third preference category, labeled "professionals of exceptional ability."[82] Unlike the first and second waves, the post-1965 immigrant community came from the urban middle class in the Philippines, who were largely influenced by American consumerist and individualist values.[83] But like the second wave, women dominated the Filipino immigrant population.

Because of the family-reunification provisions of the act, family members of Filipinos who had arrived in the US before 1965 joined these white-collar workers.[84] Between 1976 and 1988, when the implementation of the act was at its peak, family members outpaced the professionals, because the entry requirements tightened for skilled workers while the proportion of family-reunification preference immigrants rose to about 80 percent (table 2.1). As a result, more than 221,000 Filipinos immigrated to the US in 1981–85, compared to fewer than sixteen thousand in 1961–65.[85] The Filipino American community exhibited more class diversity than it had in the past.

Because the destination of professional immigrants depended on employer sponsorship rather than on the presence of preexisting communities, they tended to be more dispersed throughout the US compared to agricultural and low-skilled laborers.[86] Health-care workers such as nurses, physicians, and doctors were recruited to replenish the shortage of medical personnel in older metropolitan areas in the Northeast—such as Washington, DC, New York, and New Jersey—and in the Midwest, mostly in Illinois. Outside of occupational immigration, kinship and social networks, rather than availability of work, influenced geographic settlement.[87] Agricultural and low-skilled laborers could prioritize family reunification when choosing where to live, and they revitalized the established Filipino communities in California, Hawai'i, and Washington.[88]

TABLE 2.1. Total number and percentage of occupational preference and family-preference immigrants from the Philippines from 1966 to 1985

	Occupational preference immigrants	Family-preference immigrants
1966–70	30,350 (49.5%)	31,090 (50.4%)
1971–75	49,606 (51.5%)	46,610 (48.4%)
1976–80	19,035 (19.3%)	78,605 (79.8%)
1981–85	18,470 (19.0%)	78,431 (80.9%)

Source: Cariño et al. 1990.

But Filipinos who migrated to the US through the occupational chain had minimal ties to their pre-1965 compatriots. Settling in suburban neighborhoods such as Glendale, Cerritos, Long Beach, and West Covina in Southern California, they tended to form their own communities and organizations, which catered primarily to their class interests and needs.[89] In San Francisco, they avoided or were unaware of "Manilatown," where the International Hotel was located and where the elderly bachelors of the first wave spent the remainder of their lives.[90] Class cleavages surfaced even among the third wave of Filipino immigrants. The lives of the middle-class professionals from the occupational chain hardly intersected with those who came through family sponsorship. The former often resided in affluent, predominantly white neighborhoods, while the latter shared apartments in working-class communities with relatives who came to the US before 1965 as semiskilled laborers.[91]

In sum, whereas colonialism in the Philippines in the early twentieth century prompted the relocation of mostly low-skilled Filipino workers and war veterans to a single prime destination, the US metropole, neoliberalism has resulted in the Philippine state orchestrating overseas employment for Filipinos in new countries of destination in Asia, the Middle East, and Western Europe, heralding a process of dispersion typical of diasporas. Migrant-receiving countries such as the US and the Netherlands have also encouraged the movement of workers to address labor scarcity and to take advantage of low wages for foreigners and new immigrants. The consequence of these developments is the growth of an overseas Filipino population divided based on legal status, social class, gender, age, geographic area, and immigrant generation—factors that shape their social networks, political practices, and ideas about membership in the Philippine nation-state.

State Construction of the Filipino Diaspora

With the global dispersion of Filipinos, the Philippine state has an interest in the political project of diaspora formation. First off, Filipino migration in the context of neoliberalism reflects state failure. Through its labor export policy, "the state literally *made* a 'new diaspora'" while maintaining ties with permanent settlers in countries of emigration, to which we typically associate diasporas.[92] Incorporating its citizens by developing policies and embracing the language of diaspora to recognize their contribution to the nation allows the state to jettison responsibility for its adoption of pernicious economic programs that pushed its citizens to go abroad, to ensure the continuous flow of remittances, which accounts for 7.3 percent of gross national income,[93] and to give overseas Filipinos a sense of agency and voice in the country's economic trajectories—that is, endow them the role of a development actor. Second, with many Filipinos integrating economically and politically in the old country of settlement (the US), thereby constituting an important social base for mobilization, governments in power have sought their material and symbolic support to legitimize their regimes. Various administrations have implemented three diaspora-making strategies aimed at constituting overseas Filipinos as political actors and subjects: encouraging homeland tourism, labeling migrants as national heroes, and creating institutions to support the rights and welfare of OFWs as well as laws that "thickened migrant membership" in the Philippine nation-state.[94] These efforts pivoted on the cultivation of affective bonds to the territorial homeland and commitment to nation building.

Sociologist Shaul Kelner argues that homeland tourism is a powerful means for states to territorially root their transnational migrant communities, having the ability to offer participants "a locus for meditation on the meanings of diasporic identities."[95] States bring migrants and the succeeding generations back to the homeland for them to develop affective ties to the land and its people—essentially, to become diasporic.[96] Soon after declaring martial law, Marcos launched the *Balikbayan* Program of 1973 to invite Filipino emigrants to visit the Philippines for the holidays—from September 1, 1973, to February 28, 1974—with promises of reduced airfares, expedited visas, and tax breaks. *Balikbayan*, literally homecoming, is based on two Tagalog words: *balik* (return) and *bayan* (town or country). Thus, the program frames the act of spending Christmas season in the Philippines—a cultural tradition of such importance to Filipinos that celebration starts on September 1 and ends on Epiphany/Three Kings Day (January 6) or the Feast of the Black Nazarene[97] (January 9)—as an affirmation of one's continued membership to the nation. As Cristina Szanton Blanc argues, "being a *balikbayan* carries a special nostalgia for the home country, a sense of belonging, of still being acknowledged by the Philippine nation-state."[98]

But Marcos's main goal was to recuperate the image of his administration among Filipinos in North America, where many of his opponents were exiled to and a burgeoning movement against his dictatorship was located. He countered the critics' claims of not being able to go home again due to the chaos that his dictatorship had created.[99] By showcasing the advantages and outcomes of his regime's ideology of *Bagong Lipunan*, or "New Society," Marcos expected to earn the endorsement of Filipinos in Canada and the US, which could reverberate internationally given their diaspora positionality, which political scientist Maria Koinova refers to as "the power which diaspora political agents are perceived to amass from their sociospatial position in a specific context and linkages to other global contexts";[100] in other words, their global position could be an asset for the state. With a lot at stake, Marcos gave the program an initial budget of US$300,000 and mobilized state agencies at the local and national levels as well as consulates and embassies abroad.[101] Lina Richter describes the impressive coordination put into the program.

> Hundreds of thousands of copies of an "Invitation to a Traditional Philippine Christmas" were sent abroad to overseas Filipinos. School children were also given assignments to personally invite relatives to come home for Christmas. Local governments were charged with developing local festivities and welcoming committees. Immigration, tax, customs officials were instructed to exempt balikbayans from most requirements. Building upon the closeness of Philippines ties and the longest Christmas season in the world, the Department of Tourism constructed a tourist package for balikbayans that promised a 50 percent discount on air fare as well as concessional rates on accommodations and shopping.[102]

The program was a huge success, since it helped improve public opinion about the Marcos regime in the US, with "favorable comments on the cleanliness, beauty, and order" in the international and local press.[103] Because of this, the government developed "other specialized homecoming programs geared to influential expatriate groups."[104] As the flow of *balikbayans* continued, Marcos renewed the program every year, but the definition of *balikbayan* changed over time, limiting it, starting on March 1, 1980, to citizens or permanent residents of other countries and their families and descendants, while exempting Filipinos who worked for international organizations such as the UN and the World Bank.[105] The program was institutionalized as Republic Act 6768 in

1989 under the administration of Corazon Aquino, heralding the onset of an economy based on homeland tourism and migrant return that has shaped the urban development of Manila.[106] With a growing population of OFWs, the law expanded the term *balikbayan* to "a Filipino citizen who has been continuously out of the Philippines for a period of at least one (1) year, a Filipino overseas worker, or a former Filipino citizen and his family, as this term is defined hereunder, who had been naturalized in a foreign country and comes or returns to the Philippines."[107]

Regardless of the legal conception, *balikbayan* had entered Filipinos' everyday parlance and cultural understanding of migration, shaping the practices of migrants themselves and the repertoire of Christmas tradition in the Philippines. For instance, overseas Filipinos, especially those who cannot visit home during the holidays, send a *balikbayan* box filled with gifts and sundry items to foster intimacy and reinforce kinship ties and solidarity.[108] With the expectation of an influx of *balikbayans* arriving during the Christmas season, airport authorities in Manila, Cebu, and Davao partner with private companies to stage elaborate welcome receptions such as a Christmas choir serenading returnees and handing out *Noche Buena* (Christmas Eve) presents.[109] Crowds of family members wait for hours at the arrivals area and in parking lots, surrounded by vendors selling food and drinks to the weary *sundos* (people who pick up or fetch someone), most of whom have traveled from another province or region. The spectacle at the airports has made the holiday season almost synonymous with *balikbayan*.

Another diaspora-making strategy of the state is the discursive construction of OFWs as self-sacrificing modern-day heroes of the nation. Although Marcos's labor export policy was intended to be a temporary solution to unemployment, it has persisted to the present day. To ensure the continuous flow of OFWs, Aquino introduced ideas about nationalism that normalize out-migration and coined the term *bagong bayani* (new hero). Public consensus around the notion of migration as an expression of Filipino nationalism was not always achieved, and commentators often made distinctions between OFWs and emigrants. For some, leaving the Philippines to permanently settle in countries like the US was tantamount to a betrayal of sorts, a nonfulfillment of an obligation to contribute to the nation. Those who migrate, with no intention of return, to pursue material wealth and class fantasies in the US—such as the post-1965 Filipino immigrants to the US—were considered traitors.[110] In contrast, unable to take up residence in their host countries, Filipino labor migrants in the Middle East or Western Europe, whose lives are fraught with "loneliness, deprivation, and abuse," are the exemplary martyrs of the Philippine nation.[111]

Rooted in colonial and religious narratives, historian Vicente Rafael argues that *bagong bayani* evokes the suffering and martyrdom of José Rizal, the "first Filipino" exiled in Spain, and to Jesus Christ, both of whom were "forced to undergo humiliation at the hands of alien forces."[112] By using *bagong bayani* in their documents and programs, state institutions such as the CFO, the POEA, and the Overseas Workers Welfare Administration reinforce these cultural understandings of sacrifice for the family and the nation, often naturalized as innate Filipino traits and as a source of national pride.[113] As the principal architect of labor migration, the state invokes and politicizes role and social identities in official discourses, defining a worker, a father, or a Filipino based on their ability to contribute to the national development of the country, thus fusing culture, economy, and identity. In 1984, the POEA even launched the Bagong Bayani Awards "to recognize and pay tribute to our OFWs for their significant efforts in fostering goodwill among peoples of the world, enhancing and promoting the image of the Filipino as a competent, responsible and dignified worker, and for greatly contributing to the socioeconomic development of their communities and our country as a whole."[114] Thus, not only are OFWs valorized as heroes, they are also expected to be ideal representatives of the nation abroad.[115]

Like *balikabayan*, *bagong bayani* has entered the lexicon of ordinary Filipinos, as even businesses that target the vast market of OFWs and their families, as well as civil society groups and mainstream media critical of labor export, have all embraced the rhetoric of migrant heroism.[116] Some scholars have even compared Flor Contemplacion, the Filipina domestic worker executed in Singapore for the murder of another Filipina in 1995, to the martyred José Rizal, as observed by historian Filomeno V. Aguilar Jr. at academic conferences.[117] And with the proliferation of films that portray the daily ordeal of OFWs—dealing with workplace abuse and undocumented status in their countries of destination as well as maintaining close relationships with those left behind in the Philippines—poignantly captured in *Anak* (2008, Hong Kong), *Milan* (2004, Italy), *Caregiver* (2008, London), and *Maid in London* (2018, London), *bagong bayani* has entered the zeitgeist in Philippine cinema. Migrants themselves have consented to this state construction, although they are selective in their appropriation of the discourse. For instance, among seafarers, they espouse *bagong bayani* "to boost their image as exemplars of masculinity" through their personal sacrifice and financial contributions to their families and promote the image of "the 'heroic' seafarer—as seasoned adventurer, as sexually experienced, as provider and patron, as father and husband."[118] All these point to the cultural hegemony of *bagong bayani*, along with *balikbayan*, in Filipinos' meaning making of contemporary migration.

Finally, to guarantee that overseas Filipinos remain attached to the Philippine nation despite being located outside its geographic boundaries or having taken up another citizenship, the state has reconfigured itself, expanding its territorial reach and administrative role as well as adopting laws to build a transnational political community. A global campaign initiated by Filipino migrant advocacy organizations led to the enactment in 2003 of two laws: the Citizenship Retention and Reacquisition Act, which allows Filipinos to maintain dual nationality, and the Overseas Absentee Voting Act, which recognizes their right to suffrage. Both had the symbolic effect of blurring the distinction between the "old diaspora" of permanent settlers and the "new diaspora" consisting of OFWs, although data on voter registration and turnout since 2004 show that expressions of political membership still vary between the two groups, with the "highest in other Asian countries, where Filipinos are less likely to have university training or legal status, and lowest in the United States, where they are among the most high-status immigrant groups in the country."[119] This may be due to the former having more stake in the results of the Philippine elections given their lack of opportunities to gain permanent residence and citizenship in their host societies and the precariousness of their contract-based jobs. In short, they are more likely to go back to the Philippines for good and deal with the government in power.

In response to the execution of Flor Contemplacion, which sparked mass protests among Filipinos in the Philippines and abroad and a diplomatic row between the Philippine and Singaporean governments, the state also shifted its orientation of OFWs as citizens rather than simply clients and epitomized this in the passage of the Migrant Workers and Overseas Filipinos Act of 1995 (Republic Act 8042).[120] The law created a management and governance structure that strengthens the state's role in protecting the rights and welfare of OFWs, especially domestic workers, by attending to migrant vulnerabilities. Through the regulation of migration, creation of labor standards, and education policies, the state capacitates disciplined migrants to advocate for themselves—what Parreñas refers to as "pastoral empowerment."[121] Before prospective migrant workers can exit the Philippines, they must undergo a methodical process of certification, skills verification, and training at various agencies, including a predeparture orientation seminar. A result of going through each step is the construction of a collective identity as OFWs based on their shared experiences and rights.[122] This identity is expressed in the norms of social interaction among OFWs, whereby, "regardless of class and occupational status, [they] expect to and do greet each other as *kabayan* (compatriots) on the streets."[123] In essence, by implementing rules and regulations to safeguard the rights and welfare of temporary migrants, the state is

46   CHAPTER TWO

engaged in diaspora formation by inadvertently forming a collective identity based on ethnic/national solidarity.

Building a Diaspora from Below

The invention of diasporas can also be undertaken by migrants themselves, outside the scope of influence of the state. While the state does possess control over movement and legal membership, migrants also have choices about and power over how they associate and the identities they form. Scholars have found that to help them adjust to the norms and culture in their host societies, cope with alienation and homesickness, and maintain links with the homeland, migrants develop quotidian practices, rituals, and organizations that eventually turn into transnational communities. These include hometown associations,[124] church and faith-based groups,[125] and grassroots migrant and refugee organizations,[126] which directly or indirectly become sites for forging identities. To be sure, not all transnational communities are engaged in the political project of diaspora formation. But as migrants become increasingly tethered to these communities, they begin to recognize their collective experience—that sense of "we"-ness that comes from an awareness of their social location—and create bonds of trust, loyalty, and solidarity.

Among overseas Filipinos, we see this dynamic in migrant-led publications that provide a venue for information-sharing, literary expression, and dialogue. In her study of the construction of an "imagined (global) community" among Filipina migrant domestic workers, Parreñas examines *Tinig Filipino*, a monthly fifty-page magazine published in Hong Kong and Italy and distributed to more than a dozen countries, where migrants write articles and commentaries about their social realities.[127] With the central narratives of loneliness and homesickness in topics concerning transnational family life, work difficulties, migration laws, and general challenges women face, "readers do not just imagine the conditions of fellow domestic workers in other countries but also recognize them as those very much like their own."[128] The magazine creates a transcontinental forum whereby migrants respond to each other's needs and thus serves as a venue for emotional support against their isolation as well as for the development of counterhegemonic discourses on their subjectivities. For instance, a Filipina worker in Italy posted a criticism of the Philippine government's romanticization of overseas employment through the *bagong bayani* label and called on her compatriots to convey the truth about their pain and suffering, to which readers responded in the regularly featured columns of "Life in Italy," "Life in Saudi," and "Life in Singapore." Thus, *Tinig Filipino* functions like the newspapers and books that fostered nationalism in the early modern period[129] in that through the magazine, migrants develop a common vernacular that they use to talk and spread ideas about their situations.

The formation of a shared language that delineates membership in a collective is also observed by Martin F. Manalansan IV among Filipino gay men in New York City, where they use swardspeak, a spoken lingo that combines English, Tagalog, and elements from popular culture.[130] He shows that swardspeak is constitutive of a *bakla* (gay) identity, in which its users "deploy translation as part of their attempts to claim a space for themselves as queer citizens in both the homeland and in the new place of settlement."[131] Because its lexicon and syntax change quickly, swardspeak evades being fixed in a single territory or context and thus "creates a dissident form of citizenship that refuses incarceration to a specific geographical, cultural, and linguistic space but instead enables speakers to be 'mobile' as it were by appropriating cultural and linguistic items and imbuing them with specific local meanings."[132] Through swardspeak, Filipino gay men construct a collective identity based on alternative forms of belonging, one that is not limited by the boundaries of the Philippine or American nation-states but rather rooted in constant border crossings between two cultures.

Religion offers another site for diaspora formation, where Filipino migrants frequently encounter each other, learn about their lives, and develop shared understandings about their collective experiences. For instance, at Saint Bernadette Chapel in Paris where service is conducted in Tagalog, Filipinas, especially the *sans-papiers* (undocumented migrants), regularly attend mass not only because the church is like "an extension of their country of origin, a social space that allows them to affirm their religious and linguistic identities and symbolizes their national belonging"; it also offers them access to information and help from the Samahan ng Manggagawang Pilipino (Association of Filipino Laborers), which is connected to the chaplaincy.[133] The church becomes a space for both spiritual and social nourishment, where their identities are celebrated and validated. This is also the case among Filipinas in Dubai and Doha who converted from Roman Catholicism to Islam and born-again Christianity. Faith group meetings offer an opportunity to learn the Qur'an and the Bible while at the same time, through *salu-salo* (feast) after worship, mingling with other Filipinos, enjoying Filipino dishes that they are unable to consume at their employer's residences, and speaking openly and freely in Tagalog or other Philippine languages.[134] Thus, through religion, migrants can concurrently deepen their faith and strengthen ethnic/national solidarity.

Finally, associational life arises among overseas Filipinos either through membership in formal organizations or the occupation of public spaces, both of which become means to form affective bonds with each other and the homeland but are mediated by legal and occupational status in the host societies. In her analysis of class relations in Filipino migrant communities, Naomi Hosoda points to the emergence of the *"kababayan* street community" in Dubai where "Filipinos can be found everywhere," but most especially in Karama, Deira, and Satwa.[135] The community is made up mostly of lower-class workers, often in precarious immigration status and employment, who depend on social interactions in the streets for information about jobs and cheap accommodations. High-skilled Filipino professionals such as nurses, on the other hand, rarely go to these places; rather, they encounter other Filipinos in voluntary organizations, where the "needs of nurses for middle-class identity and meaning in life meet with domestic workers' material and moral needs."[136] Thus, in *kababayan* street community, a class identity develops among Filipinos who frequent it, while in voluntary organizations, where cross-class encounters occur, a sense of solidarity stems from their shared experience as Filipinos and immigrants in Dubai.

By no means are these the only migrant practices and sites that build the Filipino diaspora from below. But they offer insights into the ways through which collective identities emerge among a group of migrants separated geographically and divided based on class, legal status, and religion but who share common experiences of loneliness and marginalization in their host societies and nostalgia for the homeland. They also show that despite the state's hegemonic role in defining and enforcing official and unwritten norms and principles of belonging to the nation, "people continue to find ways to subvert and transgress borders, despite the difficult processes of exclusion, immobility and marginalisation that may also occur."[137]

Conclusion

Migration has played a central role in the Philippine nation-building project and in its integration into the world economy from its earliest days. From the circular movement of Filipinos between the Philippines and the US in the early twentieth century to the contemporary mass exodus of temporary workers to the Arab Gulf States, Hong Kong, Italy, and Singapore, migration has become a durable structure in Philippine society, shaping Filipinos' way of life and aspirations. While colonization instigated migration flows and put in place the infrastructure that would sustain these streams, the expansive growth of the overseas Filipino population in the last five decades is an outcome of processes related to the dominance of the neoliberal ideology—the restructuring of global capital, the surrendering of the state to the market in achieving development goals, and the normalization of migration in the broader culture. The global Filipino population is spread over six continents and exhibits heterogeneity within and across countries of destination, with the lives of permanent immigrants and naturalized citizens in North America at odds with those temporary workers in the Middle East and Asia. As David Camroux remarks, "put prosaically, to say the least, the worldview, self-identity and loyalties of contract workers in Riyadh are, to say the least, rather different from a dual-national Filipino academic in California."[138]

Thus, when we speak of a Filipino diaspora, we want to recognize its heterogeneity and emphasize the process of its construction within historical contexts. The Philippine state is a dominant actor in facilitating the movement of its citizens and in recent decades in reincorporating them. The transnational bureaucracy it created to perform its labor brokerage functions and disciplinary governance is mobilized for its diaspora-making project as well. Among OFWs, loyalty to the homeland and ethnic/national solidarity are fostered prior to migration through institutionalized regulatory and training processes and the hegemonic construction of migrant subjectivities based on culturally resonant themes and narratives. State efforts to create a Filipino diaspora are also evident in the expansion of political membership through citizenship and voting laws as well as protection of human rights and social welfare of its nationals abroad.

Migrants themselves are also engaged in diaspora formation through cultural and social practices that forge collective identities, rooted in their common experience of displacement and daily struggle for survival and dignity but anchored to their attachment and belonging to the Philippine nation. Social movements would build on and target these initiatives in their struggle to overthrow the Marcos dictatorship, achieve and institutionalize migrants' rights, and forge memories across generations. But, as discussed in the introduction, collective identities are formed not only through the interaction between activists and social movement constituents. In discursive arenas, activists try to gain a standing on par with the targets of their movement. Subsequently, they adapt their strategies according to the actions of these actors. In other words, there are power dynamics in identity construction. How do migrant activists engage with elite targets—such as states and mainstream media—and make claims about their identities in public? How do they undermine hegemonic discourses that constrain how they express their loyalty to the homeland? The next chapter deals with these questions as Filipino migrants involved in the transnational movement against the authoritarian regime framed themselves as patriots and revolutionaries.

3

Patriots and Revolutionaries

Anti-Dictatorship Movement and Loyalty to the Homeland

In the fall of 1977, the Fletcher School of Law and Diplomacy at Tufts University accepted a $1.5 million grant from the family of Philippine president Ferdinand Marcos. The donation, which came with the stipulation that they establish a Ferdinand E. Marcos Chair of East Asian and Pacific Studies, was one of Marcos's image-enhancing tactics at the height of domestic and international opposition to his dictatorship. More than one thousand students and faculty members opposed the university's action. A series of demonstrations culminated on October 27 with students surrounding a car to jeer at Imelda Marcos, wife of the president and governor of Manila, during her campus visit.[1] Six months after the confrontation at Tufts, on April 13, 1978, seven members of the Anti–Martial Law Coalition (AMLC), an alliance of Filipino and solidarity organizations in the US, staged a sit-in at the Philippine consulate in San Francisco. They called for the release of 1,500 political prisoners who were arrested in the aftermath of the National Assembly elections in the Philippines. They locked their arms and legs together and sang "Bayan Ko" (My country)[2] and "Marcos Will Be Removed." The group of seven men and women, who came to be known as the AMLC Seven,[3] refused to leave the consulate and demanded to speak to the dictator on the phone. Consul Romeo Arguelles denied their request. Instead, he summoned the San Francisco Police Department to apprehend the group, which was indicted for trespassing, disturbing the peace, and resisting arrest. In a brochure the AMLC circulated to raise funds for the trial, activists juxtaposed photos of the occupation and the arrest of Philippine-born activist Walden Bello with the statement, "The AMLC's occupation of the Consulate was indeed a necessity and a very much called-for action to unite all people to help shorten the life

PATRIOTS AND REVOLUTIONARIES

of the dictatorship. We in the U.S. have a sacred obligation to stand by our people in the homeland during this critical period."[4]

Across the Pacific Ocean, Filipinos took to the streets on September 21, 1983, to mourn the death of opposition politician Benigno "Nonoy" S. Aquino Jr. and to protest the regime. Called the "National Day of Sorrow," protesters burned an American flag and effigies of Presidents Ronald Reagan and Marcos. They called Marcos "the puppet of an American cowboy." When demonstrators tried to storm the presidential palace, government forces opened fire at protesters, killing eight and wounding hundreds. In response to the chaos, Corazon Aquino, widow of the assassinated opposition leader, said to the press, "I am sure the people around Mr. Reagan are reading what's going on here and maybe they can tell him that Marcos is not the Philippines."[5]

From the early 1970s to 1986, Filipinos in the US, who were part of the transnational anti-dictatorship movement that included the AMLC and martyred leader "Nonoy" Aquino, collectively contested the symbols and identities that denoted loyalty to the Philippines. Allegiance to the homeland is a core foundation in the creation of diasporas, but how does protesting the homeland's government convey migrants' desire for continued membership in it, especially from outside its physical boundaries? Whether real or imagined, the homeland has been depicted as an authoritative source of value, identity, and loyalty.[6] Because of its central role in the nation-building project, the state has often managed to keep other sources at bay in migrants' imagination of the homeland.[7] Unlike mobilizations to defend the integrity and sovereignty of the ancestral homeland from external forces in which the conflict between "us" and "them" is obvious, struggles that oppose the government in power are often fraught with contradictions. Challenging the homeland state might feel tantamount to betrayal of their country of origin to migrants—their ancestry, culture, and history. Even if they disagree with the specific state policies or the regime in general, they may avoid taking a stand against them in public. Depending on the circumstances that led to their migration, they may also consider participation in homeland politics, especially on divisive issues, as holding back their integration into the hostland, where they must demonstrate worthiness and allegiance.[8] Finally, the homeland state might have the infrastructure to repress its overseas citizens when they protest.[9] Social movements must therefore wrestle with framing loyalty, assimilation, and collective agency in the context of suppression if they want to encourage mobilization and counter hegemonic discourses about membership and belonging to the nation.

We know that collective identity is constructed in a dynamic and social process in multiple arenas—from the microlevel, intimate sphere of the family to meso-level interactions within communities or organizations. Because elite actors such as the state and media have extensive material and ideological infrastructures, they constitute the overarching macrostructure in this relational and interactive process of identity building. Social movement actors strive to disrupt the elite's dominance and to influence the external discursive environment that limits how activists make claims and demands in public and the identities that inform these claims. Francesca Polletta and James Jasper argue that "how a group frames its identity (exclusive or inclusive, involuntary or chosen, challenging or conventional) depends on the setting and the audience to which it is speaking, the kind of opposition it confronts, and the organizational linkages it has to other groups and movements."[10] Drawing on Erving Goffman's concept of dramaturgy,[11] Mary Bernstein contends that activists engage in "identity deployment"—they express their identities as a political strategy either to transform societal beliefs and values, to change policy, or both.[12] In public claims making, activists carefully choose and emphasize elements of their identity through both the message content and the performance or repertoire of contention. The tactics they pursue become the means to articulate and stage who they are vis-à-vis those they oppose—in other words, to negotiate "the relationship and the boundaries" between us and them.[13] Finally, activists deliberate on appropriate strategies based on interaction with target authorities, bystanders and potential allies, mass media, movement adherents and supporters, and opponents.[14] These players are themselves active agents engaged in the strategic performance of identities based on the institutional context.[15] In the processes of selection and negotiation internal to the movement and demonstration for an external audience, they form a collective identity.

In this chapter, I analyze how, through the transnational anti-dictatorship movement, overseas Filipinos constructed a collective identity as patriots and revolutionaries loyal to the homeland. Movement actors did this strategically in interaction with members of the US Congress, the Marcos regime, and non-state authorities as well as conservative leaders in the Filipino communities who exercised power over formal and informal arenas of politics. In various stages of mobilization, activists confronted these opponents and their dominant discourses, often positioning themselves as the true representatives of Filipinos abroad and staging counterevents (figure 3.1). They adapted their tactics according to the historical context in which their public claims were facilitated or hindered. They framed their demands and enacted their identities differently depending on the social norms and cultural codes that governed the field of political contention.

FIGURE 3.1. The Coalition against the Marcos Dictatorship holds a press conference at the National Press Club meeting in Washington, DC, on September 16, 1982, during Marcos's first state visit to the US in sixteen years. In front of the banner that reads "Concerned Filipinos Opposed to the Marcos Dictatorship" are (*left to right*) opposition leader Benigno S. Aquino Jr., Geline Avila of the Katipunan ng Demokratikong Pilipino (KDP), human rights lawyer Romeo T. Capulong, and Raul S. Manglapus of the Movement for a Free Philippines. (Source: KDP and *Ang Katipunan*.)

In these settings, activists challenged the state as the natural reference point for migrants' homeland-oriented collective identity. Their strategies to delegitimize the Marcos government depicted the state as an entity that does not always serve the best interests of its people. In the process, they contested the idea that the state should monopolize migrants' expression of loyalty to the homeland. In doing this, they offered an opportunity for a different imagining of national membership to flourish—one that disentangled the state (through the existing regime) from the nation (the Filipino people). This chapter, therefore, shows how migrants, in contesting the legitimacy of the regime, reconstructed patriotism and loyalty to the homeland from below.

Exiles against the Colonial State

To understand how the anti-dictatorship movement disengaged the state from the nation, I look to the Filipino émigrés in Europe during the Spanish colonial period. These elites founded the Propaganda Movement, which initially called for integrating the Philippines into Spain as a province. As they developed national culture and consciousness and simultaneously forged solidarity with other colonized nations, they realized that the Spanish state could and should not represent the Filipino people. The strategies and outcomes of the Propaganda Movement inspired and offered a blueprint for the transnational activism against the dictatorship of Marcos, a continuation of the nation-building project in which Filipinos living overseas have long had an essential role. In essence, shaping Filipino migrants' struggles against the state, colonization and the resistance against it gave rise to what Patrick G. Coy, Lynn M. Woehrle, and Gregory M. Maney refer to as "discursive legacies"—the "well-established, repetitive, restrictive, and culturally recognized ways of talking and writing about a particular issue over time."[16]

Spain had two main goals in its colonization of the Philippines from 1565 to 1898: to use the country as a hub for trade and other commercial activities in Asia, and to spread Catholicism.[17] The Spaniards governed the country through the friars, who set up primary schools and introduced formal education across the archipelago. Eventually, they founded colleges and universities, which allowed a small but significant part of the Filipino population to pursue higher education.[18] With the opening of the Philippines to international trade, the economy grew, and several elite families prospered. The simultaneous processes of expanding education and establishing commercial relations facilitated the sojourn of Filipino *ilustrados* (erudite or enlightened ones) to Europe, stimulating the "beginnings of a consciously articulated nationalism."[19]

Led by José Rizal, Marcelo del Pilar, and Mariano Ponce, the Filipinos in Europe formed the Propaganda Movement in 1872, which attracted émigrés and students influenced by Enlightenment thought, liberalism, and anticlericalism. They were also disillusioned with the Spanish Empire, since they saw social decay and political bankruptcy in Spain. Despite their disenchantment, the Propagandists wanted assimilation. They advocated for the Spanish government to apply the laws and rights of the metropole to the colony, and for the full recognition of Filipinos as citizens. Two strategies became prominent. One was to search for a culture from which a Filipino nation could spring and grow. The Propagandists traveled all over Europe and began to compare the achievements of other countries to Spain's defects and failures. They pondered the possibility of forging a nation for and by Filipinos.[20] Pre-Hispanic Philippines was their point of departure for the quest to understand themselves as people. As John N. Schumacher argues, "the search for the Filipino past was both a product of, and a stimulus to, nationalism."[21]

The publication of Rizal's *Noli Me Tangere* in 1887 was the pinnacle of this quest for a national culture. The novel represented a significant rupture from the early assimilationist stance of the Propagandists, and articulated Rizal's ambivalence toward Spain. Until then, Rizal had vehemently disapproved of the friars that governed the Philippines, but he had not expressed opposition to Spain.[22] In *Noli*, however, Rizal attacked the mother country. The novel became political propaganda against the Spanish Empire and the "charter of nationalism" that rallied the Filipino to "recover his self-confidence, to appreciate his own worth, to return to the heritage of his ancestors, to assert himself as the equal of the Spaniard."[23] Like the colonized intellectual in Frantz Fanon's *The Wretched of the Earth* who fights to disprove the "colonialist theory of precolonial barbarism,"[24] the Propagandists subverted the Spaniards' racialized construction of Filipino *indios*,[25] stripped of the ability to run their own government. At this moment, the idea of a Filipino people separate from the Spanish state became explicit.

Another strategy of the Propagandists was to forge international solidarity among colonized people to expose the Spanish state's ineptitude in governing the Philippines and thus to validate Filipinos' struggle for a nation of their own. The newspaper *La Solidaridad*, published in Barcelona, was the principal instrument for Filipinos to exchange ideas and build cross-border support with other anticolonial movements. To denounce the Spanish government in the Philippines as an incompetent ruler, *La Solidaridad* "engaged in comparative scholarship by publishing reports on German Africa, British Malaya, French Indochina, and the Dutch Indies."[26] In the process, the Propagandists created doubts among Spaniards in the metropole on the friars' ability to preside over the colony. Literature also assumed a central role in promoting anticolonial internationalism, particularly among Cuban and Filipino revolutionaries. In addition to José Rizal's *Noli Me Tangere*, they drew on the works of Cuban writer and national hero José Martí to create "a collective consciousness of resistance that would juxtapose colonized people in the Caribbean and Southeast Asia."[27]

In their anticolonial struggle, the Filipino Propagandists combined the creation of a national culture from the ground up through arts and literature and the building of international solidarity by communicating common critiques of colonial rule. In these actions and the discourses that undergirded them, they extricated the construction of the nation from loyalty to the state. The transnational movement against the Marcos dictatorship built upon and adopted the strategies of the Propagandists. While the Filipino exiles in Europe in the nineteenth century confronted a colonial state through the leadership of corrupt and abusive friars, the Filipino migrants in the US and the Netherlands fought a state beholden to Filipino and American elite interests through the regime of Marcos. In both periods, activism centered on the delegitimization of the government in power, which permitted other forms of homeland-oriented collective identities to emerge.

The Marcos Dictatorship and Its Pursuit of "National Interest"

Marcos came to power in 1965 and inherited a national economy that was one of the largest in Asia due to rapid industrialization in the Asia-Pacific region.[28] Against the backdrop of the enlargement of the Vietnam War, the US championed the election of Marcos—a staunch anticommunist—to the presidency and provided him the financial and military assistance to advance his rule for twenty-one years. In exchange, he guaranteed the United States continued use of the military bases in the Philippines—particularly Clark Air Base and Subic Bay Naval Base—for the war. During his presidency, to project the strength of his administration and vision for the country, Marcos pursued extensive infrastructure development using loans from the IMF/WB. He also made substantial progress in his programs on agricultural production and land reform. His accomplishments made him popular with his constituents, who considered Marcos to be pursuing an agenda that strengthened national interest. These material achievements and the concomitant perception of his administration's success allowed him to be reelected in 1969, making him the first Philippine president to serve a second term. By this time, Marcos had cemented his position as the champion of US foreign policy in the region, or as US president Lyndon B. Johnson called him, "my right arm in Asia."[29] Amid allegations of massive electoral fraud, he was proclaimed Philippine president on November 11, 1969, with US vice president Spiro Agnew attending Marcos's inauguration in Manila and thus signaling Washington's full support of his presidency.

Due to debt-driven industrialization that Marcos pursued in his first term and his use of close to $50 million in public funds to finance his campaign,[30] a balance-of-payment crisis occurred immediately upon his reelection, and the subsequent IMF/WB-prescribed structural adjustment program to address the situation exacerbated unemployment, which led to social unrest.[31] From Marcos's State of the Nation Address in January 1970 to the last week of March, violent demonstrations regularly took place, which authorities suppressed with brutality leading to the death of four students. During this period, dubbed "First Quarter Storm," the militant bloc of students associated with Kabataang Makabayan (Nationalist Youth [KM]) grew rapidly, especially in Manila, and the New People's Army (NPA), the armed wing of the Marxist-Leninist-Maoist Communist Party of the Philippines (CPP), pursued a protracted war in the countryside and began to receive young recruits from the capital.[32] Periodic public displays of militant opposition to the government persisted and intensified in the first two years of Marcos's second term, in which protesters targeted both the Philippine president and the US. In September 1972, Marcos declared martial law.

The White House, the State Department, and the American Chamber of Commerce publicly supported Marcos when he officially imposed martial law. By 1973, it was unquestionable that the dictator had the full backing of the recently reelected US president. A classified National Security Decision Memorandum signed by National Security Advisor Henry Kissinger on March 27, 1973, specified the new official US policy vis-à-vis the Philippine dictatorship, which highlighted the importance of maintaining a cordial relationship with the dictator "in our pursuit of fundamental U.S. interests in the Philippines and of implementation by the Marcos Administration of measures aimed at long-term stability for the Philippines."[33] Marcos assured the US that martial law would not interfere with the functioning of the bases and of the American business community.

During the martial law period, Marcos confiscated and appropriated by force many private and public businesses such as those in manufacturing, financial services, and construction; he then redistributed them to his cronies and close personal friends in the form of monopolies.[34] An economy based on "crony capitalism,"[35] a system based on close relationships between entrepreneurs and government officials, resulted in weak public institutions and an antidevelopment state.[36] These facilitated Marcos's plunder aimed at ensuring the survival and perpetuation of his regime, as he channeled the wealth of the country to the personal coffers of his family and friends in offshore bank accounts.[37] Like the Pahlavi and Somoza dynasties in Iran and Nicaragua, respectively, Marcos's rule was sultanistic, which is a type of authoritarian regime based on personal ideology and favor to maintain the autocrat in power; there is little ideological foundation for the rule except individual power.[38] From a president who purportedly had the country's best interest in mind, as articulated in his mantra "The Philippines Will Be Great Again" during his political campaign and throughout his first-term presidency,[39] Marcos turned into a tyrant who used the state to enrich himself and his network and oppress the Filipino people in the process. Activists recognized that his government no longer had the authority to represent the Philippine nation.

Linking Issues and Actors

Melinda Paras was in high school during the escalation of the Vietnam War. Born to a Filipino father and a white mother, she was raised in Wisconsin.

Her interest in learning about her father's homeland and his intense opposition to the war prompted her to move to the Philippines. There, she organized and recruited American soldiers stationed at Clark Air Base and Subic Bay Naval Base into the global anti–Vietnam War movement. Her activism led to numerous contacts with the Philippine Left, in particular the radical KM, and she eventually became a member. She served as the liaison between the KM and antiwar activists until the declaration of martial law, when she was arrested in Manila. As an American and the granddaughter of a former Philippine Supreme Court justice, her class and citizenship privileges spared her from the cruel treatment most dissidents got when they were detained by the military. After her release, she was deported and banned from future entry into the Philippines. Back home, she became one of the leaders of the burgeoning movement against the Marcos dictatorship.[40]

Bruce Occeña was also an anti–Vietnam War activist and a participant in the Third World Liberation Front strikes in 1968. The son of a former farmworker and Alaskero, he was raised in Brooklyn, New York. He was the first to go to college in his family. Originally, he went to the University of Hawai'i, where he was involved in the state's first occupations against the war in Vietnam. He later transferred to University of California, Berkeley, where he became involved in a wide range of issues from supporting the Black Panther Party to fighting evictions at the International Hotel. He also joined the Venceremos Brigade[41] and eventually went on the first organized trip to Cuba.[42] He participated in Marxist study circles in the San Francisco Bay Area and was a central figure in the propagation of Marxist-Leninist-Maoist thinking among Filipino Americans. Like Paras, he became a central figure in the transnational movement against the Marcos regime.

Augusto Espiritu claims that "cross-cultural awareness and cross-ethnic organizing was for some individuals their first 'border-crossing' political act."[43] The 1960s was a period of global political and social tensions, which paved the way for an increase in protest activities around anti-imperialism, civil rights, and decolonization. In the US, the children of Filipino farmworkers, cannery laborers, and war veterans of the first and second waves of migration were coming of age, in search of their identities. As the war in Vietnam offered Marcos the necessary US endorsement and infrastructure to strengthen his power, it also fomented multiple local and global injustices that created organizational links between Filipinos in the US and in the Philippines. The war encouraged young Filipino American activists to reexamine the migrant community's formation through the lens of the historical relationship between the Philippines and the US. They expressed solidarity with the communists in Vietnam who, in their view, were struggling for independence and self-determination. For these Filipinos, the Vietnam War was a continuation of US racist imperialism in Asia that had started with the colonization of the Philippines in the twentieth century. This analysis was crucial in developing their critique of Marcos, who they regarded as an embodiment of the United States' continued intervention in Philippine politics to serve its own interests in the region. Thus, the war became a fulcrum for Filipino activists to develop collective identities rooted in a criticism of the Philippine state's subservience to the US.

Together with recently arrived Filipino student radicals, Filipino American civil rights and antiwar activists founded an anti-imperialist newspaper called *Kalayaan International* (Freedom International) in 1971. The newspaper took its name from the official organ of the Filipino revolutionary organization established by peasant leader Andrés Bonifacio during the anticolonial struggle against Spain—the Samahang Kataastaasan, Kagalang-galang Katipunan ng mga Anak ng Bayan (Supreme and Most Honorable Society of the Children of the Nation), or Katipunan for short.[44] The collective that ran *Kalayaan* described the paper as the "answer to the need of the overseas Filipino to be aware of the multi-faceted problems of his people, both here and back home."[45] It linked contemporary struggle to the past and called for a Second Propaganda Movement through decolonization of Filipino national consciousness.[46] The *Kalayaan* collective had two interrelated and parallel agendas: one, to struggle for a socialist society in the US, and the other to support the revolutionary movement in the Philippines, led by the CPP–National Democratic Front (NDF).[47] As second-generation Filipino Americans became involved in *Kalayaan* and developed close relations with Filipino nationals, their political identities slowly veered away from their Asian American panethnic roots and moved toward Filipino nationalism.[48] But the Vietnam War was still the backdrop of national level politics, and activists tied their construction of collective identity to a critique of imperialism.

With the rise of authoritarian regimes in the Third World, the sixties and seventies also saw the growth of international solidarity. Throughout the developed world, groups that backed national liberation struggles in countries in Africa, Asia, and Latin America proliferated and developed a common repertoire of contention. These consisted of exposing events and issues not covered by mainstream media, transforming public opinion, and providing alternative analyses and explanations through public outreach, educational campaigns, and exposure trips.[49] Many of the solidarity activists were introduced to the movements they supported while they were in those countries as religious and development workers. Such was the case with many Dutch missionaries and volunteers who were assigned to the Philippines.

60   CHAPTER THREE

Relations between the Netherlands and the Philippines developed prior to the Marcos period. The Netherlands was an export destination for Filipino agricultural products and an important investor in the Philippines through Dutch multinational companies such as Unilever, Shell, and Philips.[50] These economic ties precipitated bilateral aid. The Philippines benefited from official Dutch development assistance in the mid-1960s, which focused on poverty alleviation. Starting in the early 1970s, however, in light of the ascent to power of undemocratic leaders in places where the Dutch government had aid programs, the Dutch made respect for human rights a key criterion for recipient countries, in addition to gross national product per capita and the presence of a redistribution policy.[51] Thus, as the human rights situation worsened under the Marcos regime, direct support declined. Aid was channeled almost exclusively through the cofinancing program, wherein donors, multilateral institutions, and development agencies come together to assist developing countries with a variety of projects.[52] Four private Dutch development organizations received funds from the government to undertake agricultural and rural development projects in the Philippines in partnership with Philippine nongovernmental organizations (NGOs).[53] Since Marcos basically banned NGOs when he declared martial law, Dutch funding agencies relied on Basic Ecclesial Communities[54] and the network of Social Action Centers of the Catholic Church. Aid provided the resources at the grassroots level for cooperatives and educational projects aimed at empowering indigenous peoples, peasants, and women. In essence, the Dutch government's bilateral assistance contributed to the growing grassroots opposition against Marcos by providing infrastructure for recruitment and organizational expansion.

The involvement of Dutch citizens in the movement against the dictatorship expanded and intensified through the government-run Stichting Nederlandse Vrijwilligers (Foundation of Netherlands Volunteers [SNV]).[55] In 1969, the first group of Dutch volunteers arrived in the Philippines. With educational backgrounds in engineering, social work, community development, and the medical sciences, they were assigned to teach at trade schools and state universities and to set up facilities that would improve the health and livelihood of rural villagers. Since Dutch aid did not go directly to government programs, almost all volunteers worked in church-related organizations. Despite the Dutch government's disapproval of the Marcos regime, SNV enforced a policy of neutrality and nonintervention in domestic political affairs and advised its volunteers to exercise distance and impartiality when dealing with locals. But since the volunteers were in the country before and shortly after the declaration of martial law, from 1969 to 1973, they witnessed the escalation of repression in the country and the peak of political turmoil and social unrest.

Coincidentally, most of the volunteers were assigned to rural areas of Central and Southern Philippines, which were strongholds of the NPA, the armed wing of the communist movement CPP-NDF, and thus were sites of intense military operations. They encountered NPA rebels and local organizers, to whom they offered food and temporary shelter. These interactions introduced the Dutch volunteers into the Philippine struggle. Upon their return to the Netherlands, they got involved in solidarity activism, supporting the struggle against Marcos. So, an unintended outcome of Dutch development cooperation was enlisting its citizens in the Philippine national liberation movement as conscience adherents—"individuals and groups who are part of the appropriate SM [social movement] but do not stand to benefit directly from SMO [social movement organization] goal accomplishment."[56] In other words, the Netherlands-Philippines state relations strengthened the support base of the anti-dictatorship movement by mobilizing international allies and sympathizers.

Building a Movement Constituency

Marcos's imposition of martial law in 1972 expanded the movement. Although repression increased, activists saw this as an opportunity rather than a constraint. They exploited the discursive opening that martial law provided to break the consensus among Filipinos in the US and the Netherlands, as well as the international community, about the perceived positive outcomes of the dictatorship. At this stage of mobilization, the goal was to sow conflict among overseas Filipinos that would make them question the foundation of their belief systems about loyalty to the homeland. At the same time, because Marcos relied on the material and symbolic support of the West to maintain his rule, the movement sought to educate citizens in these countries on their governments' direct and indirect roles in sustaining the regime. Interestingly, it was precisely this political division in the Filipino migrant community that allowed activists to build a movement constituency.

During the Marcos dictatorship, the Filipino community in the US was one of the largest and most heterogeneous ethnic groups in terms of education, income, legal status and citizenship, length of residency, migrant generation, and occupation. Most had settled permanently in the US. While they publicly expressed pride as Filipinos and continued to be devoted to the homeland, these actions remained in the realm of cultural heritage, often through the celebration of religious traditions and holidays. For instance, second-wave immigrants, which consisted of World War II veterans and their brides, romanticized the culture of the Philippines in customs such as hometown fiestas and cultivated a variant of Filipino nationalism that incorporated loyalty and gratitude to the US. They relished the fact that they, as immigrants from an American colonial outpost, could assimilate more easily than other immigrants.[57] Most Filipino immigrant parents transmitted and nurtured a political identity among the second generation geared toward assimilation into the mainstream. This entailed limited participation in or withdrawal from politics in the Philippines. The few immigrants who continued to be involved in homeland affairs tended to be politically conservative. How then did activists mobilize a community whose members viewed belonging to the homeland nation to be largely cultural? More importantly, how did they portray their struggle to depose a homeland regime from afar as a patriotic mission, especially since they were detached from the day-to-day suffering of those living under dictatorship?

After the declaration of martial law, several groups were formed including the following four, the largest in terms of size and scale of mobilization. The National Committee for the Restoration of Civil Liberties in the Philippines (NCRCLP) consisted of Filipinos from center to left on the political spectrum. The Katipunan ng Demokratikong Pilipino (Union of Democratic Filipinos [KDP]) was an anti-imperialist cadre organization with links to the CPP-NDF. The Movement for a Free Philippines (MFP) was founded by self-exiled former Philippine senator Raul Manglapus and other politicians and technocrats who had fled the Marcos regime. And the Friends of the Filipino People (FFP) rallied non-Filipino allies. At this stage of movement growth, these new organizations carefully navigated the political culture of the Filipino community and framed their opposition to attract a broad constituency. For instance, NCRCLP chose to limit the discourse on resistance to human rights to avoid alienating most first-generation immigrants who espoused conservative views. Grace, a Filipino American activist in the San Francisco Bay Area whose parents were farmworkers, reflects on the NCRCLP's decision despite consensus among its members that Marcos's removal from office was the best outcome. "I think it was important then to try to unite the broadest cross section of the Filipino community against the dictatorship. . . . We recognized that we needed to have a broader approach to build consensus in the Filipino community to oppose dictatorship and that was to have it pitched to civil liberties," she recalls.

One of the early campaigns of NCRCLP that appealed to Filipinos in the US was the fight against Philippine income taxes on Filipino citizens overseas.[58] In a statement published in *Kalayaan*, NCRCLP framed opposition to the policy by divorcing support for the state from love of the nation—that is, fulfilling one's duty to the homeland government in the form of taxes was not an expression of one's commitment and loyalty to the people. They also highlighted the number of Filipinos in the US and their power as a united actor to change the status quo. Their message was that Filipinos overseas, because of their critical mass, can influence political outcomes in the homeland. With this approach, NCRLP advanced a migrant agency frame:

> To pay your taxes is to support the Marcos dictatorship. Your hard-earned dollars will be used to kill our Moslem brothers, maintain political prisons, repress students and teachers, draft your twenty-year old brothers and cousins to fight in Mindanao, maintain the Marcos households in England, Switzerland and California, crush the peasant and labor movements, and in general support and prop up Marcos's rule. Let us not be cowed by the threats of the Marcos agencies abroad. There are 350,000 of us in the United States. If we unite and refuse to pay taxes, the Marcos dictatorship cannot do anything to us.[59]

Although the newly formed organizations shared the goal of ending martial law in the short term, their analyses differed on one key element of agency and identity: the role of the Filipino activists in the US in the struggle, and their membership in the Philippine nation. The contrast was starkest between the KDP and the MFP. In his speech at the MFP's founding convention, Mangalpus spoke of the significance of the forming of the MFP just a few blocks from the White House, "where it all began 75 years ago," referring to the United States' decision to annex the Philippines at the turn of the century.[60] He compared his exile in the US to the historic journeys of Filipino Propagandists to Spain.[61] MFP members saw themselves as the new *ilustrados*, "eyewitnesses, with personal experience of what martial law was like on the ground."[62]

The MFP was made up of self-exiled politicians and technocrats who had fled the Marcos regime. Although most of them were not directly connected to the communist movement in the Philippines, their opposition to the US-backed regime made their applications for asylum difficult based on the Immigration and Nationality Act of 1952 (or the McCarran-Walter Act). The act denied asylum to immigrants who espoused political ideologies opposed to American principles.[63] Some had escaped without passports or access to their funds in the Philippines, so they depended on their social network for short-term accommodations, housing, and employment.[64] Others entered a lower social class, as they joined the American workforce with precarious employment.[65] The MFP framed their journey of escape and the hardships of their immigration and class status as testaments to their commitment to the Filipinos left behind under Marcos. The activists insisted on being called "exiles" rather than "migrants" or "immigrants," for the term captured their identity rooted in persecution, forced displacement, and the goal of return. They strategically deployed this identity in organizing constituents and confronting pro-Marcos challengers in the community.

The MFP often made distinctions between Filipino nationals who were temporarily living in the US as students and exiles and those who had acquired permanent residency and citizenship and had made the US their home. In his historical account of the MFP, former activist Jose Fuentecilla regarded the post-1965 professional immigrants as having "relatively weak ties to people and institutions in the homeland" with activities limited to fundraising for infrastructure projects in their hometowns through their provincial associations, cultural and social events, and alumni organizations.[66] To the MFP, their concept of the Philippine nation was confined to their hometowns and organizational interests. On the other hand, "the younger, newest segment of this wave, mostly students—single, undecided about where to put down roots, and perhaps with plans to return home after completing their degrees" were receptive to organizing efforts related to the Marcos dictatorship.[67] The *Philippine News*, the biggest US-based Philippine newspaper in circulation, offered to publicize the MFP to the migrant community. Filipinos in the Philippines were its most important audience, while those in the US had a secondary, supportive role in the struggle.[68] The MFP urged the latter to include news clippings in letters home to inform their families of the overseas resistance.

In contrast, the KDP did not see the concerns of Filipinos who were in the US temporarily and those who had chosen to settle permanently as distinct, or as constituting two different and opposed communities. Building on the ideologies and resources of the *Kalayaan* collective, the KDP fought transnationally on two fronts: against the Marcos dictatorship in the Philippines and against capitalism in the US. It advocated for democracy in the Philippines so that Filipinos would not have to leave the country. It also fought to establish socialism in the US to combat racial discrimination and social injustices against Filipino migrants and other minorities. Connecting authoritarian rule in the Philippines and capitalism in the US, the KDP saw the experiences of Filipinos in the US as deeply entangled with the history of Filipinos in the Philippines. For the KDP, while a nationalist framework was useful in mobilizing against the dictatorship, an international approach could address the structural roots that led to Marcos's rise to power.

The KDP's organizational and ideological foundations epitomized the transnational belonging of Filipino migrants and appealed to those who considered the Philippines their homeland despite putting down roots in the US. Members also acknowledged the privilege that came with US citizenship: their social position allowed them to condemn Marcos and hold US elites responsible for his power without negative consequences. Propaganda and movement recruitment were fundamental tasks that defined the day-to-day operations of the KDP. They sold *Ang Katipunan* newspaper in churches, groceries, schools, and public places that Filipinos frequented. The KDP directly enlisted members by tapping into Filipino youth programs and networks focusing on Filipino identities and cultural heritage. The annual Far West Convention[69] of Filipino American youth on the West Coast was a major arena for recruitment, and the KDP attracted a cross section of the Filipino community, especially second-generation Filipinos with working-class backgrounds.

On December 30, 1973, more than a year after Marcos declared martial law, leading anti-dictatorship organizations in the US—FFP, KDP, MFP, NCRCLP, and the National Association of Filipinos in the US—held a "historic unity meeting" in New York. Despite ideological differences, they joined forces to denounce the regime and pressure the US government to withdraw support for Marcos. In the joint statement that the groups issued, they emphasized their solidarity with the Filipinos in the homeland, whose interests Marcos had failed to uphold. Throughout the statement, the activists juxtaposed their unity as Filipino people with Marcos's violation of the social contract, in essence framing the movement as a more legitimate representative of Filipinos' collective interests than the government:

> Today, December 30, 1973, Ferdinand Marcos's term as President of the Philippines ends under the validly ratified and operative 1935 Philippine Constitution. Filipino groups in the United States opposing the Philippine dictatorship therefore united in demanding that Mr. Marcos fulfill his contract with the Filipino people and step down from office.
>
> Since the Filipino people have been silenced by a repressive martial law rule, we take this opportunity to voice their desire for the restoration of democratic rights. . . .
>
> Since Marcos does not represent the Filipino people, we call upon the U.S. government to stop all economic and military aid to him. We also call upon the American people to oppose the use of their taxes in supporting another illegitimate government in Asia.
>
> We stand together with the Filipino people in the homeland struggling for the release of political prisoners, the restoration of democratic liberties, and the return of human rights.[70]

Not surprisingly, the movement against the dictatorship encountered resistance from Marcos's emissaries and propagandists, and from conservative and indifferent members of the Filipino migrant community who, for years, had remained dominant in the public sphere. It also faced hostility from progressive activists who believed the priority should be the Filipinos in the US—any involvement in divisive Philippine issues could undermine existing initiatives and endanger the whole Filipino population in the US. Marcos's suppression of Filipino Americans regardless of citizenship revealed the contradictions in migration and national belonging: while increased mobility often encourages a fluidity of identity, erecting both physical and symbolic borders through state policies and discourses implies that the boundaries of the nation-state remain rigid.

Surveillance by the Philippine government led to the blacklisting of 150 supposedly anti-Marcos Filipinos in the US.[71] The dictator instructed the consulates not to renew their passports.[72] The list consisted mostly of Filipinos who were US citizens by birth or naturalization or Philippine nationals with permanent residency in the US. Most were writers and editors of Filipino American newspapers critical of the dictatorship and activists affiliated with the KDP and the NCRCLP. However, the list also included leaders in the Filipino community who were not members of anti-dictatorship groups but were involved in activism on domestic issues that Filipinos in the US confronted such as employment, housing discrimination, and access to social services. This incited tensions between the anti-dictatorship activists and community leaders, as the latter concluded that involvement in homeland politics by a few Filipinos was a threat to much of the migrant population.

The Marcos regime also resorted to indirect repression and disinformation. Unable to control the press in the US, the Philippine government used a network of agents to discourage subscribers and advertisers from supporting *Philippine News* and the Chicago-based newspaper *Philippine Times*.[73] It sponsored the New York–based newspaper the *Filipino Reporter* to publish favorable news and editorials about the economic and political situation in the Philippines.[74] Marcos also fostered return tourism through his Balikbayan Program, launched on September 1, 1973, to showcase his government's accomplishments and the benefits of martial law to overseas Filipinos. Finally, Marcos's media propagandists portrayed the MFP and the KDP activists as disloyal to the nation and as "steak commandos,"[75] an attack on their identity as Filipinos and their class position. By alluding to a contradiction between protest and comfort, the term portrayed the activists as critical of the regime while at the same time reveling in the abundance that the US offered, such as the consumption of steak. Because they had the resources to leave and stay in a foreign country and were physically absent from the territory of the Philippine nation-state, they did not suffer like their compatriots. They were depicted, therefore, as lacking the lived experience to speak for all Filipinos. But this backfired, because as Ann Swidler argues, "when institutions make questions of group identity salient, they generate identity-oriented movements and a quest for identity on the part of individuals."[76]

The biggest challenge for the anti-dictatorship movement was appealing to those who remained unconcerned about the political developments in the Philippines and who chose to keep their distance—due to their desire to assimilate or because they believed the challenges of Filipinos in the US as racialized immigrants must take precedence in political organizing. To address these audiences, the MFP tapped into the history of heroism among exiled Filipinos, especially the Propaganda Movement and *La Solidaridad*. In *Philippine News*, the MFP published an advertisement for Manglapus's new book, *Philippines: The Silenced Democracy*, entitled "History Repeats Itself." It stated, "Our people back home cannot wait any longer. . . . Let us be inspired by the courage and foresight of Jose Rizal, Marcelo H. del Pilar, and Graciano Lopez Jaena who used their freedom in exile to work for the freedom of their countrymen at home."[77] The persistent use of the term "exile" in the MFP's writings suggested that Filipinos in the US, like their counterparts in Spain in the nineteenth century, were living overseas only temporarily and that the Philippines was the country to which they truly belonged. In contrast, because the KDP worked on two fronts and was the only organization that consisted of a significant number of Filipino Americans, it faced opposition from some activists with roots in the identity movements in the 1960s. These activists considered the conditions in the Philippines and resistance against the Marcos regime as separate from the fight for equality in American society.

Some of these conflicts transpired at the Far West Convention.[78] Aileen was a community leader and an organizer of the convention. She thought that participating in the anti-dictatorship movement would drain resources from efforts to address the problems of new Filipino immigrants in the US. But her reflection below also captures the ambiguities of transnational belonging among US-born Filipinos. She makes a firm distinction between issues "there" (in the Philippines and about Marcos) and "here" (in the US and about the death of Americans in the Vietnam War) while asserting her identity as Filipino.

> I [was] not going to join the KDP. Why? Why would I join the KDP given all the issues I was already fighting? I was fighting for all the immigrants who were coming into this country and thinking I was going to change their world.

68 CHAPTER THREE

> Marcos was just a name. I knew very little about him, when I started to read about it [the dictatorship]. I didn't like Nixon. I didn't like the war in Vietnam. I ran a youth program, and some of the children we had worked with were coming home in body bags. To me, *that* [pounds on the table] was an issue.... And I am very Filipino. I am probably more Filipino than a lot of them [KDP members].

The KDP encountered many community members like Aileen. Through *Ang Katipunan*, the KDP appealed to them with "a kind of moral prescription, an admonition not to forget."[79] In an editorial titled "Stand Up for the Homeland," the KDP called attention to the privilege of Filipinos in the US relative to those in the Philippines under the dictatorship, despite their marginalization:

> There is no question that Filipinos in the U.S. have many problems and suffer much hardship, especially discrimination because of national origin and even skin color. But this cannot be an excuse for us to divorce ourselves from the problems and needs of our homeland. Such attitudes are only a reflection of unpatriotic and selfish ideas. Because we are able to temporarily escape the dire poverty and oppression we faced in the Philippines, we should not ignore the conditions of our brothers and sisters who remain back home.[80]

Finally, the AMLC addressed multiple audiences with cultural activities and events that challenged state-centered discourses, beliefs, and traditions. These aimed to ensure movement continuity when mobilization ebbed and to prevent the formation of consensus in the community based on conservative groups' discourses on the dictatorship and the advocacy of those who considered the issues in the Philippines and in the US as separate. On Philippine Independence Day, June 12, Philippine consulates all over the US organized galas with Filipino and American elites to showcase the achievements of the community. AMLC countered the narratives that the Philippine state propagated during the events by organizing an alternative, often thematic, commemoration called "Philippine National Day." In 1980, for instance, the fifth annual Philippine National Day barrio fiesta paid tribute to three waves of Filipino immigration to the US and highlighted the contributions of Filipinos to American and Philippine nation building.[81] A similar strategy was used by the leaders of the Salvadoran American National Association (SANA) in the 1980s. To mobilize Salvadorans in Los Angeles to make demands upon the US and Salvadoran governments as well as the guerrillas of Frente Farabundo Martí para la Liberación Nacional (Farabundo Martí National Liberation Front) to end the civil war, SANA took advantage of *El Dia del Salvadoreño*, a weekend festival to honor the founding of Villa de San Salvador

PATRIOTS AND REVOLUTIONARIES   69

in 1525, to intervene and influence the discourse on politics in El Salvador.[82] Official holidays such as the Philippine Independence Day and *El Dia del Salvadoreño* offer an opportunity to introduce counternarratives and change the cultural scripts associated with the events; in the case of the AMLC, by centering the celebration on Filipino migrants, the holiday becomes about the people, not the state.

Compared to the US, the community in the Netherlands during the dictatorship was small and largely homogeneous, composed mostly of temporary, contract-based workers. Given the small number of Filipinos in the Netherlands, community infrastructure was initially built to alleviate estrangement and longing associated with the migration experience, and to forge ties with the Dutch population. The Catholic Church was the principal meeting venue for Filipinos, which catalyzed the formation of ethnic organizations. In 1965, the Philippine Nurses Association of the Academisch Ziekenhuis (University Hospital) was formed in Leiden. It was a cultural and social club for Filipino nurses, exclusively, to fraternize outside of work. In the 1970s, Dutch-Filipino friendship associations became a popular way that Filipino migrants could learn about Dutch culture, language, and society in the absence of any official integration program for temporary workers. The Dutch-Philippine Club was established in 1973 in Gendringen, where one of the Berghaus factories that employed Filipino seamstresses was located. Six years later, the Dutch-Philippine Association was formed in Utrecht, which spearheaded discounted cultural trips to the Philippines for Dutch citizens and formal social gatherings with support from the Philippine Embassy. In essence, most of the Filipino organizations abstained from activities related to homeland political affairs.

Two simultaneous processes changed this situation. First, former SNV volunteers and Dutch Carmelite missionaries who had returned to the Netherlands from the Philippines formed the Filippijnengroep Nederland (Philippine Group Netherlands [FGN]) in March 1975 in Utrecht. Their initial objective was to draw attention to the escalation of human rights violations in the Philippines through their monthly magazine, *Filippijnen Bulletin* (Philippine Bulletin). The FGN called for solidarity and stressed the experience of Dutch volunteers in the Philippines who witnessed the struggle of Filipinos. Since the Dutch public was relatively unfamiliar with the situation in the Philippines, the FGN piggybacked on the popularity of efforts against Latin American dictatorships and interposed the Philippines into policy discussions on human rights and democracy that were gaining traction in the Netherlands. It developed relations with other solidarity groups and personalized distant or abstract issues through life stories of ordinary Filipinos to attract the Dutch public.

The second process through which Filipinos in the Netherlands got involved in homeland political affairs was the migration of the top leaders of the CPP-NDF to the Netherlands. When Marcos intensified his campaign to quell the communist insurgency in the mid-1970s, the CPP-NDF began deploying cadres overseas both to escape persecution and to build diplomatic relations with socialist parties in Western Europe.[83] Through the help of religious congregations and a permissive Dutch asylum policy, they were able to obtain refugee status in the Netherlands and settle in Utrecht, where most of the members of the FGN lived. The lack of Filipino migrant organizations focusing on political issues in the Philippines encouraged the refugees to join the FGN and eventually set up the NDF international desk in its office. In this common space, the lines between the FGN as an international solidarity organization and the NDF as a national liberation movement blurred. The activists' commitments oscillated between the FGN and the NDF, such that one could not be engaged in the former without also being involved in the latter. Activists spun through the revolving door between the solidarity and the revolutionary movements.

With the informal establishment of the NDF, a significant portion of the FGN's work shifted. It sent periodic press releases to Dutch newspapers on the economic, political, and social situation in the Philippines and propagated the idea that organized resistance existed and therefore must be supported. The FGN portrayed the anti-dictatorship movement as a continuation of the Filipino people's fight against domination by foreign powers and domestic elites, a fight that had deep historical roots. Its activities centered on building an infrastructure of material and political support for the CPP-NDF. Although FGN did not specifically target the Filipino community in the Netherlands in their campaigns, it earned notoriety among the 1960s wave of migrants who saw their protests at the Philippine consulate and openly criticized the organization's campaign. Hugo was a SNV volunteer in the Philippines from 1972 to 1975. With a degree in mechanical engineering, he was assigned to provide teachers' training at a vocational institution. He joined FGN a few months after it was founded. He recalls his encounters with Filipino migrants in FGN's education campaigns:

> When we were invited somewhere to give presentations on the Philippines in the 70s up to the 80s, wherever there would be Filipinos, they would get very upset because we were very negative. They would say, "Why don't you talk about the nice and beautiful things about the Philippines?" We would respond, "Yeah, that's true, but we also talk about poverty, repression, human rights.... These people [victims of martial law] are struggling for a better life and we want to support them and tell their stories."

Such reaction was expected since this migrant stream left the Philippines during the early years of Marcos when economic and political conditions were robust. Many also clung to idyllic images of the homeland to cope with the daily travails of living in a foreign land. Their positive visions of the country had more to do with a few selected memories—memories that form the basis of their identities—than with the present set of circumstances. As Paolo Boccagni found out in his study of Ecuadorian migrants in Northern Italy, "whatever regret or disenchantment regarding the 'ever worsening' situation in Ecuador, one's persistent national identity is the basis for personal consistency, in the face of the drastic changes that result from migration."[84] The FGN recognized that the movement against the dictatorship would have neither legitimacy nor the capacity to expand in the Netherlands without support from the migrant population. The state's position that the Marcos dictatorship represented the interests of the Filipino people needed to be challenged publicly.

In sum, to build a constituency against the Marcos dictatorship, political entrepreneurs that included exiled members of the elite opposition, immigrant and second-generation militants belonging to the transnational network of the communist movement in the Philippines, American allies, and Dutch solidarity activists tapped into and galvanized preexisting social networks and drew on discourses on Filipino patriotism to mobilize a population that is ambivalent on home-country affairs. In the diverse Filipino community in the US, which was divided based on stance on involvement in homeland politics amid transnational repression, the movement framed its struggle within a larger historical discourse and drew on culturally resonant themes such as bravery, sacrifice, and resilience for the nation—that is, the Filipino people. Movement actors achieved this by invoking the labor and devotion of the Propaganda Movement during the Spanish colonial period in its fight for an independent Philippines as well as altering the cultural codes and scripts to understand and commemorate national events. In contrast, Filipino migrants in the Netherlands depended on the community for camaraderie and solace, in a country where there were very few of them, and their work insulated them from each other. They considered Dutch activists' anti-Marcos views to be an affront to the Philippines—to who they are as Filipinos. Thus, even at the early stage of mobilization, the movement was already engaged in the process of collective identity formation, interrogating and testing migrants' sense of loyalty. With a constituency built in both the US and the Netherlands, the objective of the movement moved toward casting doubt on Marcos's authority to represent the Filipino people among political elites in the international community.

CHAPTER THREE

Delegitimizing Marcos in Institutional Arenas

With the declaration of martial law, poverty and unemployment increased. Across the country, the communist insurgency grew rapidly, from about three thousand to five thousand party members at the end of 1976 to nine thousand in 1980, along with twenty-six guerrilla units in the countryside and united front organizations in Manila.[85] In the southern Philippines, the conflict between the military and the Moro separatist movement escalated and reached its peak in 1973–75, when the Bangsa Moro Army swelled to thirty thousand armed fighters.[86] With the help of Filipino exiles from the MFP, a resentful oligarchy tried to destabilize the regime with insurrectionary activities such as arson in the capital.[87] These developments all signaled Marcos's waning control of the country, and the dictator struggled to portray his administration to the international community as having the capacity to govern and represent the people. It is in this context that, between 1975 and 1980, the anti-dictatorship movement in the US and the Netherlands, like *La Solidaridad* in Spain in the nineteenth century, pursued the strategies of certification and decertification.

Katie Furuyama and David S. Meyer describe certification as "the process by which authorities recognize, engage, or endorse an actor or actors as representatives of some larger constituency."[88] Certification is an effective mechanism to the extent that multiple certifiers express support at critical junctures over time.[89] Since Marcos's claims to authority were being undermined in the Philippines, he sought the validation of external actors, especially the US, to maintain the illusion of legitimacy. Activists, therefore, worked to decertify Marcos in multiple arenas in order to amplify the erosion of the dictator's authority over Filipino citizens; at the same time, they also introduced challengers to the regime and depicted them as political actors who represented the genuine interests of the nation. To decertify the Marcos administration, activists, like the Filipino exiles in Spain in the nineteenth century, showed its degeneracy and incompetence to hostland governments and civil societies as well as the broader international community. Simultaneously, activists certified contenders to his authority—the communists, Muslim separatists, and elite opposition.

Certification and decertification took on different but related forms and produced varied outcomes in the two countries. Durable ties between the Philippines and the US created the conditions for foreign-policy lobbying. Strong linkages allowed activists to deploy symbols and activate narratives that alluded to the dictatorship's rise as an outcome of US colonization, grounding their claims and demands for the US withdrawal of support for the regime. Because the Netherlands had limited relations with the Philippines, foreign policy did not give activists there an established point of access into the institutionalized political system. Activists, however, recognized that despotic regimes were still vulnerable to foreign criticisms, especially in the broader sphere of global public opinion. Since the political culture in Western Europe was conducive to universalistic claims making, activists convened a nongovernmental human rights tribunal and damaged the reputation of the Marcos regime through naming and shaming, a tactic that entails publicizing human rights violations and employing pressure as the perpetrators and their actions gain attention.[90] In both strategies, activists uncoupled the nation (the Filipino people) from the state (the Marcos regime) using frames based on discourses on colonialism, human rights, and national interest.

SECURITY ALLIANCE AND FOREIGN-POLICY LOBBYING

Josh DeWind and Renata Segura argue that migrant groups can influence the posture of the US government toward their homelands and vice versa when their interests and goals converge with those of US officials.[91] To show this harmony, activists strategically frame their positions in ways that tap into familiar discourses and widely held beliefs. This is because foreign-policy lobbying entails shaping the attitudes of the public as much as the positions of elected politicians.[92] For instance, in the language it adopts, the Jewish lobby in the US represented by the American Israel Public Affairs Committee depicts its loyalty to Israel as part of its devotion to and defense of American democratic values.[93] Similarly, Greek Americans deployed frames that celebrate immigrant assimilation in appealing to the Greek community and allies to mobilize support during the Turkish invasion of Cyprus in 1974.[94] These dynamics can also be observed in the actions of Filipino Americans to decrease US aid to Marcos.

"One of the ironies of the neocolonial relationship between the United States and the Philippines is that leaders in Manila are as dependent on Washington for their power as they are on any of the sectors of the Philippine population. No ruler of the Philippines was more aware of this than Ferdinand Marcos during his more than two decades in power," wrote political scientist Stephen R. Shalom.[95] Despite differences between the MFP and the KDP in their views about the national membership of Filipino migrants, they shared the belief that US endorsement was pivotal for the regime's survival. Activists pursued foreign policy lobbying, with the specific goal of reducing allocations to the Philippines under the Foreign Assistance Act.

From May 20 to June 24, 1975, a few months after the withdrawal of US troops from Vietnam, the Subcommittee on International Organizations of the House of Representatives Committee on International Relations, headed by Democratic representative Donald Fraser of Minnesota, convened hearings on the human rights situation in the Philippines and South Korea. To activists, this signaled a transformed atmosphere for campaigns directed at US foreign policy in Asia. According to the FFP, the political climate and dynamics among the American political elite after the US left Vietnam offered an auspicious moment to advocate for overhauling US foreign policy in Southeast Asia. For the first time, the US Congress invited opponents of Marcos to testify on the political situation in the Philippines. Initially framing the situation in the Philippines as a human rights issue, the FFP and MFP used moral shocks.[96] They showed lawmakers evidence of US-supplied weapons used to suppress social movements, shut down mainstream mass media, and maintain political prisons across the archipelago, among other abuses.

Throughout their sworn statements, the witnesses, which included MFP founder Raul Manglapus and Joseph O'Hare, a cleric and associate editor of the Jesuit publication *America Magazine*, held the US accountable for the dictatorship in the Philippines. They asserted that Marcos would not have had the capacity to repress his people without aid intended to protect US interests in Asia. In accusing US politicians of acquiescence to Marcos, they put on trial America's commitment to the Western liberal democracy it had introduced to the archipelago during its colonial rule. They also argued that, as a global leader and champion of government by the people, the US needed to uphold the tenets of democracy in its former colony:

MANGLAPUS: You have heard it said so often that there is a deep reservoir of good will for America among the Filipinos. But, more and more Filipinos are realizing the role which American arms are playing in the repression of their rights. . . .

O'HARE: I find it ironic that in this country American spokesmen can easily dismiss the loss of freedom in the Philippines on the grounds that democracy was from the beginning only a foreign importation. . . .

Our concern now for human rights in the Philippines goes much deeper than the naïve prospect of reproducing an American image in another part of the world. . . .

Now, after 75 years of American dominance, for Americans to ease their conscience about the disappearance of constitutional government in the Philippines by the view that the will to self-rule was only a foreign American importation, this may be the ultimate condescension and the final betrayal.[97]

Activists then shifted their framing—from human rights and colonialism to national interest—when they targeted the US-Philippines Military Bases Agreement. Movement leaders knew that as long as US politicians considered the military bases crucial to the national security of American people, lobbying efforts founded on moral shocks and human rights would be futile. A challenge for the activists was to portray the bases as unnecessary for the protection of US economic and military interests. In the context of the Cold War, the Subic Bay Naval and Clark Air Bases in the Philippines became the most strategic among all overseas basing facilities, allowing the US to project its forces into both Pacific and Indian Ocean regions and thus maintain dominance across the whole Asian continent. For US politicians, fortifying the bases in the Philippines was imperative, especially because after the Vietnam War, the Soviet Pacific Fleet established itself in the naval facilities of Cam Ranh Bay in Vietnam and the airfields of Cambodia.[98]

However, since the suspension of base talks during the Ford administration, public consensus on overseas military installations began to change. US academics, journalists, and former generals began to challenge the importance of the bases. Editorials, opinion columns, and news reports expressed consternation over how much politicians would yield to Marcos's demands to keep the US bases in the Philippines at the expense of American taxpayers and the sovereignty of the Filipino people.[99] These policy challenges provided an opportunity for anti-dictatorship activists to target the fiscal foundation of the bases and appeal to US national interests. FFP portrayed the bases as a misappropriation of government funds that could otherwise be allocated to programs and services for American citizens. In a hearing on aid to the Philippines by the House Appropriations Committee held on April 5, 1977, FFP members James Drew and William Goodfellow delivered a statement in which they attempted to create further doubts among the political elite on the continued value of the bases: "We believe that these distant installations are of no vital strategic importance and only serve to corrupt traditional American values by being pawns of the Marcos regime in its demands for more U.S. dollars in order to sustain itself."[100] In essence, maintenance of the bases in the Philippines meant violation of liberal democratic principles that constituted the cornerstone of American government.

But Marcos received military aid at a continually increasing rate despite numerous congressional hearings on the Philippines, the enactment of legislative measures to curtail aid to authoritarian regimes, and the election of Jimmy Carter, who pledged to administer a foreign policy based on human rights. Lobbying efforts declined in the 1980s as the Iranian and Nicaraguan revolutions in 1979 overthrew the Pahlavi and Somoza regimes, respectively, altering the political climate for the movement against Marcos. With the US bases secure, talks about Marcos's human rights obligations dissipated. The Philippine president used the fall of his fellow autocrats to strengthen his position vis-à-vis the US executive and legislature. Although the movement found new supporters in the US Congress, Carter became more intransigent to their demands than ever before and lobbying to cut aid produced bleak results.

In sum, strong intergovernmental linkage—manifested primarily in the Military Bases Agreement—provided Filipinos in the US an accessible institutional target for claims making. While a conservative US foreign policy on the Philippines and executive dominance in decision making indicated closed opportunities for influence, these did not preclude activists from pursuing hostland state engagement. This is because in the US, a coherent and unitary foreign policy is unlikely. Congress—an arena that is permeable to constituency influence and thus provides an opening for movements to exploit conflicts within the US foreign-policy establishment—has a crucial role in decision making.[101] Although movement goals diverged with US strategic interests as defined by the executive, activists were able to make proposals in areas that required congressional roles, such as cutting economic and military aid to Marcos in the Foreign Assistance Act. Activists engaged policy makers in defining the foundation of US national interests in a language that celebrated American liberalism and democracy. Homeland-hostland linkages allowed activists to intimate that the rise of the Marcos dictatorship was an outcome of US colonization of the Philippines, enabling them to use familiar symbols and narratives and grounding their claims and demands for the US withdrawal of support to the regime.

TRANSNATIONAL ADVOCACY NETWORKS AND REGIME ISOLATION

Across the Atlantic, the asylum of CPP-NDF leaders Luis Jalandoni and Consuelo Ledesma in the Netherlands and the deployment of CPP-NDF cadres to Europe instigated a chain migration of refugees and their families who, like their counterparts in the US, were from elite and upper middle-class backgrounds in the Philippines. Dutch asylum policy in the 1970s, based on the 1965 Aliens Law, inadvertently facilitated the transplanting of activist mobilization resources from the Philippines to the Netherlands. The act made no distinction between aliens (who left their home countries for non-persecution reasons) and refugees (who fled their homeland because of oppression).[102]

Since there were no *asielzoekercentra* (asylum seeker centers) in the Netherlands until the late 1980s, asylum seekers had to find their own places to live.[103] This empowered members of CPP-NDF to live close to each other in Utrecht, where almost all the Dutch solidarity activists resided.

Spatial proximity facilitated the creation of a social movement community.[104] The city provided a physical and conceptual space where activists shared, nurtured, and maintained movement symbols, rituals, and ideology through everyday activities, from attending celebrations of life milestones to hosting political discussions in their homes. The offices of the FGN and the NDF became movement community centers that offered mutual aid and support. For both Filipino refugees and Dutch solidarity activists, their personal and political lives converged in Utrecht. These cross-cultural intersections helped crystallize a political refugee identity and a group narrative among Filipinos based on discourses on national loyalty and internationalism. A transnational advocacy network (TAN) focused on the Marcos dictatorship and human rights in the Philippines emerged within the community. The TAN consisted of Filipino refugees, European solidarity activists, church-based NGOs, and academics who pursued naming and shaming through the arena of nongovernmental human rights tribunals.

In 1978, Filipino and European solidarity activists filed a complaint in the Lelio Basso Foundation's Permanent People's Tribunal[105] based on traditional legal standards and those enshrined in the 1976 Universal Declaration of the Rights of Peoples. The activists wanted the tribunal to serve as a venue to express appeals to public conscience, to apply established rules and principles of international law, to delegitimize and politically isolate the Marcos regime in the international community, and to mobilize support for the Philippine national liberation movements. From October 30 to November 3 in 1980, the tribunal on the Philippines met at the University of Antwerp, Belgium, to examine appeals presented by the NDF and the Moro National Liberation Front (MNLF) on behalf of the Filipino and Bangsamoro[106] peoples, respectively (figure 3.2). The jurors[107] evaluated more than three thousand pages of secondhand comprehensive reports on the economic and political situation in the Philippines. Six witnesses from the Philippines testified (a peasant, a student, a writer, a union leader, a former civil servant, and a member of a tribal minority), and one witness from Italy (a domestic worker). The jurors saw visual evidence gathered by the joint preparatory committees on the tribunal. An estimated five hundred people attended the session, most of whom were members of solidarity groups in Belgium, Britain, Canada, France, Germany, Hong Kong, Ireland, Italy, Japan, the Netherlands, Sweden, and the US.[108]

FIGURE 3.2. Luis Jalandoni, spokesperson for the National Democratic Front, addresses the jurors and audience members at the Permanent People's Tribunal on the Philippines, held from October 30 to November 3, 1980, in Antwerp, Belgium. (Source: Chris Pennarts.)

The legal brief accused Marcos and his military of "violation of the rights of peoples, violations of human rights, and crimes under international law including genocide."[109] The prosecution also put on trial the US government, the IMF/WB, and various multinational corporations[110] for participating in transgressions against the Filipino people through direct aid and loans. The tribunal informed the governments of the Philippines and the US of the charges against them through their embassies in Italy, where the tribunal was incorporated, and in Belgium, where the session would take place. Both were invited to send representatives to the tribunal to respond to the allegations, but neither did so.[111] The tribunal considered the joint complaints of the NDF and the MNLF separately but framed the judgment in identical terms. In its final verdict, the tribunal found "that the Marcos regime by its reliance on 'permanent' martial law and numerous blatant abuses of state is deprived of legitimate standing as a government in international society and lacks the competence to act on behalf of the Filipino or Bangsa Moro people."[112] The decision acknowledged and affirmed the authority of the NDF and the MNLF as rightful representatives of their respective peoples. As representatives, they had the dispensation to pursue the liberation of their peoples from the regime

PATRIOTS AND REVOLUTIONARIES

even through armed struggle. This recognition enabled the revolutionary movements to legally receive assistance from established government and other international bodies.

The delegitimization of the Marcos regime and the endorsement of the NDF and the MNLF by the international community presented a unique opportunity for broadening the movement beyond the campaign against the dictatorship. During the tribunal, the network of movements and constituents diversified. It brought together, for the first time, solidarity organizations, political parties, national liberation movements from other countries, church groups, and trade unions across Europe to support the Philippine revolutionary struggle. Through their solidarity manifestations read in the plenary, the diverse network of activists played an instrumental role in backing the two contenders of state power—the NDF and the MNLF. The tribunal also enabled the parallel processes of certification and decertification as more than six thousand letters and petitions arrived in Antwerp from private citizens across Europe, North America, and the Asia-Pacific region, calling for the condemnation of the US-Marcos dictatorship and the international recognition of the NDF and the MNLF.[113] Finally, it connected the US anti-dictatorship movement to its counterparts in Europe, making the event a tangible moment of transnational collective action. Upon learning about the initiative, the 1979 AMLC National Conference held in Seattle passed a resolution supporting the efforts of activists in Europe and designating the International Association of Filipino Patriots (IAFP) to liaise with them. The IAFP instructed all chapters of the AMLC, the FFP, and the KDP to sign and send postcards to Belgium, indicating endorsement of "the efforts to have the plight of the Filipino and Moro people be heard."[114]

The tribunal further delegitimized Marcos by connecting the suffering of OFWs to the regime. Including a migrant worker as a key witness in the tribunal gave OFWs stature as not only victims of the dictatorship but as agents in the revolutionary struggle, too. In her testimony, Celia Soliman, a Filipina migrant worker and organizer in Rome, identified two mutually reinforcing systems—global capitalism and authoritarianism in the Philippines—that created the conditions for exploitation of Filipino workers in their hostlands and the complacency of the Philippine state.[115] Her statement below demonstrates frame bridging, whereby activists deploy frames that connect their issues to the broader discourse.[116] She elaborated on the connection between labor migration, the insecurity of OFWs in Europe, and authoritarian rule in the Philippines:

> The dream of finding better conditions abroad than in the Philippines becomes a nightmare . . . the hard work and the inner pain; the incomparable

sadness; the separation from home and loved ones; the adjustment to a new culture and a new language; legal papers to worry about; anxiety about the police; the low and inadequate salary; the debts incurred to come and which have to be repaid. . . .

From among the migrants, the seeds of their organization [are] already beginning. They realize that only in organizing themselves will they be able to fight to defend their rights, to work for better working conditions and to be able to face the world with dignity and self-respect.

The roots of the problem remain, however. These are:

1. Marcos' political and economic policies which force thousands of Filipinos to go abroad to find jobs due to unemployment at home.
2. The policy of using migrant labor to get foreign exchange.
3. The collusion between the Philippine government and legal and illegal travel and employment agencies.
4. The inadequate information and protection given by the Philippine government to Filipino workers abroad.[117]

Bridging macrostructures in the homeland and microlevel processes in the hostlands provided a framework on which to construct the oppositional consciousness necessary for the mobilization of migrants. Activists built upon Soliman's testimony to create an identity that contradicted Marcos's construction of OFWs' heroism and sacrifice. As will be explained in chapter 4, in mobilizing overseas workers, activists strategically used a class ideology to frame the experiences of those who suffered dislocation from the homeland and marginalization in the host society. A collective identity as migrant workers—an imagined transnational community based on shared experiences of migration, separation, and exploitation, all products of the Marcos regime—separated the state from the nation.

The tribunal propelled the Philippine conflict into the international public sphere. By delegitimizing the Marcos regime and holding the US accountable for its support of authoritarian rule based on legal and moral standards as well as rallying support for national liberation movements, activists were able to leverage public opinion to press for reforms in human rights at the minimum and to put Marcos and the US under increased public scrutiny. But the institutional norms of the tribunal, combined with a narrower multiorganizational field composed mostly of TANs, limited the ways by which activists could make public identity claims. Although the tribunal supported the agenda of the liberation movements, including their tactic of armed struggle, activists downplayed nationalistic frames. Rather, activists used a class-based identity that fused cosmopolitan ideals and particularistic attachments based on the oppression and agency of migrants as both Filipinos and workers in the global economy.

Thus, in the unsettled cultural period of the dictatorship where the definition of and division between patriots and traitors—between "us" and "them"—became malleable, the movement altered the tool kit from which Filipinos draw to make sense of the political situation. In both foreign-policy lobbying and naming and shaming, activists decertified Marcos, such that acts of resistance against his regime would no longer be considered unpatriotic, paving the way for new articulations of loyalty to the homeland. Eventually, political conditions in the Philippines and around the world offered the impetus for Marcos's downfall. The dictator nominally lifted martial law in 1981. When the Marcos-aligned Philippine Congress amended the constitution to change the system of government from parliamentary to semipresidential, Marcos called an election and won. Despite Marcos's democratically sanctioned extension of power, the activists in the Philippines and overseas saw the oligarchy splintering. The regime gradually lost elite support after the election, and activists recognized an opportunity to advance the revolutionary work. The assassination and martyrdom of exiled opposition leader Benigno S. Aquino Jr. on August 21, 1983, finally fractured the elite opposition, which made the NDF and the MNLF the only viable actors who could topple the dictator. And on February 22–25, 1986, over two million Filipinos held demonstrations in the capital of Manila, which led to the overthrow of Marcos. Unlike other sultanistic regimes that were defeated by a revolutionary movement or ousted by a military coup d'état, a massive crowd of largely nonviolent protesters finally brought down the regime.

Loyalty to the Homeland

If a diaspora is created through activism, and that activism undermines the homeland regime, how does it forge a collective identity that fosters migrants' continued belonging to the homeland? Is allegiance to institutions of power such as the state necessary in diaspora formation? We saw in this chapter how, in the movement against the Marcos dictatorship in the US and the Netherlands, Filipinos challenged the idea that loyalty to the regime was fundamental to their attachment to the Philippine nation. Activists framed protesting a government that had lost legitimacy from its citizens as an expression of love for the homeland. The framing strategies varied due to the distinct relationships the Philippines had with the US and the Netherlands, as well as the different demographics and resources of the respective migrant communities. But in both cases, activists depicted the Marcos government as no longer representative of the Filipino people. To contest the state, then, was to demonstrate unity with the nation.

In each stage of mobilization, activists disrupted the hegemony of the government in migrants' imagination of the homeland—in essence, to show that, as Corazon Aquino said in a quote at the beginning of the chapter, "Marcos is not the Philippines." In essence, the anti-dictatorship movement had three interrelated outcomes that contributed to Filipino diaspora formation: it denaturalized the relationship between the state and the nation, it contested the idea that resistance to the state is an act of disloyalty to the people, and it opened opportunities to imagine and articulate alternative ways of belonging to the homeland. In other words, activism led to the construction of diaspora based on an oppositional collective identity whereby patriotism is combined with revolution.

4

Workers and Minorities

Mobilizations for Migrants' Rights and Ethnic/National Solidarity

Joyce was only twenty-one when she went to the Netherlands as an au pair in 1990. She lived with a young, highly educated couple and their four-year-old child. Despite earning less than a Dutch nanny and receiving no benefits, she felt satisfied. Her life in Amsterdam was better than it had been in Manila, where a degree in commerce from a private university had produced no job prospects. After the au pair program ended, Joyce decided not to go back to the Philippines, and she became an undocumented worker. She worked for various families, cleaning houses and taking care of children. She also waited tables, and when I talked to her, she was working at a restaurant popular with tourists in the Amsterdam city center.

When I first met Joyce, she said she immediately felt comfortable with me because "you are not like the Filipinos from the US who come to Amsterdam for travel." Confused, I asked her to elaborate:

> Filipino tourists from the US come to the restaurant because it's so near the museums. I get excited. But whenever I ask in Tagalog, *'Taga saan kayo sa atin?'* [Where are you from in our own (land)?¹], they would respond to me in English, 'Oh, we're Americans.' But I know they understood me. Maybe because they don't want to be associated with me. *Sus, kunwari pa!²* [Really, how pretentious and snobbish!] We are all the same, perceived lower by the Dutch and Americans.

"But why can you let your guard down with me?" I asked. "Because we came from the same background," she replied. I had mentioned to her that my mother is an OFW. I realized that for Joyce, there was more to solidarity than shared culture. Social class mattered, and for that reason, she considered me kin. But Joyce also regarded US-based Filipinos as like her—insofar as they were in an inferior position in the racial hierarchy and thus subjected to identical treatment.

Allan, Roy, and Nelia were also undocumented, but unlike Joyce, they entered the Netherlands as tourists. Before they left the Philippines, they were employed in professions such as education and technology industries. They already had relatives and friends from their hometowns who had been in the Netherlands for years, which was how they got short-term visas. This social network was invaluable in finding employment, too, especially when their visas expired. All of them were active in the movement campaigning for undocumented workers' rights such as health care, occupational safety, and social security. As they enthusiastically explained to me their upcoming events and activities, Roy said their fellow activists were like his family. "I trust other undocumented migrants regardless of race and ethnicity more than Filipinos who are Dutch citizens or who have papers. They don't know the struggle," he said in Tagalog. Nelia chimed in, recounting the experiences that convinced her, in the words of anthropologist and writer Zora Neale Hurston, "All my skinfolk ain't kinfolk." She told me of how a Dutch Filipino took advantage of her, hiring her to do numerous personal errands and household chores but not paying her the proper wages. When she demanded her salary, the Dutch Filipino threatened to report her to the police and deport her, and even blackball her in the community so she would never find work again.

At first, she thought she was just unlucky, but after meeting activists in the movement, she learned that her Indonesian and Moroccan peers had had similar incidents. She realized that legal status defines social relations among co-ethnics. Nelia concluded her anecdote by telling me, in Tagalog, how she felt about Filipinos in the Netherlands in general: "We speak Tagalog, go to church together, eat the same food—that's all." Joyce's, Roy's, and Nelia's stories reveal that their idea of community acknowledges and combines difference and similarity.

As discussed in chapter 2, Marcos's labor export program stimulated the dispersal of Filipinos abroad, producing three interrelated effects on the composition of the overseas population. First, for the first time, diversity based on social class and legal status characterized the migrant workforce. Highly trained professionals such as engineers relocated simultaneously with low-skilled, often undocumented laborers in the same country. Second, most Filipinos who migrated were unable to settle in the places of destination due to the contractual nature of their employment and the citizenship laws in these countries. So, they continued to be under the authority and control of the Philippine state. Third, until the mid-twentieth century, the main destination was the US colonial metropole—an idealized land in the national imaginary.

The decade that followed the implementation of the policy, however, saw the emergence of countries in Europe as sites where Filipinos dreamed social mobility was possible.

With such heterogeneity in the occupational and legal statuses of Filipino migrants, building solidarity across borders is a complex process. For professional workers and permanent settlers, the presence of low-skilled, undocumented laborers is a source of national shame and dishonor. They tarnish the reputation of co-national/co-ethnics who have "made it" in the hostlands and undermine the international image of the Philippines. Overseas travel and employment are no longer the exclusive possession of Filipino elites and the middle class, so regular social encounters in public spaces—an avoidable situation in the class-segregated cities and neighborhoods of the Philippines—have heightened anxieties of ethnic and national lumping among professional-class workers and permanent settlers in these foreign lands. In response, many have set up "social and discursive boundaries to segregate themselves from domestic workers"—as the experience of Joyce shows—that efface "the undifferentiated quality of liminal beings undergoing the ritual of economic pilgrimage."[3]

Since the late 1970s, the number of Filipinos making this odyssey has been vast. But a diaspora is more than just a demographic actuality. It is defined by social relationships mediated through and epitomized by practices, symbols, and discourses. And while homeland orientation is essential, it is not sufficient to explain the formation of diasporas. Migrants also need to create bonds with their co-ethnics/co-nationals who have left the homeland and settled elsewhere. As James Clifford argues, "a shared, ongoing history of displacement, suffering, adaptation, or resistance may be as important as the projection of a specific origin."[4] While perceived attachment based on ideas about common culture can draw migrants together initially, it cannot sustain these ties when schisms based on their daily realities surface. To understand the formation of diasporas, we must interpret the persistence of sameness alongside difference, especially how "the boundaries of difference are continually repositioned in relation to different points of reference."[5] This means that social ties are continuously created, negotiated, and renewed to account for migrants' multiple and variegated circumstances that change and evolve depending on historical and objective conditions and their location in the migration life course—from recent arrival to full assimilation. We cannot therefore speak of one static migrant narrative that encompasses all experiences. How do people who are different and physically separated identify with each other and think they are somehow the same and connected? If diasporas are social constructions, what discourses encapsulate similarity and diversity so that migrants can build solidarity across time and space?

"We Filipinos are the Jews of today" says Thelma, a live-in caregiver in Tel-Aviv in Claudia Liebelt's study of Filipino domestic workers in Israel and their appropriation of the discourse of victimhood in their organizing to assert legal, social, and cultural inclusion not in the Philippines but in their new home.[6] Social movements play a central role in the discursive processes through which migrants see themselves as part of a collective. They provide a space and constitute practices that allow migrants to encounter each other and share their stories. They also intentionally pursue consciousness raising in these social interactions that often lead to the participants' and their own cognitive liberation—when they "collectively define their situations as unjust and subject to change through group action."[7] With cognitive liberation, actors interpret, generate, and attach meaning to events, relationships, and experiences that lead to them feeling that they need to do something, and this will make a difference. Fostering solidarity through social movements therefore means that the formation of a collective identity is strategic as much as it is discursive. It is also transformative at the individual level, for "participation in social movements frequently involves enlargement of personal identity for participants and offers fulfillment and realization of self."[8]

In his study of the undocumented youth movement in the US, Walter Nicholls argues that activists carefully and persistently use a discursive strategy that transforms a group of individuals into "a common political subject with common worldviews, aspirations, and emotional dispositions."[9] They emphasize certain proclivities, values, and beliefs to shape identities based on their assessment of the political context and the goals of the movement.[10] Because migrant communities are heterogeneous, activists draw on discourses that speak to the lived experiences of a range of actors. They single out recognizable frames that weave together their personal stories, often changing the meanings of well-known symbols and narratives. But fundamental to these discourses and frames, which emerge and develop in the context of oppositional interaction, is the political agency and efficacy of individuals as one group so that ideas are actualized into practices. Solidarity is thus constituted through collective action whereby identity formation is both a process and an outcome in conflictual relations, as shown by Rick Fantasia in the emergence of class consciousness among workers in the US.[11]

But this sense of solidarity need not be rooted in direct ties—that is, it does not have to emerge from material and visible connections such as when people belong to a movement organization and regularly see each other at meetings or protests. Otherwise, nations would not have been formed. As Benedict Anderson has famously put it, solidarity at this level is based on "imagined communities,"[12] with people who have never met—and possibly

WORKERS AND MINORITIES

never will—bound together by their ideas about their relationship to each other. In fact, Francesca Polletta argues that in institutions of government, business organizations, and social movements, people have worked together based on relationships they did not actually have; rather, they invoke the obligations of culturally familiar relationships (e.g., family member, neighbor, co-worker) in different settings.[13] In essence, ties need not be real but invented. Through what Polletta calls "relationship schemas," actors can draw on norms, expectations, and emotions to guide how they interact in situations rife with uncertainty and how they see the character of the bonds they forge.

I saw these processes of engaging with discourses and generating frames as well as using relationship schemas in how the movement for migrants' rights built solidarity and constructed a collective identity of Filipinos as workers and minorities at a period when they were scattered across the world due to the Philippine government's labor export policy. Through their activism, migrants tapped into preexisting relationships, networks, and communities rooted in their countries of settlement. They acquired an organic understanding of how the social structures in the US and the Netherlands shape the life chances of their co-ethnics/co-nationals. In the process, they questioned their multiple identities and social roles—Filipino, migrant, refugee, worker, family member, and so on—and recognized shared and contradictory experiences, grievances, and goals. These personal transformations enabled activists to understand the dialectics of solidarity and conflict in the formation of a community.

Activists' experiential knowledge then shaped the discursive strategy they employed in various campaigns and avenues for migrants to make sense of their individual experiences. As political entrepreneurs, they interpreted and articulated these experiences and developed what I call a "displacement, marginalization, and empowerment" frame based on these three themes or propositions: economic insecurity in the Philippines that dislocated Filipino migrants; racial boundaries of belonging in the US and the Netherlands that marginalized them; and migrants' economic contributions to the homeland and the hostlands that empowers them. At the same time, activists drew on fictive kinship, a relationship schema familiar to Filipinos with its cultural roots in both indigenous and colonial Philippines and its strong anchor and influence in contemporary social relations—from patron-client bonds in local politics to support networks among overseas Filipinos as discussed in chapter 2. They used this to nurture commitment not only to the movement but to their fellow migrant workers, who rely on each other like family members in the hostile environment of their hostlands. In essence, solidarity with co-ethnics/co-nationals arose from the movement for migrants' rights through the following process: in strategic campaigns and day-to-day organizing, activists generate discourses so that migrants think of their individual struggles as part of a collective experience—that is, their problems are rooted in their similar structural location and are not due to their own personal faults; with group action to address these issues and better the situation for all Filipinos abroad, not just for movement participants where they are, they allude to their relationship with each other as their family in their countries of settlement, for as minority workers undergoing the same difficulties such as separation from and longing for their biological kin, they are united based on their shared struggle and perceived common fate.

We can observe this dynamic play out more prominently with the global dispersion of Filipinos and the emergence of a discourse that linked the difficulties of OFWs to the political developments in the homeland, compared to when Filipinos were going only to the US as colonial migrants and when mobilizations occurred to target solely the immigration policies of the US state. But the use of fictive kinship as a relationship schema to create a sense of obligation to each other has long existed among Filipinos in the US in the unions, cooperatives, and mutual aid networks they built to protect themselves from the racist attacks of the native-born population, to educate and rally members, and to deal with loneliness and alienation. Thus, like the Propaganda Movement of Filipino exiles during the Spanish colonial period influencing the anti-Marcos dictatorship movement in the US discussed in chapter 3, past organizing has also shaped contemporary activism in two ways: it established discourses and frames that captured the lived experiences of Filipino migrants as racialized workers, Third World peoples, and community members; and it anchored the concerns and issues of migrants to other social movements.

Building Solidarity in Early Periods of Mobilization

In his semiautobiographical novel *America Is in the Heart: A Personal History*, Filipino author and labor leader Carlos Bulosan recounts how he endured discrimination and hostility from the American white population that rudely awakened him to the class and racial structures that pervade American society. When he applied for jobs in San Diego, California, in the early 1930s, restaurant and hotel owners physically assaulted him. Bulosan initially held responsible his fellow Filipinos' cultural traits:

> I put the blame on certain Filipinos who had behaved badly in America, who had instigated hate and discontent among their friends and followers. This

misconception was generated by a confused personal reaction to dynamic social forces, but my hunger for the truth had inevitably led me to take an historical attitude. I was to understand and interpret this chaos from a collective point of view, because it was pervasive and universal.[14]

Bulosan's reflections illustrate that individuals see themselves as part of a collective when they understand their personal ordeals as a product of their social location and historical development. Once settled in the US, the predominantly male Filipino population from the first wave of immigration faced segregation, antimiscegenation laws, and exclusion from naturalization and other opportunities. Because few could vote, they used labor organizing to advance economic and political interests.[15] According to Dorothy B. Fujita-Rony, unionization was an opportunity for Filipinos "not only to connect with other groups of color but also to interact with the European American population, whether in confrontation or in alliance."[16] From the 1930s to 1960s, unions thus became the main locus for Filipinos to express, question, and negotiate different aspects of their identity. These included the Filipino Federation of Labor, the Filipino Labor Union, the Cannery Workers' and Farm Laborers' Union (CWFLU), the International Longshoremen's and Warehousemen's Union (ILWU), and the Agricultural Workers Organizing Committee.[17]

Although wage increases and favorable working conditions were important issues to Filipinos, active ethnic unionization was also a vehicle to combat overt racism from the majority white population. Physical isolation and antimiscegenation laws created state-imposed bachelorhood among Filipinos. But they found spaces for everyday forms of resistance,[18] such as in pool and taxi dance halls. In these places Filipino men could interact socially with white women, often leading to interracial relationships and marriages.[19] The increased visibility of Filipinos in these physical and symbolic realms heightened white male resentment. Filipinos were not just accused of "taking jobs away" from them; they were also considered a threat to their masculinity.[20] Social and economic tensions fomented anti-Filipino sentiment, which came to a head in the Watsonville anti-Filipino riot of 1930. Labor militancy among Filipinos intensified in the San Joaquin Valley and the Salinas-Watsonville area, where vigilante mobs operated and local politicians exploited the violence for electoral support.[21] During this period, class oppression became a reality for Filipinos through their subjugation based on race and nationality.[22]

Fusing cross-class, national loyalties even among Filipinos in the unions posed a challenge. Ethnic and linguistic differences, and mythic constructions of the inferiority or supremacy of particular provincial and regional cultures, often provoked animosity within their ranks.[23] Bulosan observes critically that a "tribal" orientation "had obstructed all efforts toward Filipino unity in America."[24] The lack of a common language hindered the formation of social bonds. The Philippine national language emerged only after World War II. Early Filipino immigrants in the US spoke a variety of languages and dialects, and proficiency in English was limited. Filipino union organizers had to carefully navigate the factionalism in their community, often prioritizing ethnic and national solidarity at the expense of class unity with other racial groups. For instance, in the CWFLU Local 18527, Filipino union activists only targeted Chinese and Japanese contractors to show their co-ethnics/co-nationals they were "one Filipino race."[25] However, as they recognized that a similar class status was applied to Filipinos in the US despite different regional origins in the Philippines, they eventually overcame these divisions and cooperated.[26]

While Filipino unions fought for labor representation and rights in the US, they also strived to forge and maintain a national consciousness tied to the homeland.[27] Newspapers were key in this endeavor. They featured news from the Philippines and reports from Filipinos in different cities of settlement in the US. Hometown associations—that is, associations of migrants who hail from the same town or province—also proliferated in the 1930s and formalized the process by which goods could be sent to the Philippines, facilitating transborder exchange.[28] Few organizations served the needs of the Filipino community, so the unions also provided mutual aid and social support for their members. Migrants built fictive kin relationships in unions and reinterpreted "family" as "an expansive concept that included not only immediate relatives or members of the extended family but also townmates and other Filipina/os met while traveling, working or going to school."[29]

The role of the union as a space for the formation of a collective identity rooted in class and racial oppression continued with second-generation Filipinos. For instance, male teenage children of Alaskeros[30] spent summers in the Alaska canneries working low-paying jobs like their fathers, even though their families had achieved middle-class status. According to Jason, the son of an Alaskero from Seattle, through this "rite of passage," he personally witnessed and directly encountered racial and sexual discrimination, dangerous working conditions, and widespread corruption in the unions. Such experiences inspired Filipino Americans to commit to a lifetime of union organizing as they joined CWFLU and ILWU Local 37.[31] But they also grew up during a period of social unrest due to continued racial oppression of minorities and US imperialism in the Third World—conditions that gave rise to the civil rights and anti–Vietnam War movements. As the US-born descendants of immigrants from the first and second waves sought to understand the political and social conflicts they confronted, they turned to struggles in education, and the locus of identity construction shifted from the unions to student organizations.

The civil rights and antiwar movements mobilized Filipino Americans initially, but their political socialization intensified on campuses, especially on the West Coast. Those who grew up in predominantly white neighborhoods in San Diego, San Francisco, and Seattle and in ethnically mixed and segregated communities in California's Central Valley encountered each other at institutions of higher education. Through the Educational Opportunity Program and special admissions for disadvantaged students, they were the first to attend college in their families. They went mostly to state schools that were hotbeds of dissent and rebellion such as San Francisco State College, the University of California, and the University of Washington.

While the Vietnam War served as a springboard for the emergence of an oppositional consciousness among Filipino Americans, the Third World strikes[32] cemented a transnational radical identity. They learned about the common oppression and fight for national liberation among colonized peoples in the US and other countries. From November 6 to March 21, 1968, the Third World Liberation Front (TWLF)—a coalition of the Black Student Union, the Mexican American Student Coalition, the Latin American Student Organization, the Pilipino American Collegiate Endeavor (PACE), the Intercollegiate Chinese for Social Action, and the Asian American Political Alliance—mobilized thousands of students at San Francisco State College in the longest student strike in US history. They demanded that the histories, struggles, and triumphs of people of color be taught on their own terms, and that the university establish a school of ethnic studies with a faculty and curriculum chosen by their communities, along with open admissions for all nonwhite applicants.[33] Through the strikes, Filipino Americans constructed a collective identity that transcended ethnic, cultural, and national boundaries—that is, they saw themselves not just as Filipinos but also as part of an international movement against white supremacy.

After the TWLF strikes, Filipino American activists established themselves at Kearny Street, the heart of Manilatown in San Francisco. The area earned the moniker "Red Block" and became a thriving movement center for the radical left arm of the Asian American movement, where ideas that guided the national liberation struggles in Africa, Asia, and Latin America circulated.[34] In this space, Filipino Americans were introduced to a radical reading of Philippine history through the writings of Filipino nationalists José Rizal, Andrés Bonifacio, and members of the Propaganda Movement as well as leftist historian Renato Constantino and José María Sison, founder of the CPP. These works inspired the young militants to immerse themselves in the local Filipino community.

Ryan is a second-generation Filipino American whose parents were farmworkers. He was a student leader in a university in the Bay Area in 1968. When I met him in 2014, he was in his late sixties and still involved in various forms of activism. He recalled that the strikes of 1968 paved the way for him to analyze more deeply the interconnections of various struggles across the world that shaped his political subjectivity:

> As we began to figure out what we were going to offer in these ethnic studies classes that were now given, so began my introduction to the whole intellectual history of nationalism and the progressive current in understanding Philippine history. . . . For me, personally, I was focused on the Cultural Revolution, the war in Vietnam, and the Cuban Revolution, and pleased to find this comparable tradition in the Philippines.

On Kearny Street, other Filipino Americans, like Ryan, learned for the first time the long history of Filipino radical activism in the US, including protest repertoires and the rich oppositional culture nurtured by previous generations. In 1968, the *manongs*[35] of the first wave of immigration lived in the International Hotel (or I-Hotel), a luxury accommodation built in 1907 in the city's center for visiting dignitaries. The city government later transformed it into a residence for Asian male laborers. The *manongs* told tales to young Filipino Americans about their hard lives in the Philippines before they left for the US, the trauma of being uprooted and trying to make it in America despite racism, the solidarity forged with other ethnic and racial groups due to a shared fate, and the hope and challenges of collective resistance through union organizing. According to Filipino American activist and historian Estella Habal, upon learning the life stories of the *manongs*, who were like their *lolos* (grandfathers), the second generation discovered "the ancestral roots of their own radical impulses, allowing them to recover their own sense of historical connection."[36] They traveled to Delano, California, on weekends to investigate the problems that the *manongs* and other farmworkers confronted and to understand further the history of struggle of Filipinos during the first wave. As those involved in the TWLF strikes developed an awareness of the experiences of the immigrant generation in their communities, they became embroiled in mobilizations to fight the destruction of Asian enclaves from the late 1960s to the 1970s, especially since their colleges and universities were situated in cities undergoing rapid gentrification.[37]

The itinerant lives of the first wave of Filipino immigrants in the US mainland prevented them from establishing a place of ethnic concentration. In response to racist attacks, however, they set up community centers and organizations in cities and towns where many Filipinos lived, such as Salinas, Seattle, Stockton, and Yakima.[38] The American branches of Philippine fraternal and Masonic orders were "the most formal, largest, and long-lived of these Filipina/o American religious, political, and community organizations," which served as a surrogate family and support network for the thousands of single men.[39] Filipinos also joined other Asians in the Chinatowns of San Francisco and Seattle, which functioned as a safe haven against racial violence and a way station for new immigrants.[40] In San Francisco, the I-Hotel area eventually housed the first Filipino community in the city.[41] But urban renewal projects and government revitalization programs threatened these spaces of refuge during a period of social unrest.

Filipino American activists were at the forefront of the struggle to save their neighborhoods. The most famous was the mobilization against the eviction of elderly Asians tenants, including the *manongs*, at the I-Hotel. At that time, the revolutionary philosophy of Mao Tse-tung influenced political groups and alliances in the US such as the Red Guard Party, the Black Panther Party, and the Asian American movement. "Serve the People" became an inspiring rallying call for Filipino Americans to join the anti-eviction movement, especially since most of the tenants at I-Hotel were Filipino. PACE was among the first student organizations to be involved in the movement through its community outreach and action programs, and Filipino Americans who participated in the mobilizations achieved cognitive liberation, as captured in Habal's reflection: "In the radical upsurge of 1968, we began to realize that we were not middle class; that we were actually from working-class backgrounds, although we were more privileged than the *manongs*, and we formed our own organizations."[42] In essence, as Filipino Americans developed class consciousness in the anti-eviction movement, recognized their historical affinity to the I-Hotel, and developed kinship with the *manongs*, they also saw themselves as members of the community they were defending.

In Seattle, Filipino Americans also participated in community activism and coalition politics to create better living conditions in the Chinatown–International District (CID). Home to Chinese, Filipino, and Japanese laborers who settled in the city in the early twentieth century and to poor whites and Blacks who migrated there during World War II, the neighborhood was in danger of deterioration, especially after the city constructed the Interstate 5 freeway, splitting the district. In 1970, the construction of the King County

94 CHAPTER FOUR

Multipurpose Domed Stadium[43] adjacent to the CID divided the community, with Asian business organizations supporting the project and young Asian Americans opposing it. Second-generation Filipinos felt attached to King Street in the district, where their parents and ancestors sought sanctuary upon first arrival in the US. To them, preserving the CID was not just protecting the physical space from decay, but more importantly, saving their people's history from erasure. Labor organizer and son of Alaskero Silme Domingo wrote, "In Seattle, history for Filipinos begins at King Street in Chinatown (now referred to as International District). For others, it may be just another street. But for the thousands of Filipino males who came to the U.S. during the 1920s and 1930s, King Street was where life began."[44]

In sum, Filipino immigrants' early mobilizations in the US connected local, community-based struggles to global movements where they and the second generation constructed identities that melded working-class internationalism and Philippine nationalism. In reclaimed autonomous spaces—college campuses, ethnic enclaves, cannery shop floors, and pool and taxi dance halls—they developed and circulated hidden transcripts, "discourse that takes place 'offstage,' beyond direct observation by powerholders."[45] Movements intersected, diffused, and spilled over in these physical and ideological spaces, and activists linked issues, formulated common protest repertoires, and developed kinship ties. The sites allowed social encounters among Filipino immigrants that revealed their common marginalization as workers and minorities at the bottom of class and racial hierarchies, regardless of their perceived group position in the Philippines. For US-born Filipinos, these spaces provided an institutional base to connect with other oppressed groups, learn about the forgotten histories of their people, and reject the cultural codes that reproduce power relationships. From their first forays into antiwar protests to their habitual interaction with the tenants of I-Hotel on Kearny Street or cannery workers in Alaska, the young Filipino American activists developed multilayered, rich, and textured identities. In addition to their individual, family, and community experiences, discourses on nationalism, panethnicity, Third World liberation, and working-class solidarity combined to root their identities, connecting the movements among immigrants from the first and second waves to those of second-generation Filipino Americans coming of age during a tumultuous time in global history. In all these mobilizations, actors drew on discourses and developed frames that point to their displacement (e.g., destruction of ethnic enclaves) and marginalization (e.g., employment discrimination and social exclusion of farm and cannery workers as well as alienation from knowledge among college students), and

WORKERS AND MINORITIES   95

drew on a relationship schema (e.g., fictive kinship) that was familiar to them to enact their commitments to social change.

But as Marcos's labor export policy came into full effect in the late 1970s, colonial and permanent immigrants in the US no longer dominated the Filipino overseas population. This demographic change impacted the type of movements that arose in the communities and the discourses that animated them. The interconnected and parallel movements against the dictatorship and for migrants' rights produced a master frame[46] that identified the Philippine state as the cause of Filipinos' displacement and marginalization in their countries of temporary residence or permanent settlement. This common antagonist wove together spatially bound experiences and catalyzed bonds of kinship and solidarity among Filipino migrants across borders.

Anti-Dictatorship and Migrants' Rights Movements

If diffusion to two or more countries is an important characteristic of diasporas, then the source of this scattering is fundamental to the discourses that inform migrants' collective identity. In *Diasporas*, Stéphane Dufoix suggests that the violence of the slave trade has led to two equally important ways all people of African descent imagine their attachment with Africa and constitute the meaning of the "Black/African diaspora": their link is imagined either as "continuity with or rupture from the origin" or as "the absence of an origin and the development of a common culture precisely founded on hybridity."[47] In contrast, Khatharya Um argues that the genocide by the Khmer Rouge has produced tenuous ties among dispersed Cambodians and deep yet tormented connection to their ancestral homeland, making the struggle to understand and deal with the historical trauma as constitutive of the Cambodia diaspora.[48]

Among Filipinos, colonialism initially caused movement to the US and shaped the daily experiences of immigrants and the subsequent political socialization of their children. But colonialism did not directly produce the exodus of Filipinos as temporary workers from the 1970s onward. In fact, as Filomeno V. Aguilar argues, "Once Filipino workers began to disperse themselves around the world, the edifice of Philippine-US binarism began to crumble. . . . No longer is the United States the sole Philippine Other."[49] To be sure, discourses on colonialism are powerful in defining and constituting kinship among Filipinos in the US, as E. San Juan Jr. argues.[50] But they are not paramount in the formation of a collective identity that promote cross-border solidarity among the rest of the dispersed Filipinos. "My first sight of the approaching land was an exhilarating experience. Everything seemed native and promising to me. It was like coming home after a long voyage, although as yet I had no home in this city," wrote Carlos Bulosan upon reaching Seattle in 1930. This is not the feeling for the thousands of OFWs arriving at various airports in Asia, the Middle East, and Europe.

When the massive outflow of labor peaked during the Marcos dictatorship, the role of the Philippine state became salient in discourses on migration. As a labor broker, the state determines and designates who can move to which country and with what skills.[51] It also stipulates how migrants should behave in their countries of destination, putting limits to their agency. The state, therefore, creates not only the objective conditions of OFWs; it also controls the narrative about their migration and shapes their political subjectivity based on ideals of heroism and sacrifice imposed upon them. Thus, with the 1974 Labor Code, the government has actively participated in the discursive construction of the diaspora. State discourse was a point of departure in how social movements developed frames to create cross-border solidarity, even for those who permanently settled and gained citizenship in other countries.

In the Netherlands, anti-dictatorship activists discussed in the previous chapter were the first to get involved in the economic and political issues confronting Filipino migrants. In contrast, migrant activists in the US had been mobilizing for decades, but they made the connection between their situation and developments in the Philippines only when the anti-dictatorship movement gained traction in the US. But how did activists develop solidarity based on two seemingly conflicting struggles—one homeland-oriented, the other aimed at the countries of destination?

As anti-dictatorship activists in the US and the Netherlands mobilized to hold Marcos and his regime accountable for plunder and human rights violations, they learned about the grievances of Filipinos based on their experiences as migrants. From this, they gained real-life understanding of the dynamics in the communities and the multilayered identities of their co-ethnics/co-nationals. These insights transformed how they saw themselves and the movement, for social forces impinge on personal lives, expanding or restricting an actor's set of choices. I saw in the experience of members of the KDP in the US and the NDF in the Netherlands how the intimacy they formed with Filipino migrants in their organizing for the anti-dictatorship struggle unsettled their worldviews and identities—that is, in their interactions with movement constituents in their countries of settlement, they experienced cognitive liberation on issues that affect and resonate with migrants.

In the US, KDP was the only movement organization that deliberately connected the campaign against the Marcos dictatorship and the struggle for rights of Filipino migrants. This dual approach was as much strategic as it was ideological. KDP did not view the Filipinos in the US as an exile community that would return to the Philippines once the political situation improved. A huge proportion of Filipinos in American society were permanent immigrants and a growing second generation, keen on settling or maintaining a home in the US. In addition, the membership of KDP was disproportionately composed of US-born Filipinos who tended to be more interested in domestic rather than homeland issues.[52] Thus, the demographic composition of KDP also defined its framework.

Antonio was a student activist in the Philippines. After his arrest at a demonstration in front of the US embassy in Manila during Vice President Spiro Agnew's Philippine visit in 1969, his parents pressured him to move to the US. He was able to migrate through the family-reunification provision of the 1965 Immigration and Nationality Act. Upon arrival, he immediately joined the KDP. During our interview, he reflected on the primacy given to the issues of Filipinos who had settled in the US alongside the overthrow of Marcos since the organization's inception. He considered mobilizing Filipinos on their concerns as workers and minorities as both ideological and instrumental:

> We needed to organize Filipinos on the basis of their problems here and strategically you can't say the solution is revolution in the Philippines. That won't be enough. That's part of the solution. But even if there's a revolution in the Philippines, their problems here of discrimination and inequalities still have to be resolved. And for that, the context of your analysis and proposals or resolutions has to be based on the United States. It is not dependent on the Philippine situation. . . . We would organize Filipinos on [their] issues in the United States and then win them over to the national democratic position in the Philippines. . . . [Our goal was to] create a real left-wing, if not socialist position, in terms of their concerns in the United States . . . like labor, discrimination, gender, race.

A key strategy of anti-dictatorship activists was lobbying legislators in Congress to decrease aid to the Philippines. To strengthen their leverage with politicians, especially those who represented states with a sizable number of Filipinos such as California, Hawai'i, and New York, activists organized ethnic constituents and established linkages with preexisting social movement networks and local civic organizations. Aside from convening public forums and holding demonstrations outside the Philippine consulates to display resistance, they also met with Filipino immigrants in spaces of daily social interaction. Activists distributed the KDP newspaper, *Ang Katipunan*, at Asian grocery stores that Filipinos visited regularly. Since most Filipinos in the US

98 CHAPTER FOUR

were Catholics, they also went to churches every Sunday and to restaurants where parishioners celebrated the Sabbath with their families and friends. Finally, they attended events and activities that focused on Filipino identity and cultural heritage, such as hometown fiestas, political holidays, and religious celebrations.

While the initial goal for anti-dictatorship activists was to mobilize a Filipino constituency around foreign-policy lobbying, exposure to the issues and problems that Filipinos encountered every day in these public spheres was an unintended outcome. Like Antonio, Juana, relocated to the US when Marcos's repression of activists had intensified. As a minor child of a naturalized citizen, she was granted permanent residency that enabled her to leave the Philippines immediately. She remembered how her anti-dictatorship activism brought her to political spaces where Filipinos were organizing for concerns related to their position as immigrants.

> Being an immigrant, I was initially just involved in the anti-Marcos campaign, but in the meetings, I met Filipinos who were active in some local issues such as problems with the FACLA [Filipino American Community of Los Angeles]. I got to know who they are, then I started going to their events. In these events, I met other Filipinos involved in the concerns of nurses, which I knew nothing about. Then, after a few months, I started going to more and more meetings. . . .
>
> Most of the anti–martial law work was done by [Filipino] immigrants. On the other hand, the Filipino American group tackled issues regarding youth, students, labor, and so on. . . . At that point, I became more "aware"—let us use the term "educated" instead—of the other issues facing Filipinos in the US. So, I got involved with the issues around immigration and solidarity work.

In large cities such as Los Angeles, New York, San Francisco, and Seattle, where Filipinos lived in ethnically and racially mixed neighborhoods, grassroots organizing for the anti-dictatorship movement laid the foundations for inter-ethnic and multiracial collaborations and civic engagement beyond Filipino communities. Activists joined Third World solidarity committees and the activities of groups such as the Central America Resource Center. They saw similarities in their struggles and understood how the US created the conditions that led to their displacement and migration. By establishing political and social relations with a segment of the US population they would otherwise not interact with intimately, they developed a network of experienced leaders and allies from which they learned how to frame their issues and identities.

In the Netherlands, the settlement of Filipino activists in Utrecht offered an opportunity for them to establish links with Dutch social movements.

While their counterparts in the US prioritized foreign-policy lobbying due to the US government's role in sustaining the dictatorship through bilateral aid, the activists in the Netherlands focused on international efforts to delegitimize Marcos in the realm of public opinion. Since they possessed college degrees and spoke English fluently, they had the cultural capital needed to act as brokers or bridge builders between the Filipino migrant community and organizations within Dutch civil society, particularly the ecology, antinuclear, peace, solidarity, autonomous, and women's movements.

To anchor the anti-Marcos movement to the global struggle against dictatorship and imperialism in the Third World, the activists linked with country-specific solidarity groups such as those for national liberation in East Timor, Nicaragua, Palestine, and South Africa. The movement communities were sites for social learning and strategic adaptation. Activists became incorporated into these networks and socialized into the political culture and "the local 'rules of the game,'" enabling them to "readjust their activist skills and experiences accordingly,"[53] including how to use collective identity strategically in the public sphere. Janet entered the Netherlands as an asylum seeker in the late 1970s. Despite having years of experience organizing for the communist movement in the Philippines, she was unfamiliar with protest repertoires in the Netherlands, which made her feel disheartened and frustrated. As she attended several events of the solidarity movement, she discovered practices that resonated with the Dutch public.

> We learned a lot from the Eritreans who were here before us. Many of them were members of the Eritrean People's Liberation Front. . . . When they have activities like a forum, there's a lot of singing—very festive. And people from the audience, even if they are not Eritreans, go up [to] the stage and give them money. So we said it's very important to study movements that have a lot of support here. We thought we cannot just replicate our strategies in the Philippines here. We have to know what makes them [the Dutch citizens and other immigrants] come out and back us too.

In both the US and the Netherlands, migration issues and solidarity work provided activists with a space to nurture their values, identity, and political vision especially during periods of abeyance,[54] when activists have less visible and fewer interactions with target authorities either due to abatement of conflict in the homeland or a nonreceptive hostland environment. When the protest cycle declined, activists in the anti-dictatorship movement were still actively engaged in organizing and thus could sustain commitment and achieve a sense of purpose in spaces where they organized and on issues that affected Filipino migrants daily. As Antonio from earlier reflects,

100 CHAPTER FOUR

We were always waiting for something to happen in the Philippines. But there was a big ebb from the declaration of martial law until the Ninoy Aquino assassination. . . . There was no upsurge. . . . So, here, the approach was, while we would have periodic protests and programs, most of our day-to-day work was actually organizing Filipinos on the basis of democratic rights—police brutality, licensure discrimination, racism, stuff like that.

Within the intersection of anti-dictatorship, migrants' rights, and solidarity work, activists interrogated their definitions of immigrant, citizen, Filipino, and other dominant identities. They questioned primordial ethnicity and modern nationalism as foundations for migrants' collective identity. They had regular contact with co-ethnics/co-nationals from different social locations—"Filipinos they would have never even developed friendship with in the Philippines because they live in the bad side of town," according to Josephine—which prompted them to reflect critically on their own class positions in both the homeland and the hostlands. In these spaces, their identities, privileges, and sometimes contradictory social roles were challenged. The experiences of Carolyn and Eduardo capture this dynamic.

Carolyn rarely interacted with Filipinos outside of her social class in the Philippines. She was from a middle-class household and was educated in private Catholic schools. When she moved to the Netherlands in the 1980s, her social circle consisted mostly of Filipino anti-dictatorship and Dutch solidarity activists and exiled intellectuals from other countries. Tasked with recruiting Filipino domestic workers—most of them women—to the movement, she attended social functions organized by labor migrants. In these spaces, she grappled with her class identity. While she was initially indifferent to the norms in the weekly gatherings, her attitude gradually changed as she developed friendships and learned about the women's lives. She recalled one "eye-opening experience":

The women invited me to their holiday party. I went wearing only a T-shirt and a pair of jeans. I noticed that all the women were dressed in formal gowns that they had ordered months earlier from the Philippines, and I just thought how ridiculous that was. When I talked to one of the attendees wearing a gown, I was so ashamed. And it stayed with me. Until now. She said that the annual Filipino Christmas party was the only thing she looked forward to all year—that she was excited to wear a gown with all the other Filipinos in the Netherlands. I thought to myself, "How shallow." Then she said, "It makes me feel good about myself. Wearing something nice at the Filipino party. Because, you know, the rest of the year, I scrub toilets every day, wearing dirty clothes."

I felt slapped. I was so arrogant, thinking that I am above this trivial stuff because I know better, because I am an intellectual and this is beyond me. I

WORKERS AND MINORITIES 101

was so elitist. And I was supposed to organize them. Since then, whenever I attend an event, I really dress up because it [the event] is important to them.

Frequent interactions with Filipino labor migrants had taught Carolyn about the demobilizing effect of their lowered class position. Some anti-dictatorship activists regarded OFWs as apolitical by choice. But Carolyn saw the role of structure in their decisions not to participate in homeland politics. As economic migrants forced to leave the Philippines to support their families, their objective was to earn as much as possible and save for their eventual return. Moreover, OFWs were under the authority of the Philippine state via the embassies. The embassies encouraged migrants to be proper guests in the Netherlands. They prohibited participation in protests. When OFWs joined demonstrations, consulate representatives confiscated their passports and work permits. Thus, OFWs had neither the class privilege nor the migrant status to participate in transnational activities. Since her first meeting with Filipino domestic workers in 1985, Carolyn has been involved in the movement for migrants' rights, particularly on the legalization of undocumented workers and assistance to victims of sex trafficking. Her work immersed her in dense networks of activists, where she developed a migrant identity based on her perceived common fate with other migrant groups in Dutch society, despite her privileged status in the Philippines.

Eduardo went through a similar transformation. Before he migrated to the US in 1980, he was part of the underground movement against the Marcos dictatorship. He was reluctant to move to the US through family reunification in the first place, and originally had decided to stay there only temporarily. Eduardo became a member of KDP and lived with other activists in a commune in Oakland, California. There, he recognized his differences with other Filipinos due to his class upbringing, despite similarities in political ideology and ethnic culture:

My parents were not wealthy, but rich enough for us to have a good future. I was used to having maids in Manila, so I had to overcome my class background. . . . For example, we had to take turns cooking, and all I could cook was this *ginataang manok* (chicken in coconut milk) that another activist taught me. I would make that every time it was my turn. They finally got fed up and they said, "No, we're not going to eat this anymore." . . . There was another time, in the beginning of my stay with the collective, they would ask, "Do you want coffee?" And I would say, "Yeah, sure." They would ask, "Oh did you make it?" "On second thought I don't want coffee." . . .

I was not challenged by my comrades [about my class] in the Philippines the same way [I was by] my comrades here in the US. Even though a lot of the Filipino activists here were part of the underground movement in the

102   CHAPTER FOUR

Philippines, they were all petit bourgeois, highly educated. But there are a lot of the Fil-Am [Filipino American] activists here. Their parents were farmworkers. So, there was also a little bit of cultural clash between the two [Filipino nationals and Filipino Americans].

At first, Eduardo's commitment to the KDP was confined to the antidictatorship movement, where he organized demonstrations and established links with the US Left. But living with US-born Filipino activists made him more aware of his co-ethnics' struggles; he wanted to learn about "this part of Filipino history that was not taught to us in the Philippines." He became involved in the struggle to save the I-Hotel, and his interactions with the *manongs* inspired him to travel to Delano, California, to investigate the problems that immigrant farmworkers of various nationalities faced.

Activists also learned how the Dutch and American racial structures limited choices for those at the bottom of the racial hierarchy. Coming from the Philippines, which they consider racially homogenous, most of the activists belonged to ethnolinguistic groups with economic and political power such as the Tagalogs. As such, they were "not sensitive about race," said Cristina. Conrado agreed, "it was not part of our upbringing." They met Filipino migrants who regularly experienced workplace discrimination. Their involvement in anti-dictatorship activism became their introduction to racial politics, and they began to develop a lens through which to see their own racialization, as in the case of Leonora:

> When I was in the Philippines, my knowledge of race was theoretical. I would read about it, for instance, in the case of Palestinians in Israel. But it was not my day-to-day experience growing up. Classism, yes, not racism. Because I did not belong to an ethnic minority. I am Kapampangan, one of the largest groups in the Philippines. So, in New York, where I first settled, I did not really think much about race, because my reference point was still the Philippines. Then when I talked to Filipino nurses and doctors [who are on work visas] about the Marcos dictatorship, I learned that they were discriminated heavily by management and patients because they were not white. Slowly, I began to see race in my day-to-day experience. I started to notice I would be the only nonwhite person in my class in NYU [New York University] and professors treated me differently because I spoke with an accent.

As the Philippine-born activists developed associational life in the US and the Netherlands and developed multilayered and intersectional identities, they began to contest the discourses of resistance into which they were socialized in the anti-dictatorship movement back home. Their main critique was the primacy put on a purely nationalist struggle, where confronting the racialized experiences of overseas Filipinos in their countries of settlement is largely ancillary. Certainly, nationalism easily evokes emotions such as love, loyalty, and pride, especially during periods of conflict. But the territorial nation-state as a basis for collective identification and solidarity can also be called into question as the processes of migration, displacement, and resettlement often lead people to reconfigure the boundaries of the imagined community and/or to seek belonging in other communities to find meaning in their experiences.

For Luisa, a political refugee in the Netherlands, the perspective that social change in the Philippines should be the central concern of migrants in their activism is not grounded in the economic, political, and social realities that they faced every day. Luisa was a government employee in the Philippines, who became part of the underground movement against Marcos in the early 1980s. When repression became severe and the threat to her life imminent, she reached out to members of the CPP and the NDF who were already in the Netherlands to help her escape and seek asylum. Upon arrival, the CPP-NDF assigned Luisa, like Carolyn, to organize OFWs to support the revolutionary struggle in the Philippines. She grappled with both ideological and organizational problems that stemmed from the ambiguous role of Filipino labor migrants in the revolutionary struggle. The goal of the CPP-NDF was "to arouse, organize, and mobilize overseas Filipinos in Europe . . . to support and play an active role and have direct participation in the Philippine revolution."[55] It, however, set restrictions on who to mobilize among Filipinos abroad:

> Overseas Filipinos, both settled and migrant, are generally considered as potential internal forces of the Philippine revolution, if they belong to one of the national democratic classes and if national identification with the Philippines is still principal to them.[56]

As she carried out the day-to-day tasks of organizing, she learned that Filipinos—mostly low-skilled workers in Amsterdam and Rotterdam with temporary or undocumented status—were ambivalent about joining the anti-dictatorship movement. But their networks were easily mobilized on issues related to their migrant and worker statuses—their main collective identifications. For instance, the Filipino community provided support to seafarers of all nationalities who went on strike for six weeks at the port of Rotterdam in the winter of 1978. The seafarers were demanding fair wages and decent living conditions from their employer, Tropwind Trading. Other Filipino migrants supported the strikers by being present in the site, raising resources to maintain their daily needs, organizing food distribution centers, and providing first-aid and emergency care, thus at once creating and expressing "cultures of solidarity."[57] Luisa was involved in the strikes and strongly identified as a "working-class immigrant" despite her entry to the Netherlands as a refugee. For her, the strikes were pivotal, because they made her question the ascendancy of identification with the Philippine nation-state in the CPP-NDF's ideology, rather than with workers and minorities irrespective of nationality.

As anti-dictatorship activists learned firsthand the struggles of overseas Filipinos in the US and the Netherlands in their daily organizing, which resulted in the interrogation and transformation of their own selves, they extended the bedrock for the construction of a minority worker identity, intertwining multiple narratives about the challenges of the structures of class, race, and nationality on migrants' agency. As Stephen Valocchi contends, activists who embody and articulate multiple identities "do mobilizing work that tries to reconfigure or revalorize different understandings of social marginality."[58] Thus, the claims and demands they made in their activism on migrants' rights often expressed what Paul Gilroy describes in *The Black Atlantic* as the "desire to transcend both the structures of the nation state and the constraints of ethnicity and national particularity."[59]

With this learning process, anti-dictatorship activists became actively involved in local campaigns to address the immediate needs of the communities informed by multilayered and intersectional identities. For instance, KDP activists on the East Coast organized Filipino nurses and the Filipino community to protest exploitative recruitment practices and discriminatory licensing examinations. Their mobilization peaked during *US v. Narciso and Perez* (1977), a federal court case in which two Filipina migrant nurses, Filipina Narciso and Leonora Perez, were criminalized and framed by the Federal Bureau of Investigation for poisoning and murdering patients at the Ann Arbor Veterans Affairs Hospital in Michigan (figure 4.1).[60] Activists on the West Coast also reformed the FACLA and the Filipino Community of Seattle, which were mired in political conservatism and corruption. In the Bay Area, the struggle to save the I-Hotel lasted from 1968 until its demolition in 1981. KDP members also helped recent Filipino immigrants confront prejudice and alienation in their neighborhoods and workplaces through the Filipino Advocates for Justice, formerly Filipinos for Affirmative Action. Finally, in advocating support for the presidential candidacy of Jesse Jackson in 1984, KDP published an article in *Ang Katipunan* calling for unity with other minority groups in the US, emphasizing historical continuities regarding the experiences of previous Filipino migrants:

Deep down, Filipinos realize that no matter what, they are still part of the voiceless, powerless and disregarded sectors of the population that Jackson speaks for and about.

Many Filipinos may have forgotten their predecessors in the 20s and 30s were exploited in the backbreaking jobs in California and Hawaiian farms, forbidden to marry outside their race and confronted by "No Filipinos Allowed" signs in restaurants and hotels. The truth is, even today race and national oppression—a system that has victimized Blacks, Native Americans, Mexicans, Asians and other minorities—are still part of the Filipino experience in America. Only the forms have changed.[61]

Like the campaigns of the 1920s and 1930s, these campaigns revealed Filipino immigrants' struggle to integrate and their demands for inclusion in the multicultural nation. Thus, they reflect continuity in the construction of solidarity based on discourses of marginalization in the country of settlement due to the rigid boundaries of racial belonging.

In the Netherlands, one of the oldest Filipino organizations, the Filiippijnse Arbeiders Vereniging Nederland (Philippine Workers Association of the Netherlands [also known as Samahan[62]]), captured migrants' collective yearning for inclusion despite the challenges of integration. An editorial entitled "Who Are the Filipino Workers in the Netherlands?" in Samahan's first newsletter in March 1983 expressed the sentiment well: "We want to be here

FIGURE 4.1. At a community protest in San Francisco in 1977, Filipina nurses express support for Filipina Narciso and Leonora Perez, who were charged with the murder of ten patients at the VA Hospital in Ann Arbor, Michigan. (Source: KDP and *Ang Katipunan*.)

in the Netherlands. Many of us have been here for a long time—so, we feel more or less very much at home—and we know how to live in another country. There are also some of us who are still adjusting to life here, who still do not know Dutch, who still do not have friends."[63] Samahan activists framed the notion of the Netherlands as home, whether temporary or permanent, as an invitation to be active in Dutch political life—to stake their claim and to exercise their citizenship.

As Bridget Anderson argues, citizenship is no longer viewed simply as a legal status given by the state; it is also constructed by migrants themselves through action.[64] This means being aware of problems confronting all migrants, having a venue to collectively analyze these problems and to speak as one community, and engaging in public. According to the Samahan editorial board, "We need a newsletter for the quick and widespread dissemination of information. . . . Through our own publication, we can voice our concerns and our positions on issues that affect us . . . we can debate amongst ourselves."[65] When writing about discrimination and racism toward migrants in the newsletter, the authors persistently used a class lens. While members of Samahan acknowledged the importance of maintaining "our own culture as true Filipinos," they also promoted unity "to fight for our welfare and rights as workers in the Netherlands,"[66] encouraging solidarity across ethnic and racial lines and creating a community based on a minority worker identity.

The Commission on Filipino Migrant Workers (CFMW), an organization founded by Filipino migrants and Italian missionaries in Rome in 1979, with an office in Amsterdam, also built solidarity based on the collective identity as migrant workers. CMFW recognized that most of the Filipinos in Europe were of middle-class status in the Philippines. They had been teachers, civil servants, bank employees, or other professionals before migrating. From the point of view of activists, the process of labor migration had "subproletarianized" the Filipino workers, meaning they were doubly exploited, first by the ruling class in the homeland and then by the people in their host societies.[67] With this analysis, CFMW and the Philippine Seafarers' Assistance Program (PSAP)—one of the earliest port-based migrant organizations in the Netherlands, based in Rotterdam and established in 1981—led mobilizations around Philippine Executive Order (EO) 857 in 1985. The order required Filipino labor migrants to remit 50–70 percent of their basic monthly salary to their beneficiaries in the Philippines through the Philippine banking system.[68] The CMFW and PSAP found this policy egregious, given the precarious living conditions of OFWs, with the contractual nature of their employment and limited social safety nets in their countries of destination.

The issue of compulsory remittances resonated among Filipinos in

WORKERS AND MINORITIES

Europe, the Middle East, and Asia, and appealed to the minority worker identity generally for three reasons. First, overseas Filipinos regularly dealt with exploitative banks that charged high fees, thereby reducing the actual remittance to their families. Second, compliance with EO 857 curtailed their right to the money they themselves earned. Finally, the provision included penalties for violation, which implied the Philippine government's indifference to the economic difficulties that migrants encountered in foreign lands.

CFMW relied on the discourse of displacement due to economic hardship in the Philippines to mobilize migrants in the campaign against EO 857. The message was that millions of Filipinos were forced to work overseas because of abject poverty and rising unemployment in the Philippines. In a report published in *Kababayan* and circulated to Filipino migrant workers in various countries, CFMW stated,

> Overseas workers' remittances totaled US $1B in 1983 displacing the country's traditional exports.... Even if 100% of the remittances were coursed through official banking channels it would not readily mean solving the chronic payments problem. Deceptively, the workers' remittances are being used by the government to boost its dollar reserves in order that new foreign loans be granted. This would only further put the Philippines in deeper financial difficulties.[69]

As transnational migrant organizations like CMFW activated their networks and partnered with local groups, the opposition to EO 857 spread to every country where there were OFWs, and in March 1985, Marcos withdrew the decree.[70] With this victory, migrants felt a sense of political efficacy, emboldening them to step up their organizing even in times of an ebb in protests.

Serin Houston and Richard Wright argue that "movement into exile forces the reinvention of tradition," where some may be "consciously reconstructed for their political utility."[71] CFMW and PSAP promoted the narrative of forced displacement even during Philippine celebrations such as Christmas and Lent—gatherings that promoted togetherness—against the backdrop of longing for the family and the homeland. On such occasions, the unity with other Filipino labor migrants becomes an "'identity reservoir' one cannot be stripped of, whatever the difficulty one may face in the country of settlement."[72] Feelings of nostalgia for people, places, and practices during holidays juxtaposed with narratives of sacrifice and oneness evoke the unbroken relevance of the homeland and solidarity with other displaced Filipinos. In its holiday issue of *Kababayan*, the newsletter of CFMW, the editors elaborated on the minority worker identity during a time of revelry and camaraderie. They connected the affective dimension (e.g., yearning for home) with the political

108   CHAPTER FOUR

and social dimensions (e.g., marginalization in the host country) while emphasizing that solidarity was the best way to cope with the challenges:

> Working in another country is no picnic. It entails sacrifice. The biggest sacrifice is being away from loved ones for a long time. And the hardest challenge is facing a new culture, especially adjusting to the norms of foreigners. But more often, the problem of the majority is discrimination and the absence of rights of migrants.
>
> In the face of all these, CFMW and *Kababayan* believe that unity accomplishes a lot to improve the condition of Filipino workers in other countries.
>
> For example, Christmas is near. Every Filipino would be happy to spend it with his or her loved ones.
>
> Nonetheless, even though one is far from the homeland and his or her loved ones, Christmas will be a wonderful one if celebrated with other Filipinos.[73]

The newsletters featured stories and poems penned by migrants that often chronicled the destitution that led them to go abroad, the alienation in the country of settlement, and the ambivalence about continued belonging to the homeland. In this serialization of the OFW experience, the authors conveyed a sense of "we"—that they are going through the same ordeal together. In essence, they developed a common language to build solidarity. Boyet R.'s two-part account of his life entitled "Is Holland Really Heaven?" articulates the devotion to the Philippines as home, despite a source of anguish and painful memories. His narrative also appeals to migrants' identities as children, siblings, and parents. But Boyet R.'s story resonates with OFWs because of what Aguilar refers to as the "ritual of a labor contract pilgrimage," a ritual that doesn't end until "the economic journey reaches its completion with the return to the homeland"[74]:

> I have been in Holland for nine years, and I have not gone home to the Philippines even once. I am very eager to see our country once again, and I have planned to go home. But it looks uncertain right now. So allow me to write in Tagalog. This way, I feel like I am in the Philippines, even if I may not be able to go ahead with my plans.
>
> It was December 1974 when I arrived here. I was only fourteen then, but I felt I was ten years older. This is probably because of the hardship that I went through taking care of four younger siblings. We lost our mother at a young age. I was only ten years old then. Since I was the oldest, it was only natural that I stood as both mother and father for my siblings. My father was not with us then. As a seafarer, he worked in different countries, and he persevered so that we could all come here in Holland.

When we were on the plane, I did not want to revisit the cruelty of our relatives to me and my siblings. I did not want to think about that perhaps they want our plane to crash. I just wanted to feel that unsurpassed joy. Finally, I thought, we would be rich and would no longer experience maltreatment in life.[75]

These literary texts cultivated the narrative that Filipinos endure the hardship they experience in their host countries to improve the conditions of their families left behind. *Kababayan* became a venue for disseminating news and inspiring overseas Filipinos to work hard for their kin and the whole country. It also provided information on affordable ways to send remittances and goods to the Philippines. Thus, through the newsletters, migrants linked blood, family, and nation together.[76] But while the collective identity was serialized in publications, by and for overseas Filipinos, migrants nurtured bonds of trust through routine activities, engaging every day in meaning production. For instance, they often met to enjoy Philippine culture in the form of food, songs, dances, movies, and gossip. The cultural group Alay sa Bayan (Gift to the People [ALAB]) took advantage of these ordinary practices to politicize the discourses associated with them. ALAB performed folk songs such as "Bayan Ko," which echoed the patriotic sentiments of Filipinos. The group also staged the play *Oratoryo ng Bayan* (The nation's oratorio)[77] throughout Europe. In a concert tour proposal in 1984, ALAB wrote,

> Songs by Filipino artists . . . have radically changed the past decade. This field used to be dominated by imported pop music which in the majority of cases border on escapism. The new school of Filipino singers consciously work for social relevance and artistic value in all their compositions. . . .
> This group [ALAB] is committed to the search for national identity. We believe that this cannot be found in the mere nostalgic love for the past or an idealized view of our traditions and history. National identity should be based on the present social realities and on a critical assessment of our national historic past so that we may trace the roots of those realities.[78]

ALAB's framing of the evolution of Philippine arts and its group identity validate Stuart Hall's argument that while cultural identities have origins, "like everything which is historical, they undergo constant transformation."[79] Thus, in their strategies to promote solidarity, activists do not appeal to a recovery of the past based on some primordial essence of groups; rather, they punctuate current shared experiences and reinterpret history so that migrants themselves make sense of their location in the structures of power.

This imputation of meaning is crucial to the formation of diasporas through collective action, for dynamic processes call for actors' recognition and exercise of their human agency.

Minority Worker Identity after the Dictatorship

After Marcos was ousted, social movement organizations in the US and the Netherlands took different paths with regard to solidarity building. Mirroring events in the Philippines, Filipino Americans sought reconciliation and unity in the community, which had been divided on the dictatorship for fourteen years. Filipino activists, professionals, and elected officials met at a Filipino American Unity Conference in San Francisco in September 1986 to restore friendly relations with each other and to build a unified leadership in the community. The meeting produced the Filipino American Council. Participants envisioned the council as the main institution representing Filipino interests in the American economic, political, and social arenas, similar to the National Association for the Advancement of Colored People and the Japanese American Citizens League.[80]

KDP members who had been introduced to the problems of Filipino migrants while mobilizing against the dictatorship began to focus full-time on the struggle for migrants' rights, especially with the enactment of the Immigration Reform and Control Act of 1986. Others continued with labor unions such as the ILWU and the Service Employees International Union (SEIU), while a few committed to forming a new communist party in the US through the Line of March. Some engaged in local politics like Velma Veloria, who was involved in organizing nurses and other medical professionals through SEIU and was the first Asian American woman to be elected to the Washington State Legislature in 1992.

In contrast, while activists in the Netherlands persisted with building cross-border solidarity, they sharpened the displacement, marginalization, and empowerment frame. This is because the Aquino government did not cease but rather intensified Marcos's labor export policy, so the deployment of OFWs to Europe continued. In a communiqué to Aquino published in *Kababayan*, CFMW framed overseas Filipinos as important actors in the newly democratized Philippines as a result of their power derived from their structural location in the national economy: "Filipino migrant workers contribute millions of dollars to the government coffers to prop up the Aquino government's sinking economy. Hence, it is not only proper but justified that their welfare occupy a top slot on the list of the Aquino government's priorities."[81]

WORKERS AND MINORITIES

As in the past, CFMW perpetuated migrants' attachment and responsibility to the Philippines and solidarity with other Filipinos by publishing migrant workers' poems and stories. In 1986, activists started distributing *Kababayan* to OFWs in countries where CFMW had networks as well as to organizations in the Philippines. It remained a venue not only to learn about issues and events that affect Filipino migrants, and the potential to act collectively, but also to lay claim to national belonging through affect. For instance, in a poem entitled "Tunay Ka Bang Pilipino? [Are You a Real Filipino?]" the author—an OFW in Saudi Arabia—roused feelings of pride and honor to remind OFWs that service to the nation and unity is at the core of being Filipino:

> A question so easy
> Not difficult to answer
> Are you a real Filipino?
> In appearance and in action
> There are so many Filipinos
> Who became leaders in our country
> But all they did was enrich themselves
> And steal from the coffers
>
> A real Filipino
> Is not through blood and color
> Is not through birth
> In our own nation
> The responsibility of each
> Is to serve the country
> With devotion in your heart
> While you are living
>
> The Filipino race
> Has the blood of the brave
> Most of the heroes
> Have nationalist aspirations
> There were some who defended
> So freedom could be achieved
> But it was not written in the stars
> These acts so brave
>
> If you are a real Filipino
> Behold our Motherland
> Looking for care
> So that she can be enriched
> It is time to bond
> Together we can remedy

> So our country can break free
> From its poverty
>
> So Filipino, wake up
> You, Filipino, should wake up
> It is time to unite
> In spirit and in emotion
> If that is achieved
> Happiness is obtained
> Your country will be great
> Poverty will diminish.[82]

In the serialization of the OFW experience, activists showed that collective identity was an ongoing, dynamic process influenced by and adapted to historical conditions. And because migrants were still in the same structural locations in the Philippines and in their countries of destination, they shared an unchanging destiny and were part of an ongoing collective struggle.

Activists recast the Philippines' position in the global order in the national imaginary as well, through accounts of domestic and world politics that affected OFWs such as the imposition of sanctions on Libya by UN in 1992 and Iraq's payment of war reparations to Kuwait in 1993. As Aguilar notes, "as a result of Filipino global migrations, today there is virtually no major world event . . . that does not directly involve or affect someone from and in the Philippines. For Filipinos in the Philippines, the diaspora has become the major prism for apprehending news on the rest of the world."[83] The parallel and connected mobilizations against the Marcos dictatorship and for migrants' rights made the figure of the OFW as simultaneously connected to events, people, and memories in the homeland, on the one hand, and in countries where co-ethnics/co-nationals were present, on the other, reflecting the erosion of borders in the construction of a Filipino transnational community.

As democratic transition progressed in the Philippines, homeland-oriented mobilization in the US and the Netherlands abated. Activists became further embroiled in issues that directly affected and resonated with OFWs. These issues included the Schengen Agreement in Europe, a treaty that led to the creation of Europe's borderless area in twenty-six countries; the trafficking of Filipino women; and the continuation of the double taxation scheme.[84] CFMW opposed the treaty, which would create a "Fortress Europe" that facilitates the movement of nationals in the European Community and prevents foreigners from developing countries from entering for employment and asylum. ALAB, which by the late 1980s had become popular among OFWs in the Benelux area (Belgium, the Netherlands, and Luxembourg)

WORKERS AND MINORITIES   113

owing to persistent media coverage of its shows,[85] changed its focus to mi-grant issues as its membership composition diversified. During this period, Filipinos constituted a large proportion of trafficked women to the Neth-erlands through marriage migration. The language of trafficking in main-stream public discourse focused on victimhood, which defined the women not as political subjects, "but rather the objects of negotiation."[86] Since ALAB traveled around the country, it offered a space for the women to articulate their experiences and to advocate for their rights. These women often lived in small towns and did not speak Dutch and thus felt physically and socially iso-lated. Eventually, some of them joined ALAB as actors, writers, and produc-tion staff. According to Zeny, a founding member of ALAB, this gave them "a sense of purpose and dignity." She adds that this change in the organization's composition also altered its issue priorities. ALAB's performances became a community-building project for overseas Filipinos "looking for opportunities to serve their *kababayan*." As Zeny recalls,

> At a certain point, we had members who were mail-order brides. They started talking about their trafficking experience. So, for us, we thought, "Why do we keep just talking about the situation in the Philippines while what's going on here is relevant?" We just read in the newspapers stories of those who were trafficked. But they're right here with us. They trust us and share us their sto-ries. Why not focus on their issues? . . .
> There was a certain point that ALAB had so many invitations. Seafarers started volunteering to help us. For example, they would build our sets, carry our props. You could really see their *pakikisama* [fellowship]. We all felt like one family.

During the Marcos era, the discourses of displacement, marginalization, and empowerment guided activists in their campaigns and thus in the con-struction of collective identity as workers and minorities. Although structural victimization was still a predominant theme, especially in analyzing the traf-ficking of women, the period of democratization saw a considerable emphasis on the agency of migrants and their capacity to mobilize on their own behalf. Mail-order brides themselves identified problems, developed injustice frames, motivated action, and articulated multilayered identities—as migrants, labor-ers, Filipinos, women, and so on. In addition, they engaged in everyday forms of resistance; they continuously pressed, tested, and probed the boundaries of what was permissible in different institutions in Dutch society.

Jocelyn, for instance, who met her Dutch husband through a pen pal ser-vice, refrained from cooking Filipino food in their house because her partner found the smell offensive. Eventually, she slowly and incrementally started cooking Filipino food, first making dishes with only a small amount of fish sauce to see if her husband noticed the odor. In this way, she felt that she gained a certain amount of control in the household. Jocelyn was also empowered to speak Tagalog and Bisaya, another Filipino language, openly and loudly with her friends on public transportation in Amsterdam, sharing stories about their experiences with their husbands and in-laws. Like those of the anti-dictatorship activists, Jocelyn's story reveals the personal transformative effects of collective action. In the case of mail-order brides, their participation in groups like ALAB catalyzed the development of what Aldon Morris and Naomi Braine calls oppositional consciousness, "an empowering mental state that prepares members of an oppressed group to act to undermine, reform, or overthrow a system of human domination."[87]

In the early 1980s the Philippine migrant community was bifurcated by ethnolinguistic groups, legal status, and social class. But in the latter part of the decade, these groups mixed to a greater degree. This intermingling meant more connections between activities and services toward Philippines concerns, such that social and recreational events were no longer considered to be completely outside the domain of politics. Nonpolitical groups like Barangay sa Holland (Village in Holland), Dutch-Pilipino Association, Damayan (Mutual Aid), United Filipino-Dutch Association, and Samahan sa Netherlands became prominent in the migrant community through programs and projects in the Philippines for construction and improvement of infrastructure, microenterprise and development, and disaster relief and recovery. Such initiatives appealed to OFWs who wanted to improve the economic and social conditions in their barrios and advance their status in the homeland in the process. However, these actions, which are often celebrated by politicians as testaments to OFWs' enduring attachment to the nation, further validated the Philippine state's discourse on the heroism and sacrifice of overseas workers. The initiatives legitimized rather than contested the hegemonic construction of their political subjectivity and normalized labor migration in the national imaginary. By the early 1990s, as Aquino pursued national policies to consolidate democracy, hometown associations emerged as the dominant form of organization that could partner with state institutions in local plans. This emergence reinvigorated identities rooted in loyalty to ethnolinguistic group and province, recalling early periods of mobilization.

Building Solidarity

In her study of Pan-American Nikkei communities, Ayumi Takenaka claimed that "the nature of diasporic solidarity is often unexamined, because members of a diaspora are assumed to undergo similar experiences."[88] This is often due to presumptions about commonalities based on ethnic and national origin, or the persistence of a grand narrative of migration, often based on the experience of the first or largest cohort of immigrants in one country of settlement. The stories of migrants and activists in this chapter illustrate that these are not enough to build solidarity among dispersed co-ethnics/co-nationals.

To think of a third-generation accountant in Seattle, whose grandparents went to the US after World War II, as having an instinctive and natural affinity with an itinerant seafarer on board a ship in the port of Rotterdam— because they are both Filipinos—is to suggest that ethnicity and nationality have an essence that every member of the group possesses. Assuming that these are immutable and dominant flattens the formation of collective identity and hides the multiple structures of power that migrants subvert or justify in this dynamic process. This does not mean that affinity based on ethnicity and nationality is unimportant. We saw how overseas Filipinos declared their kinship with each other through poems and short stories. But these expressions of solidarity were products of their interpretations of who they were as workers and minorities based on their lived experiences, in interaction with other social actors. To imagine being part of a community, actors negotiate and reconfigure boundaries of belonging to understand their everyday struggles. In these processes, social class and legal status may be more salient in their perception of their identities.

Filipinos' collective identity as minority workers in their countries of permanent settlement or temporary residence grew out of mobilization, particularly through the discursive strategies of activists. Through anti-dictatorship and migrants' rights campaigns, Filipino activists drew on discourses as well as developed and amplified frames that evinced shared struggle and a common fate. Despite their differences, when overseas Filipinos recognized that they all occupied the same structural location in their host societies, they saw themselves as bound in a shared destiny. This understanding became more pronounced in times of political contention, when events, issues, and policies affected their lives as strangers in a foreign land or excluded them from the racial borders of belonging. Activists who were themselves migrants developed an organic understanding of the multifarious grievances and interests of overseas Filipinos. They saw how migrants navigated the new environment, and how they confronted challenges that often disrupted the social relationships and individual beliefs shaped in the homeland. Because the activists themselves underwent the same process in the course of mobilization, they grasped the complexity of human agency among migrants, particularly the contradictory and idiosyncratic ways that structures influence their actions.

From these social encounters, activists reflected on their own experiences as migrants and movement actors, from which a displacement, marginalization, and empowerment frame emerged. They adapted this frame to global historical conditions—shifting from subverting (during the Marcos dictatorship) to validating (during the democratic transition under Aquino) the state's construction of OFWs as heroes and martyrs sacrificing for the nation. Still, they alluded to a collective experience as minority workers.

From the CFMW's opposition to compulsory remittances, to push back against the Schengen Agreement and ALAB's cultural performances, activists and migrants serialized the OFW experience. They articulated a sense that "we are in this together," a sense of oneness based on shared ordeals with alienation, disenchantment, and longing, and on the tenacity in overcoming struggles. Like books and other media during the nation-building period of Philippine history, these narratives circulated in the Philippines and in other places where Filipinos resided and provided for the imagination of a transnational community.

5

Storytellers and Interlocutors

Collective Memory Activism and Shared History

On September 21, 1987, around seventy Filipinos and Dutch solidarity activists gathered in Dam Square in Amsterdam to honor the victims of the Marcos dictatorship and to protest the abysmal human rights condition in the newly democratized Philippines. They delivered speeches and answered questions from bystanders about the recently installed government of Corazon Aquino and the continued struggle for a "truly sovereign, just, and democratic society."[1] Carrying funeral wreaths and photos of slain Filipino student leader Leandro Alejandro[2] and singing patriotic hymns such as "Bayan Ko," the protesters staged a memorial service at the National Monument. The cenotaph built in 1956 symbolizes the struggle against fascism in the Netherlands during World War II. Every year on May 4, Dutch people come together at the site for the Remembrance of the Dead ceremony, which commemorates all civilians and members of the armed forces of the Kingdom of the Netherlands who have died in wars or peacekeeping missions. In choosing the National Monument as the place for Filipinos in the Netherlands to remember the declaration of martial law fifteen years ago, the beginning of a dark period in the Philippines, they connected the histories of the two countries and laid claim to the famous Dutch landmark as a space for the cultivation of a collective memory of the Marcos dictatorship and the resistance against it.

In the middle of Tufts University in Medford, Massachusetts, also lies a site of remembrance among Filipino Americans: the Cannon, a replica of an artillery piece used on the deck of the warship *USS Constitution* launched in 1797 by the US Navy. Since its return to campus in 1977,[3] students have started a tradition of painting messages of resistance, solidarity, and celebration on the Cannon. The first brushstroke was on October 27, 1977, when Imelda Marcos visited Tufts, and students and faculty protested the authoritarian regime in the Philippines, as discussed in chapter 3. And on October 31, 2018, as the government of Rodrigo Duterte escalated its War on Drugs and its repression of dissent, Filipino American students gathered at the Cannon to paint "Never Again to Martial Law." One of the participants, Timothy Manalo, a graduate student in studio art, reflected on the importance of their actions: "Those of us now working to raise awareness about Filipino issues and human rights wanted to honor and continue that legacy by drawing attention to injustices that exist in the Philippines today."[4] For Timothy and other young Filipinos at Tufts, the Cannon is not just a sculpture or a custom; it is a symbol of the historical continuity of resistance and an anchor for unmoored memories of the past among those who did not experience it. These two protests staged at different times and places with similar claims and demands encapsulate how social movements are key actors in the processes of remembering and narrating, showing that collective memory is indispensable in the making of a diaspora.

Diasporas are multigenerational. It is not sufficient that migrants feel and maintain connection to the homeland and kinship with dispersed co-ethnics/co-nationals in other countries; these emotive and material constructions must also be continuously nurtured and passed down from one generation to another. Yet the passage of time brings with it the threat of forgetting, and the bridge between the past and the present—between the old and the new generation—becomes progressively unstable. This is because with generational change, "we not only see a change of guard in the public sphere, but we can also see a shift in the frames of relevance and reference,"[5] especially since people of different age cohorts recall historical events based on whether they experienced these in their adolescence and young adulthood.[6] But even if each generation's sociohistorical environment varies, intergenerational transmission allows for memories to be appropriated and used in ways that encourage shared identification of experiences.[7] The way the past is remembered to interpret and fit the present is, thus, important in constituting and sustaining a community, especially one that is transnationally imagined. Diasporas form when different "generational units"—whose members, according to German sociologist Karl Mannheim, are "'similarly located' . . . in so far as they are all exposed to the same phase of the collective process"[8]—are connected through the continuous (re)telling or silencing of history.

Aleida Assman and Linda Shortt assert, "The file of memory is never closed; it can always be reopened and reconstructed in new acts of remembering."[9] In pluralistic societies, numerous and contested memories of the past emerge. While power holders do maintain hegemony by upholding some readings of history over others, collective memories are themselves malleable, since symbols are often multivalent and multivocal,[10] and the "dialogic nature of discourses always contains the potential for subversion."[11] Because collective memory hinges on persistent affective and cognitive (re)interpretations through group interactions, social movements have engaged in various forms of activism to transform the field of memory. In their struggle for social change, activists become counterhegemonic actors in the memory regime, embroiled in mnemonic battles,[12] where they reclaim and reconstruct memories and contest official representations and practices of remembering.[13] They assume the role of mnemonic agents: either as memory entrepreneurs who "actively invoke content from memory repositories and express them through repertoire to produce meanings that help to mobilize people," or memory challengers who "disrupt the same memory process by contesting the account of memory repositories and/or repertoires," or both.[14] Finally, they stage their protests and memory-related activities in historically significant locations and on symbolic days.[15] In other words, amid hegemonic discourses and a cacophony of marginal narratives, activists construct collective memories by developing common frames to guide the understanding of historical events and facts.

Due to the paradigmatic cases of Jews, Armenians, and Africans in theorizing about diasporas, we often associate diasporas with the collective memory of trauma from expulsion and dispersal from the homeland due to ethnoreligious persecution, cultural genocide, and slavery. In the construction of these diasporas from the migrant generation to the subsequent ones, we see how various actors—not just social movements—engage in memory work so that the significance of the event or phenomenon that instigated massive dislocation remains in the transnational imaginary. For instance, the Armenian genocide of 1915 and the denial of Turkish governments have sustained the ties of Armenians in the US to those in Armenia and Nagorno-Karabakh, giving the former "a sense of peoplehood, cultural rebirth, and historical continuity" even as the generation of those who escaped the genocide has passed on.[16] In migrant groups consisting mostly of survivors of these harrowing events, the trauma itself constitutes the foundation for identity formation, entwining national and personal histories, as captured by Khatarya Um's reflection on how Pol Pot's Year Zero has shaped the lives of Cambodians in their countries of settlement: "For communities such as the Cambodians and the Chams, the layering of historical traumas—war, genocide, occupation, and forced dispersal—has evoked a sense of loss so acute, and of an unimaginable magnitude, that it stirs not only a personal feeling of dislocation but also a collective sense of anxiety about national survival."[17] In all these diasporas, there is that one historical event that migrants and their descendants refer to in making sense of their common past, present, and future.

Along with loyalty to the homeland and solidarity with co-ethnics/co-nationals, a group's shared history, often interpreted based on collective memories transmitted intergenerationally, is an important element in the construction of a diaspora. Sociologist Lorenzo Zamponi asserts that collective memory has a "regulatory function: it defines, through its mechanisms of selection and removal, the boundaries of a group's membership and the plausibility and relevance criteria for the group identity."[18] Collective memory and collective identity are thus constitutive of each other, with the former serving as a channel for the connection of past experiences with present ones in the process of the latter's formation.[19] For a group of mostly permanent immigrants and contract-based foreign workers, whose relocation overseas was not due to a historical event that led to large-scale expulsion or persecution of the population, what memory informs their collective identity? If a diaspora must endure through generations, what stories about the migrant group are passed down? In this chapter, I show how, in the context of widespread and overwhelming support for populist politician Rodrigo Duterte, who was elected as Philippine president in 2016, collective memory of the Marcos dictatorship and the resistance against it has facilitated the continuous reimagining of Filipino migrants' and their descendants' unbroken connection to the homeland. During the period of the authoritarian regime, intense and polarizing violent conflict in Philippine history fractured the purported unity of overseas Filipino and tested their loyalties. It was also the time when cross-border migration peaked and dispersion of Filipinos to numerous foreign lands commenced due to the government's labor export. As such, it was a pivotal juncture for transnational community formation.

Since Duterte had expressed his desire to run for president in 2015, former anti-dictatorship activists in the US and the Netherlands became memory entrepreneurs or challengers who mobilized memories of the past to counter dominant discourses and persistent narratives about the "golden years" of the dictatorship. During his campaign, Duterte had no qualms calling himself a dictator. He expressed admiration for the achievements of Marcos in terms of economic development, enforcement of law, and maintenance of order. Through the small transnational memory movement in the US and in the Netherlands that started in 2015 and continued to grow as Duterte was elected to the presidency in May 2016, I explain how Filipino migrants strategically used the interweaving of individual and collective narratives to rally Filipinos abroad to reclaim and safeguard the outcomes of the anti-dictatorship struggle and to ensure that subsequent generations do not forget the Marcos regime's transgressions—as Timothy and the Filipino American students in Tufts proclaimed, "Never Again." As they engage in memory activism, defined as "the strategic commemoration of a contested past outside state channels to influence public debate and policy,"[20] migrants intervene in official memory processes and puncture the image of Marcos that elite and state-centered discourses and visual representations have created. They become storytellers and interlocutors—making past events and abstract concepts related to the dictatorship come alive and gain relevance in the present, thus stimulating the dialogue and debate necessary in collective identity formation. By sharing their stories at protests and in personal and organizational memoirs, they assert their physical and symbolic presence during an important chapter of nation building—when Filipinos in the Philippines and other countries were deeply divided on their stance toward the government, yet they were able to forge and mobilize a collective identity to fight an entrenched regime. Thus, memory activism was not only about not forgetting the Marcos dictatorship but also remembering the resistance of Filipinos overseas, both of which underpin collective identities based on loyalty to the homeland and solidarity with co-ethnics/co-nationals.

In their stories, they create dramatis personae, which allow the audience or the reader—often members of the post-dictatorship generation—to select and identify with a role to find meaning in the past, to understand the present, and to look forward to the future with a new sense of purpose. As Francesca Polletta explains, "All stories have characters and a point of view or points of view from which the events in the story are experienced. Characters need not be human or even living. But we expect to experience the moral of the story throughout characters' fates. The person who tells us his story expects to gain our empathy and we judge him by assessing his actions in the light of the character they reveal . . . storytellers make it possible for listeners to identify with different perspectives and, at the same time, to recognize each one as incomplete."[21] This practice of building empathy through presenting relatable figures—actors with a capacity to make difficult personal choices considering shared interests—is especially important in bridging generations and creating shared discourses to interpret collective experiences. Migrant activist stories about this divisive period in Philippine history help us unpack the process of multigenerational transmission of shared history and memory, which is vital to constituting a diaspora.

Myths and Memories of the Marcos Dictatorship

In a meeting with a group of farmers at Concepcion, Tarlac, on February 8, 2016, during his campaign, Duterte delivered an impassioned speech that articulated his views about Marcos: "In the hindsight [sic], if I go back in time, in the past and at present . . . if only he did not stay too long as president, if

he did not become a dictator for so long, the best president that came by—
Marcos!"[22] The crowd burst into cheers as he continued to salute Marcos's accomplishments that benefited Filipino farmers, such as Masagana 99, an agricultural program launched in 1973 that aimed to increase rice production. A
familiar adage says, "Madaling makalimot ang mga Pilipino" (Filipinos have
a short memory). Indeed, as Filipinos prepared for the thirtieth anniversary
of the 1986 People Power uprising, a political renaissance of the Marcos legacy was underway, with ordinary citizens claiming that "life was easier under
Marcos" because it was "a time our economy was booming"; thus, "Marcos
was our best president."[23]

Such assertions are emblematic of the paradoxical outcomes of the regime
change that occurred, where truth, reconciliation, and transitional justice
were pursued but not achieved. The absence of these processes has led to lin-
gering support for authoritarianism, particularly in the forms of strongman,
single-party, and military rule,[24] thus enabling the Marcoses and their allies
to seize the opportunity to distort history when popular doubts about liberal
democratic values arise. Myths that envisage the Philippines to be in its heyday during the dictatorship include, among others, that the military was the
most advanced and the Philippines the richest and most literate country in
Asia; that more than fifty thousand bridges were built; and that it was an era
of discipline, peace, and order.[25] These historical fictions have not only made
Marcos a demigod with a cult of loyalists; they have also propagated the belief
that authoritarianism was beneficial to Filipinos. A network of pro-Marcos
aides and allies has utilized traditional media to consistently boost the "great-
ness" of this dictator.[26] But with the increasing use of social media platforms
such as Facebook and Twitter in the Philippines, propaganda and disinformation about the dictatorship have become widespread or "viral," causing young
Filipinos to doubt documented evidence of repression from sources such as
Amnesty International, Human Rights Watch, and the UN, as well as testimonies and firsthand accounts of martial law victims.[27]

The transition to democracy shapes how the authoritarian regime is remembered, and memory work during this time is urgent and transformative.
This is because "a mere change of regime cannot in and of itself usher in a
new social contract."[28] In his research on democratization in Portugal, Antònio Costa Pinto speaks of the concept of "double legacy" as a framework that
informs how Portuguese people talk about the country's authoritarian years
and the revolution that followed.[29] This entailed focusing on both how the
dictatorship ended and how the new government implemented democracy
through seeking accountability from regime actors and instituting mechanisms for transitional justice, with the latter encompassing truth commissions

and documentation and education about the regime. In the Philippines, while the government of Corazon Aquino sought the recovery of ill-gotten wealth accumulated by Marcos, his immediate family and relatives, and close associates through the Presidential Commission on Good Government, it failed to adequately address transitional justice issues such as reparations to the victims of human rights abuse, institutional reforms to dismantle the power of Marcos's cronies, and truth-seeking initiatives. In fact, no administration since the restoration of democracy in 1986 has attempted to legally codify and formally establish mechanisms and practices to memorialize those who suffered and lost their lives during the two-decade authoritarian rule.[30]

Commemorative projects have centered on paying homage to key actors in the three-day People Power revolt that overthrew Marcos. It is not a memory of suffering, but of resistance, relief, and euphoria—"the memory of something that cures the traumatic aspects of the recent past."[31] Since 1987, which was the first anniversary of the EDSA People Power Revolution,[32] both festive and solemn rituals serve as a reminder to Filipinos not only of the corporeal dimension of the struggle against a firmly rooted dictatorship but also of the complex layers of emotions contained in the revolutionary process. The annual holiday commences with the ringing of church bells at dawn on February 15. Throughout the day, parades and street dances, under a rain of yellow confetti, allow people to gather publicly in a carnivalesque fashion, reminding them of the symbolic significance of the occasion while also invigorating them to continue fighting for the "spirit of EDSA"; thus, the commemoration is both a social catharsis and a social catalyst.[33] Meanwhile, one of the highlights of the celebration, *Salubungan* (encounter or convergence), is a reenactment of the historic meeting between the military rebels and civilians that precipitated the toppling of the dictator. In the ceremony at Camp General Emilio Aguinaldo marked by speeches and flag raising, presidents salute the soldiers for defying orders and answering the pleas of the clergy and the devout masses—a celebration of the moral victory of People Power.[34] Due to their communal character and what Émile Durkheim terms the "collective effervescence"[35] that arises from being in groups, these acts of memorialization are in themselves also mechanisms for collective identity.

While acknowledging the centrality of ordinary people in the revolution, the memory repertoire of official mnemonic agents in public commemorative celebrations continues to privilege elite actors and discourses, constraining activists and other citizens from telling their stories in their own words.[36] Since 2010, when the son of Marcos, Ferdinand "Bongbong" Marcos Jr. was elected to the Philippine Senate, storytelling became the dominant memory repertoire that enabled subaltern voices to enter the discursive space of remembrance.

Because of its ability to "generate empathy by highlighting areas of unanticipated agreement . . . equaliz[e] by engaging each participant's experience as valid regardless of their social status; and perhaps most importantly . . . link particular experiences with more general normative concerns, transforming individual troubles into social problems with possibilities for collective redress,"[37] storytelling contributes to collective identity formation. Susan F. Quimpo and Nathan Gilbert Quimpo's family memoir *Subversive Lives: A Family Memoir of Marcos Years*, Jo-Ann Q. Maglipon's edited volume *Not on Our Watch: Martial Law Really Happened; We Were There*, and *Tibak Rising: Activism in the Days of Martial Law*, a collection of essays by former anti-dictatorship activists edited by Ferdinand C. Llanes, recast the language and discourse of remembering the dictatorship. Rather than pivot on state structures and processes in how activists narrate their experiences, they weave together events, objects, and relationships, revealing rich, textured, and dynamic portraits of themselves that ultimately inspire readers. For instance, while tales of arrest and torture convey agony, despair, and defeat, they also relay hope, community, and "triumph of the human spirit," especially when recounted based on their identities and the choices they have made as daughters, fathers, neighbors, teachers, and so on. Aimed at educating young Filipinos about the dictatorship and encouraging them to avoid the mistakes of the older generation, the stories also foster nostalgia, often "alluding to their youthful selves having been more interesting, more colorful and more adventurous than their older counterparts of the present" and emphasizing their agency as individuals and members of communities.[38] These memoirs of former anti-dictatorship activists have served as a catharsis for the authors who personify the collective experience of ordinary Filipinos who lived under the dictatorship.[39]

To be sure, civil society initiatives to preserve a historical record of Marcos's atrocities have existed prior to the publication of these memoirs. The collection of documents, objects, photographs, and videos at libraries offer spaces for remembrance and memory activism.[40] As the oligarchic elite who supported Marcos began to assume elected positions in local, provincial, and national governments, demonstrations by social movements and other civil society actors also became part of the repertoire of the annual People Power commemoration. However, the construction and circulation of counterhegemonic discourses through activist memoirs have constituted a key strategy of the small and nascent transnational memory movement that emerged in response to Marcos Jr.'s candidacy for vice president and Duterte's immense popularity in the polls despite his publicly expressed admiration for the dictator.

During the celebration of the thirtieth anniversary of People Power in 2016, collective storytelling as a memory repertoire became more established, with ordinary Filipinos coming out and sharing their own remembrances of the past. Rather than focusing on just the narrator, storytelling is presented as a dialogic performance, thus fostering empathy, and creating bonds with the audience. Because memory constitutes both objects (symbols and narratives) and processes (collection and transmission), the cogency and resonance of stories rest on both the content and the emotions that they arouse. Affects, after all, galvanize us to do something and, in the process of mobilizing, we feel a sense of generational belonging and commitment to the group.[41] This repertoire continued after the commemoration as activists engaged in memory work in the run-up to the elections, as fear of Marcos Jr.'s election to the vice presidency heightened. For instance, in a four-minute video recording in Tagalog made by the Campaign against the Return of the Marcoses to Malacañang and posted on Facebook before the May 2016 elections, martial law victims interviewed Filipinos aged nineteen to twenty-two, where the latter shared their favorable opinions of Marcos.[42] A first-time voter asserted, "He was really strict. Like how your parents are strict because they love you." The video then segues to foreground the personhood of the recipients of Marcos's tough love. "Let me now take this opportunity to introduce myself. I am Danilo Mallari dela Fuente. I am a victim of martial law," said an elderly man with white hair, as he reached out and shook the hand of the adolescent across the table. He then proceeded to tell details of his torture through electrocution. The video ends with the message: "To this day, the true story of Martial Law is not being taught in schools. It's time to rewrite our history books." While the video was meant to reveal the truth about what happened to ordinary Filipinos during martial law, this form of exposé—a dialogue between the two generations—also shows the importance of developing common codes or frameworks of remembrance across groups through discourse. As Maurice Halbwachs says, a common framework is needed "to connect within a single system of ideas our opinions as well as those of our circle."[43]

Microblogging has also developed into a familiar and accessible form of storytelling, promoting what sociologist of mass media and culture Timothy Recuber calls "prosumption of commemoration."[44] By engaging in prosumption, wherein users are both the producers and consumers of online content, they work through their trauma and hope that posting their story would offer "a measure of closure by describing a world in which one's nation, one's family, and even oneself have suffered, but have nonetheless transformed that suffering into something positive."[45] In websites that emerged to remember the Marcos dictatorship, such as "*Hindi Kami Ulyanin* (We Are Not Forgetful): Remember Who We Are"[46] and "The Martial Law Chronicles Project,"[47] prosumers, who were former anti-dictatorship activists, juxtaposed the cathartic and transformative aspects of sharing grief and pain with foreboding images of misery and violence, imploring readers to heed their stories. In their telling of tales of disappearance and torture, they aim to achieve healing and restoration as well as to enlighten and motivate action; as such, they develop collective identities as survivors, as witnesses, and as agents of change. They characterized their memory activism as historical continuity connecting the movements of the past to the present: "We will continue the legacy of the brave who, even in death, inspires [*sic*] us to demand justice, and to keep the fire of courage burning ever brighter. *Ang ating puso't isipan ay ang mga tunay na duyan ng magiting* [Our heart and mind are the true cradle of courage]." On Twitter, users participated in the commemoration of the thirtieth anniversary, sharing messages, photos, and videos using the hashtags #NeverAgain and #EDSA30. Indeed, since the thirtieth anniversary of People Power, the internet has become a virtual meeting place for Filipinos to talk about the past—a field of contradictory and competing narratives that give meaning to historical events such as the declaration of martial law and the People Power uprising as well as processes such as revolution and democratization.

In sum, although Filipinos have officially celebrated annually the fall of the Marcos regime in 1986 through symbolic rituals that evoke struggle, victory, and unity, former anti-dictatorship activists only laid the foundation for an organized movement to forge a collective memory of the dictatorship in the mid-2010s when the Marcoses were elected to national office, auguring the possibility of their return to Malacañang; when a potential dictator (Duterte) has gained popularity in the lead up to the 2016 elections; when access to the internet has enabled ordinary Filipinos to partake in collective storytelling and share their recollections of life under an authoritarian regime in their own words; and when a group of memory entrepreneurs or challengers with cultural and symbolic capital has developed discourses to connect seemingly disparate, individualized stories of the past and tether them to the goals in the present. In social movement parlance, the movement only emerged when political opportunities were favorable, resources were available, and collective action frames to anchor grievances were introduced. The memory repertoire of this burgeoning movement in the Philippines would guide Filipino activists in the US.

Collective Memory-Making among Overseas Filipinos

As in previous official celebrations of the People Power Revolution, the thirtieth anniversary event at the Philippine consulate general in San Francisco on February 25, 2016, comprised a Catholic mass and a reception to honor

STORYTELLERS AND INTERLOCUTORS 127

the memory of those who fought the dictatorship to remind Filipinos in the US of the need to continuously "protect the legacy of People Power" and defend freedom and democracy in the homeland. With the theme "Pagbabago: Ipinaglaban N'yo, Itutuloy Ko!" (Change: You fought for it, I will continue [the fight]!), the commemoration centered on the role of Filipino Americans in keeping the memory of EDSA alive, with Philippine ambassador to the United States Jose L. Cuisia Jr. highlighting in his remarks that the quest for social change cannot be achieved "without engaging the next generations of Filipinos, without harnessing the hearts and minds of our youth." Building on Cuisia's call to action, keynote speaker California State Assembly member Robert Andres Bonta,[48] who immigrated to the US as an infant two months after the declaration of martial law, drew parallels between the People Power uprising and the California farmworkers' movement, saying, "Our Filipino leaders, *manongs* like [Larry] Itliong and [Philip] Vera Cruz, were driven by a dedication to do what's right—driven by values like sacrifice, inclusion and justice—the same values of the People Power movement." He also stressed the significance of developing wisdom from previous struggles to take steps as a collective, thereby linking the generation of the *manongs* to the younger ones through activism: "Together, our community can own our past, control our present, and shape our future. Together, we can recognize the leadership of our ancestors and create opportunities for Filipino activists of tomorrow."[49]

To actualize the theme of engaging Filipino American youth in working for change, the Philippine consulates and embassies and the Philippine American Writers and Artists, Inc., based in the San Francisco Bay Area, launched a national essay-writing contest with the motif "Recapturing the Spirit of 1986 People Power Revolution and What It Means to Me as a Filipino-American."[50] In his acceptance of the award as first-place winner, Joshua Severn from Pismo Beach, California, read a portion of his essay in the form of a letter to his grandparents. Similar to Bonta's juxtaposition of the anti-Marcos movement in the Philippines to the union organizing of *manongs* in the US, Severn delineates the contemporary struggle of Filipino Americans in the realm of culture as opposed to politics and economics for those who were in the Philippines during the Marcos dictatorship; they, however, both grapple with erasure and obfuscation of their stories in national history:

> Ours is not a physical conflict against an individual regime or tyrant. But a cultural struggle against anonymity and history and invisibility in society. Our conflicts are not waged in revolutionary language with great public displays. But with a quiet determination in the halls of government, behind our cameras, and with our pens. In speaking with the youth, our children, and telling

of your stories, we honor our people, we honor our culture, and those who fight for their beliefs. We are the offspring of Filipinos, but we are also Americans. Our charge might not be to overthrow the government, but like the revolutionaries, we must change the minds and hearts of people who do not know about us. We must save our cultures from disappearing into the shadows of history, lest we ourselves forget. We owe our lives to the sacrifices of men and women like you. Without you, I would not be here, able to enjoy the benefits of this great country. I hope our young people are up to the challenge of honoring their grandparents, great grandparents, and the spirits of those who were in EDSA in 1986. But we are in different arenas. We both fight for our right to relevancy and visibility in our national stories.[51]

While both Bonta and Severn, 1.5- and third-generation Filipino Americans, respectively, invoked a defining moment in Philippine history, their allusion to the comparable struggle of Filipinos' campaigns for rights and recognition in the US suggests that memory activism must not only deal with the temporal dimension of remembering but also the spatial elements. Like their counterparts in the Philippines, Filipino memory entrepreneurs/challengers overseas needed to disrupt the image of the "golden years" of the dictatorship that is widespread in Filipino communities abroad, and to mobilize the generation born after martial law and outside the Philippines to uphold the victories of the anti-dictatorship movement. Likewise, their memory activism entailed binding generations through individual, family, and community stories, situating personal and collective experiences within a broader historical and structural context. But they also must contend with the threat of forgetting—of historical neglect of their contribution to regime change and, in essence, Philippine nation building, while simultaneously participating in movements to assert their citizenship in their countries of settlement. In other words, for Filipino activists in the US and the Netherlands, their stories intend to mobilize memories that bridge then and now as well as to traverse here and there.

In their own annual commemorations of People Power outside of official events by the consulates and embassies, Filipinos in the US instituted memory repertoires that consisted of artistic performances and exhibits, candlelight vigils, protest marches, and storytelling by former anti-dictatorship activists aside from the usual religious services that typify events by a largely devout community. A triumphant mood characterized the early years, celebrating the actors in the Philippines who played a central role and validating the moral and spiritual tenor of the uprising. For instance, during the first anniversary, Reverend King Vaho described the ouster of Marcos at a Catholic mass in National City in San Diego County as "the ultimate expression of what love can do and what prayer can achieve" and that "power comes from not what man possesses but what is inside man: his indomitable spirit." Filipinos also shared their ambivalent views about the Marcos dictatorship. Jim Jimenez, an accountant, left the Philippines because "there was no future there for himself or his wife and two young children, at least while Marcos was in power." But he also reckoned that "at first, the martial law was good, but then it became a dictatorship, like all dictatorships," and he felt "glad democracy has gotten back to the Philippines."[52]

The jubilant atmosphere dissipated through the years. In its stead were anger and resentment, as contemporary Philippine politics defined the context of commemoration, and second-generation Filipino Americans born after the dictatorship and radicalized through the US branch of the CPP-NDF's transnational network assumed prominent roles in organizing the Filipino migrant communities. In 2008, Anakbayan New York/New Jersey, Bagong Alyansang Makabayan (New Patriotic Alliance [BAYAN]) USA, National Alliance for Filipino Concerns, Filipinas for Rights and Empowerment, New York Committee for Human Rights in the Philippines, and Bayanihan Filipino Community Center staged a protest march in Woodside in Queens, New York City, known for its concentration of Filipinos and thus earning the moniker Little Manila. The march ended with a candlelight vigil and singing of the Philippine national anthem and "Bayan Ko." The event was less of a remembrance of the People Power uprising and more of a critique of its outcomes—the democratization process that essentially cemented the hold of the oligarchic elite over state power. Drawing on the memory of the Marcos regime, the protesters criticized Gloria Macapagal Arroyo for being a "corrupt, anti-people, and fascist president and leading puppet of US imperialism."[53] The euphoric climate of commemoration was restored during the thirtieth anniversary, with former anti-dictatorship activists from the KDP and Ninoy Aquino Movement sharing personal stories of repression and resistance and framing the overthrow of Marcos as a result of unity among Filipinos all over the world—in essence, People Power forged across borders.

Because the protest infrastructure built during the mobilizations against the Marcos dictatorship has endured in the US, memory activism in the country is relatively more dynamic and sustained compared to that in the Netherlands. In late 2016, a group of mostly first-generation migrants, who went to the Netherlands as political refugees and graduate students, formed the Filipinos against Corruption and Tyranny (FACT), a loose network of individuals and organizations that regularly organize events to educate and mobilize Filipinos on the political situation in the Philippines, especially on Duterte's War on Drugs and extrajudicial killings. FACT commemorated annually the

130   CHAPTER FIVE

People Power Revolution, where it defined the meaning of the four-day uprising and the phrase "Never Again!" based on an understanding of how the
past has shaped present historical conditions—to the point of the past persist-
ing and being reproduced in the present. The alliance also framed collective
identity in terms of its foundation in the struggle against and continuation of
resistance to tyrannical rule, whether this be in the form of formal dictatorship like the Marcos regime or Duterte's illiberal democracy. For instance, in
its statement for the thirty-fourth anniversary in 2020, it declared,

> The revolt at EDSA may have lasted mere days, but it was the culmination of
> the years of the Filipino people's valiant resistance against repression and hu-
> man rights violations. When we celebrate EDSA People Power, we celebrate
> the heroism and sacrifices of ordinary men and women through that dark
> time. When we commemorate EDSA People Power, we remember to what
> depths an evil regime can sink into, and we vow to ourselves: Never Again!
>
> Never Again! This phrase has never been as meaningful as it is today. Be-
> cause today, our nation is again in the grips of a regime that is dictatorial in
> every way. The presidency of Rodrigo Duterte has mocked and attacked our
> democratic institutions. . . .
>
> All in all Duterte has been the Marcos blueprint of the immoral accu-
> mulation of powers, of undermining—if not weaponizing—democratic in-
> stitutions, and widespread and intensifying human rights violations. We re-
> main true to the spirit of the EDSA revolt and say to these all: Never Again!
> We remain true to the spirit of People Power and uphold that Filipinos have
> the right to topple a murderous dictator. If saying Never Again! means Oust
> Duterte! then so be it.[54]

Although activists in the US and the Netherlands have persistently asserted their role in the revolution, the thirtieth anniversary celebration was a
watershed in their memory work as they anticipated the election of Duterte
and Marcos Jr. and the historical revisionism that would ensue, undermining
and erasing their stories.

MARCOS'S BURIAL AS A CRITICAL EVENT
FOR COUNTERMEMORY

On August 7, 2016, one of Duterte's first directives as president was the burial
of Marcos's embalmed body at the Libingan ng mga Bayani, saying that the
former dictator was qualified to be buried at the cemetery due to being a
former president and a soldier.[55] As part of Duterte's agenda to promote national healing and reconciliation, the burial of Marcos's remains at Libingan

ng mga Bayani was his attempt to maintain the dominant discourse that the Philippine nation is steadily progressing toward a stable future that has come to terms with the chaotic past rather than being stuck and mired in it. The government proposal and the homeland mobilizations against Marcos's interment produced emotional responses among first- and second-generation Filipinos in the US and the Netherlands. This is often the case with critical events because they make unequivocal individual and collective grievances, as well as the social cleavages and power structures that produce them.[56] Since public attention is high during these times, migrants and their descendants often cannot escape situations where they must confront questions related to their relationship with their country of origin. The events thus compel them to reflect on and (re)assert their roots and multiple belongings by engaging with their co-ethnics/co-nationals in their social networks and in the public sphere, as well as participating in targeted collective action.[57]

The campaign against the interment galvanized Filipinos worldwide, and activists in the US and the Netherlands mobilized both old and new protest infrastructures for the struggle, with (re)constructing a collective memory of the Marcos dictatorship as a core movement strategy. Marcos's burial offers a site for what Michel Foucault refers to as "countermemory," where power relations—expressed materially and symbolically—in memory cohere, as with any discursive practice.[58] National cemeteries are zones that epitomize the nation's roots. Thus, the debates surrounding whether the body of the former dictator has the right to a state-sanctioned space and to lay claim to the national discourse of heroism became an opportunity for unleashing marginalized memories. These remembrances themselves challenge knowledge that privileges certain stories over others, that favors specific bodies (literally) in national memory, and that looks at history only in terms of continuity, not breaks and ruptures.

Upon learning of Duterte's plan to lay to rest Marcos at Libingan ng mga Bayani and the mobilizations in Manila on August 14, 2016, to oppose it, the Justice for Filipino American Veterans (JFAV)—a broad national alliance of veteran, youth, student, and community organizations advocating full equity under the law for Filipino Americans who fought alongside US armed forces during World War II—issued a press statement stating that Marcos is undeserving of a heroes' burial.[59] JFAV reminded Filipinos that Marcos had fabricated his own military accolades and medals in the war against the Japanese occupation of the Philippines[60] to construct himself as the messiah of the nation—a necessary strand in his depiction of the dictatorship as the pinnacle of Philippine progress. But despite the symbolic capital of the veterans in the

Filipino community, which has facilitated multigenerational, cross-class mobilization for their cause, their participation in the fight to derail Duterte's proposal was limited. Since most of them left the Philippines before the dictatorship, they could not invoke personal and collective lived experiences to delegitimize state-sponsored discourses of heroism beyond Marcos's fraudulent war honors. Thus, regardless of their standing in the community and the information they possessed to challenge the Marcoses' and Duterte's claims, the veterans alone were unable to perform the role of political entrepreneurs. Through the Kontra Libing (Anti-Burial) Coalition in the US and FACT in the Netherlands, former anti-dictatorship activists, as memory entrepreneurs and challengers, destabilized official discourses that underpin the rhetoric of a hero's burial for Marcos as a collective expression of moving on from the baggage of the past and advancing the nation toward a hopeful future. They also inspired the young generation born in the US and the Netherlands to learn about a contentious period in Philippine history in ways that inform their understanding of their location in the societies they live in.

Since memory activists were based in cities where anti-dictatorship groups were active in the US in the 1970s and 1980s, they quickly mobilized old networks of movement constituents and adherents to be part of the Global Day of Protest on September 7, 2016, with the call "Never Again to Martial Law" and #MarcosNotaHero linking the synchronized protests. The curation of photos in social media under the same rallying cry and hashtag created a transnational community based on memory. In the San Francisco Bay Area, the Kontra Libing Coalition was comprised of groups that cut across age, class, ideology, and migration cohort. Experienced activists in anti-Marcos organizing from the Coalition against the Marcos Dictatorship (CAMD) and KDP joined organizations affiliated with the NDF, whose young members are predominantly US-born (Anakbayan Silicon Valley, BAYAN Northern California, and GABRIELA [General Assembly Binding Women for Reform, Integrity, Equality, Leadership and Action] San Francisco). Cultural associations and social circles (EDSA People Power@30 Committee, Filipino Arts and Cinema International, Filipino-American Book Club, Global Filipino Diaspora Council), local student and youth leagues (PACE of San Francisco State University), national alliances on civil rights issues (JFAV and Association of Widows, Advocates, and Relatives for Equality), and the recently formed political caucus Friends of Akbayan USA also joined the coalition. In a statement published in the *Northern California Asian Journal* on September 2–8, 2016, the coalition countered the Philippine government's framing of Marcos's burial as an act of accepting the past to move into the future and

STORYTELLERS AND INTERLOCUTORS

redefined it as a smokescreen for retrogression rather than as a means toward progress:

> A hero's burial erases from memory the sins of the Marcos dictatorship, and re- moves another obstacle in the path of the Marcos family's political ambitions. Most importantly, a hero's burial for Marcos negates hard and important les- sons learned from the negative example of his dictatorial rule. The Filipino people deserve to move on—away from corruption, away from the old politics of patronage and people's disempowerment, away from tyranny and abuse of power, away from the sordid state of affairs that was the Marcos era, and into a new politics of principles, reform, social justice, human rights, genuine de- mocracy, good government and accountability.[61]

Likewise, the coalition deployed agency and identity frames that attest to the role of Filipino Americans in the historic uprising against Marcos, mak- ing them part of the national imaginary. Activists emphasized multigenera- tional continuity in collective struggle in the construction of a transnational Filipino community:

> During the years of the dictatorship, Filipinos here in the U.S. refused to be cowed, and constituted a resounding voice opposition against the dictatorship in their homeland. And despite the U.S. government's support of Marcos, al- lies here in the U.S. stood with Filipino activists to call for an end to the dicta- torship. We call on everyone once again to oppose the attempt to rehabilitate the image of this fascist and plunderous dictator.[62]

Personal testimonies and stories comprised the memory repertoire of the Kontra Libing Coalition, whereby activists concretized the dictatorship, a pe- riod in history that was individually experienced even by Filipinos outside the physical territory of the Philippines (figure 5.1). At the protest in front of the Philippine consulate in Los Angeles, former KDP members Carol Ojeda- Kimbrough and Florante Ibañez and leader of the Los Angeles chapter of the NCRCLP in the Philippines Enrique dela Cruz drew on their experiences in the anti–martial law movement to appeal to the young generation to "bear placards and protests [sic] on this issue."[63] Ojeda-Kimbrough, who left the Philippines to escape repression, shared the abduction and murder of her husband. In 1986, she became part of a class action lawsuit filed in Hawaiʻi on behalf of the ten thousand torture victims or their surviving relatives. The case was settled in 2011, where she was awarded a check for $1,000, to which she asked, "Is that the value of the life of a Filipino?"[64] Other survivors such as Lolita Andrada Lledo, who works at the Pilipino Workers Center in Los

FIGURE 5.1. Former anti-dictatorship activists who are members of Kontra Libing (Anti-Burial) Coalition gather in front of the Philippine consulate in San Francisco on September 9, 2016, to protest Marcos's interment at the Libingan ng mga Bayani (National Heroes Cemetery). Founding leader of Katipunan ng Demokratikong Pilipino Melinda Paras carries a sign that reads "I was in a Marcos prison camp and I won't forget." (Source: Rick Rocamora.)

Angeles in charge of assisting and advocating for Filipino caregivers to assert their rights as workers, and Myrla Baldonado, who is with the same organization, recounted their arrest and incarceration. Baldonado carries the scars of physical and mental torture and sexual abuse, admitting to the public that she has stayed unmarried and that "twenty years after that harrowing experience, I had to seek rehabilitation counseling because I couldn't escape its psychological impact."[65] Thus, activists' disclosure of intimate details about their lives recasts remembering and forgetting as processes that punctuate "the local, the immediate, and the personal," as "counter-memory starts with the particular and the specific and then builds outward toward a total story."[66]

In Washington, DC, former members of the MFP and CAMD joined the US Pinoys for Good Governance in a protest in front of the Philippine Embassy, where they displayed a replica of a coffin alongside black-and-white photographs of victims of Marcos's repression, including opposition leader Benigno S. Aquino Jr. who was self-exiled in Boston prior to his assassination in 1983. Like the commemoration in Amsterdam discussed at the beginning of the chapter, the dramatization of a funeral is part of the dominant protest repertoire among

Filipino activists that culturally resonates with their co-ethnics/co-nationals, symbolizing not only death and injustice under the regime but also the denial of respect toward the deceased's body. This is especially the case for those whose bodies were never found or were mutilated beyond recognition, therefore also precluding families from properly honoring the remains of their loved ones through a traditional funeral. Such repertoire thus rebuffs the Marcoses' claims of maltreatment of the dictator's body, as the "state of perpetual embalming had been the proof of the family's narrative of state cruelty against them: for disallowing a proper burial for Ferdinand, for the desecration of the dead."[67]

While former anti-dictatorship activists led the mobilizations in the US, migrant organizers were at the forefront in other countries of destination for Filipinos. The international network of Migrante, a global alliance of grassroots organizations of overseas Filipinos and their families in twenty-four countries, rallied OFWs and Filipino immigrants in Hong Kong, Thailand, Taiwan, Japan, South Korea, United Arab Emirates, Qatar, Saudi Arabia, Australia, New Zealand, Italy, Canada, United Kingdom, and the Netherlands not only to publicly express their opposition to the Marcos burial but also to counter Marcos's heroism by invoking the state construction of OFWs as the genuine heroes of the nation (figure 5.2). In its statement, Migrante identified

FIGURE 5.2. Overseas Filipino workers in Qatar protest Marcos's burial at the Libingan ng mga Bayani. (Source: Migrante International.)

FIGURE 5.3. In Sydney, a delegation from Migrante Australia (NSW) holds a demonstration in front of the Philippine consulate. Members also presented a statement to Consul Melanie Diano, which declared that the real heroes are those who fought against the Marcos dictatorship and the overseas Filipino workers whose remittances fuel the Philippine economy. (Source: Migrante International.)

the real heroes as "our *bagong bayani*' who continue to bear the brunt of Marcos' labor export policy that continues to exploit our OFWs' cheap labor, separate us from our loved ones and place us in dire and dangerous conditions."[68] Outside the Philippine consulate general in Sydney, protesters juxtaposed the signs "Justice for All Victims of Martial Law! Never Forget! Never Again!" and "The Regime That Started It All #LaborExportPolicy #ForcedMigration #NeverForget #MarcosNoHero," thus linking the anti-dictatorship and migrants' rights movements of the past to the present mobilizations (figure 5.3). In the end, although many groups mobilized against it, on November 18, 2016, Marcos's body was in fact interred at the Libingan ng mga Bayani.

But protests continued despite the outcome, even in places where the number of Filipinos was small and memory activism remained inchoate. In the Netherlands, the Filipinos in the Netherlands against the Marcoses and Their Return to Power (FLAME), an impromptu alliance of Filipino migrants across the political spectrum that eventually evolved into FACT, transformed the campaign against Marcos's burial into a sustained effort to address historical revisionism on the dictatorship. In a protest in front of the Philippine

Embassy in The Hague on November 25, 2016, a week after Marcos was finally interred in Libingan ng mga Bayani, FLAME sang "Bayan Ko" and carried signs such as "Do Not Forget the Victims of Martial Law" and "Marcos Is a Dictator, Not a Hero #NeverForget," fusing patriotism as articulated in the song to appeals for remembering the casualties of Marcos's authoritarian rule (figure 5.4). Behind a painting of Philippine national hero José Rizal inside the embassy, a representative of FLAME read the group's statement. He recounted the crimes committed by Marcos and his cronies, including "mounting foreign debt, rural poverty, widespread unemployment, low wages, and food insecurity," which instigated the large-scale cross-border migration of Filipinos to countries such as the Netherlands, and ended with, "We remain vigilant. We will never forget. Marcos is *geen held* [not a hero]."[69] Like the migrants' rights movement discussed in chapter 4, by relating the Marcos dictatorship to the forced relocation of Filipinos abroad, whether temporary or permanent, activists recognized Filipinos outside the Philippine territory as actors in memory processes. By broadening the definition of the violation of human rights to encompass social and economic injustices, OFWs become part of these narratives about the dictatorship in ways that point to both their victimhood and agency.

In sum, the burial of Marcos as a critical event offered memory activists in the US and the Netherlands a physical and symbolic site to anchor their narratives in ways that challenge state discourse on the dictatorship, particularly Marcos's purported heroism, and lay claim to the movement that overthrew his regime—that is, assert their historical presence in a period of economic

FIGURE 5.4. Even after Marcos's burial at the Libingan ng mga Bayani on November 18, 2016, Filipinos in the Netherlands continue to stage protests in front of the Philippine consulate in The Hague. (Source: Aldo Gonzalez.)

and political strife for Filipinos. Through utilizing the discourses and repertoires of the anti-dictatorship and migrants' rights movements, memory activists linked past struggles to present ones, thus enabling the multigenerational reproduction of collective identity based on resistance. At the same time, the use of the same frames (e.g., "Marcos Not a Hero," "Never Again," and "Never Forget") that were also hashtags enabled diverse social movement groups and organizations as well as unaffiliated individuals to act in concert during the Global Day of Protest, linking Filipino transnational communities to each other and to the homeland and simultaneously engaging in the construction and articulation of a collective identity centered on memories of the dictatorship.

Although the burial spurred mobilization that hinged on collective memory-making, it was ephemeral, as in any episode of collective effervescence. In periods of abeyance, when the excitement generated by crowds and other social gatherings subsides, activists nurture commitment, sustain goals and tactics, and cultivate a sense of mission or purpose through everyday habits and practices.[70] In the case of the memory movement, these were life writing in the form of memoirs. American sociologist Randall Collins argues that activists regularly gather to recreate the collective effervescence of initial mobilizations and to sustain the emotions that instigated them.[71] A memoir is a significant site of ritual participation infused with emotional dynamics. In times of dormancy, it can be "the place activists evaluate the effects of movement adherence or participation on their lives, reconciling the space between what is and what they would like to be."[72] Thus, for activists, memoirs are crucial in the continuous process of collective identity formation.

MEMOIRS AS SPACES FOR IDENTITY CONSTRUCTION

On February 2, 2018, former members of the KDP unveiled their organizational memoir *A Time to Rise: Collective Memoirs of the Union of Democratic Filipinos (KDP)* at the University of the Philippines Diliman, the hub for radical activism during the dictatorship. Several cadres of the KDP first met each other at the university through the student organizations Kabataang Makabayan (Nationalist Youth) and Samahang Demokratiko ng Kabataan (Association of Democratic Youth). At the event, coeditor of the book Cindy Domingo explained that their main goal in publishing the memoir was to inspire the next generation of Filipino Americans and other Asian Americans to continue the fight against discrimination and fascism and to strengthen the solidarity of Filipinos around the world. Armin Alforque of the AMLC,

STORYTELLERS AND INTERLOCUTORS   139

which KDP was a part of, showed photos of Filipino exiles in various contentious activities and asserted that "a Filipino exile should play a key role in the
discussion taking place here in the Philippines even though they're abroad."
Historian of the Philippines Ricardo Jose commented that the memoir is "'in-
tensely personal, riveting, and revealing' as it gives us a glimpse of the lives
led by people who were united by a common concern for country and for the
community" and that it deserves to be read especially by Filipinos in the Philippines and around the world.[73]

From Manila, KDP activists traveled back to the US in March to introduce *A Time to Rise* to a largely Filipino American audience. This time, the
venue was the historic International Hotel (I-Hotel) in San Francisco. Several
authors read excerpts from their stories, mostly focusing on their political
socialization—how global historical conditions in the 1970s and their experience and interpretation of them thrust them into activism. Isabella Borgeson,
the daughter of former KDP activists, ended the event honoring the movement community that helped raise her and celebrating her mother with "For
My Militant Mama," a poem depicting her mother's experience of growing
up in the province of Leyte in Central Philippines. In both book launching
events, *A Time to Rise* served as a spatial and temporal bridge—between activists in the US and in the Philippines and between the older and younger
generations of Filipinos.

Along with former KDP member Mila de Guzman's *Women against Marcos: Stories of Filipino and Filipino American Women Who Fought a Dictator*, *A Time to Rise* came out as Duterte consolidated his illiberal democratic
rule in the Philippines, with historical revisionism of the Marcos dictatorship as a key component. In the prologue of *Women against Marcos*, de Guzman writes, "The process of recalling this traumatic period in Philippine history has become more urgent because so much is at stake. Thirty years after
the overthrow of Marcos, the Philippines is on the cusp on another national
election, scheduled for May 2016. Marcos's son, Ferdinand Jr., an apologist
for martial law is running as a candidate for vice president. Young Filipinos,
who did not experience martial law, do not have a collective memory of that
era." Although the aims of the authors in writing their stories and in publishing them in a memoir were to document their contributions to the transnational "fight against *isms* that oppress us,"[74] the processes of life writing[75] became a vital part of group identity construction. The two-decade dictatorship
and the People Power Revolution were collective events. But they were also
individually experienced. The former activists gathered in meetings and writing retreats to talk through and lay out the goals of the book, and then wrote

stories about their personal lives during the dictatorship, especially their involvement in the movement. As such, they developed a shared frame for interpreting their experiences—experiences that bind them together—and a common language for conveying what they went through and who they are as people.

In life writing, authors are not only chronicling an event or describing the way they lived through a certain period; they are also engaged in various rhetorical acts that include "justifying their own perceptions, upholding their reputations, disputing the accounts of others, settling scores, conveying cultural information, and inventing desirable futures, among others."[76] As both object and subject, writing from externalized and internal standpoints, they "place themselves at the center of the stories they assemble and are interested in the meaning of larger forces, or conditions, or events for their *own* stories."[77] Although they sometimes incorporate documented evidence in their narratives, for the most part, they rely on personal memories and invest authority in their experiences. In fact, they become "readers of their experiential histories, bringing discursive schema that are culturally available to them to bear on what has happened."[78] This meaning making from their lived experience—an outcome of the interaction between macrostructural dynamics of historical events and mesolevel processes in their small groups—is what authors of *A Time to Rise* and *Women against Marcos* hope readers distill and relate to in the stories. In their accounts, they intend to show that the personal is political and that activism is often messy, fluid, and volatile because the choices that activists make as part of a collective impact their individual lives. As sociologist Gary Alan Fine contends, "narrative creates social spaces in which audiences are encouraged to identify with the situations, problems, and concerns of others. . . . By making experiences immediate, concrete, and dramatic, narrative by its expression provides unarguable proof of the claims of movements."[79] Personalizing distant or abstract issues through individual life stories enables the audience to vicariously experience the situations of injustice and collective efforts to address them.[80]

As an instrument that unites multiple generations through the transmission of messages that center on struggle, community, and hope, the memoirs fulfill a critical role in diaspora formation. They reinvigorate and add to existing discourses about the history and social life of the migrant community through the sharing of new narratives and the retelling of old ones. Although *A Time to Rise* and *Women against Marcos* focus on the authors' reminiscences of their activism, they also offer an opportunity for second-generation Filipino Americans to pass down the stories of their ancestors, thus promoting the intergenerational reproduction of cultural and social ties that constitute the

STORYTELLERS AND INTERLOCUTORS   141

diaspora. Thus, memoirs could fulfill the desire of Joshua Severn—winner of the national essay-writing contest during the thirtieth anniversary of the People Power Revolution mentioned in the previous section—to "recapture the unique story" of his grandparents, as *A Time to Rise* did for Rebecca Apostol, US-born daughter of immigrant activists with the KDP:

> Like many red diaper babies (as KDP activists' children are affectionately called), I grew up learning of my parents' activism and the movement through community storytelling. Each new recitation revealed new details. Since my parents' love story is intertwined with activism, my favorite tellings came from their fellow KDP activists with whom they remained close friends; these versions usually gave away juicy information that many parents had forgotten or chosen not to reveal....
>
> In my short twenty-seven years, and through the passing of my Auntie Nonie Briones and some of my parents' other KDP activist friends over the years, I have learned that our legacies lie in our stories—the ones we tell and, eventually, the ones that are told about us. For my unassuming father, I honor his legacy by retelling his story as he told it while I was growing up....
>
> This is my father's extraordinary immigrant legacy.[81]

The narratives of individual activists in both memoirs, which took years to write in conversation with other actors (e.g., family members, community organizers, and academics across generations), capture the social nature of life writing; self-reflection, expression of identity, and dialogue with an audience guided how they tell their stories. Interspersed with their own analyses of their response to unique conditions based on their social location, their accounts show how their identities influenced their rhetorical style of writing. Although memoirs are often produced not for mass consumption but largely for movement adherents and general supporters within the public, stories are polysemic, permitting multiple readings and interpretations.[82] In the case of *A Time to Rise* and *Women against Marcos*, three dominant frames allow for overseas Filipinos, regardless of their involvement in social movements, to relate to the stories and build empathy with the characters thus facilitating the discursive construction of the diaspora: cultivating courage to confront precarious situations, making difficult choices at decisive turning points and developing their sense of self, and yearning for and defining home.

Exiles and migrants wrestle with charges of national disloyalty, which generate feelings of anxiety, bitterness, and guilt.[83] For those who challenge the government in their country of origin, they are compelled to exhibit their standing as patriots and continued belonging to the homeland. Through sustained performances of their national identity, they counter the fear of being forgotten and the guilt of becoming too contented in their place of settlement with the passing of time. In recounting their experiences during the dictatorship, the migrant activists draw on feelings of torment and remorse for leaving the Philippines, particularly family members who continue to struggle with the day-to-day impact of the authoritarian regime and their comrades who continue to fight despite repression. These emotions shape how they narrate their departure and journey, with anecdotes centered on an airport scene. In describing their inner turmoil as they go through the rigmarole of checking in and passport control, the airport embodies a liminal point where they negotiate the here and there and come to terms with the past, present, and future. Like the case of Eritreans in Milan whose journey to Italy serves as a "frightening and painful ritual through which one becomes part of the Eritrean diaspora,"[84] the tearful goodbye scene at the Manila International Airport[85] marks the beginning of an emotional odyssey that overseas Filipinos share—a rite of passage into the diasporic life. In storytelling, this journey then evokes two processes: "the experience of movement through places and hints at how identity is shaped through movement" and "the way experiences are transformed as they become narratives."[86]

Like Boyet R.'s tale of migrating to the Netherlands to escape poverty and join his family in the previous chapter, memory activists expressed in their stories the pain, trepidation, and hope about leaving, often having second thoughts in the moment but recognizing the limited range of choices they have, given the structural conditions in the Philippines. Geline Avila, a former KDP activist born and raised in the Philippines, conveyed this emotional quandary in *Women against Marcos*:

> At the airport on departure day, I was still wracked by doubts about whether I was making the right decision. After saying a tearful goodbye to my family and friends, I walked slowly towards the gate of my flight. I became apprehensive when I saw two uniformed men in the pre-departure area. They were carefully checking the names of all passengers against a list, ostensibly to prevent activists and other people deemed "suspect" by the government from leaving the country. When they got to me, they looked at the long sheet of names and, much to my relief, waved me in.
>
> When the plane took off at mid-morning, I felt the same emptiness that engulfed me when my brother died. I felt disoriented, as if I was losing control of my life.
>
> ... While I remained anxious about my future in a foreign land, I knew I was about to begin a new chapter in my life as an activist.[87]

Connected to confusion is the dialectic of fear and courage as activists took legal risks when they exited the country. These anecdotes center on the

STORYTELLERS AND INTERLOCUTORS

willingness to take risks and the ability to prevail over a dangerous situation as activists encountered the possibility of arrests and incarceration and made spontaneous decisions often based on individual instincts. For instance, in the story of Jeanette Gandionco Lazam, a second-generation Filipino American, she recounts in *A Time to Rise* how she overcame her terror and triumphed when she escaped and smuggled anti-Marcos propaganda out of the Philippines during one of her trips to see relatives in Leyte just after martial law was declared. Although the experience of OFWs is qualitatively different from Avila and Lazam, Filipino labor migrants in Italy or Singapore, especially those who left without proper documentation, could identify with the fear of brushing with authorities and the courage and hope they need to muster to be able to reach their destination and achieve their goals for their families.

> The inspector looked at me long and hard. He immediately summoned representatives from the armed forces. All in all, fifteen men with rapid-fire machine guns surrounded me. I could barely move. Next, a government official came and seized my passport folder. He rifled through it, taking my passport. . . .
>
> I quickly got my wits about me and demanded to know why they were detaining me; after all, I was an American citizen. They explained that they had found antigovernment propaganda in my carry-on; they wanted to know who had given it to me and why I was in the Philippines. All in whole my mother stood outside the gates of the airport wondering why my plane hadn't taken off.
>
> Stalling for time, I demanded to speak with American embassy officials and have them present during my interrogation. The inspectors denied my request. . . .
>
> As I ran down the tarmac; I took one last, long look at the Philippines and my poor mother standing outside the gate. I cried out, fearing that I would never see her or my brother again. That was the longest seventeen-hour ride back to the States.[88]

In the US, anti-dictatorship activists endured hardship as an outcome of their movement participation. In their storytelling, they adopt the rhetorical devices of the classic tale about immigration to the US, often popularized by mainstream mass media. In the story, the immigrant—the hero or heroine—toils and overcomes hardships in pursuit of the American dream. The experiences of destitution and discrimination become the basis of an immigrant identity. Many anti-dictatorship activists from the Philippines disproportionately come from upper-middle-class backgrounds and being forced to contend with the challenges of a lower-class position is a common theme in their life narrative, such as Avila's in *Women against Marcos*:

144   CHAPTER FIVE

> When I first arrived in the U.S., I stayed with my sister in the Bay Area and worked at entry-level jobs. My parents followed me shortly, and the three of us rented an apartment in San Francisco. I became the family breadwinner on my clerical salary. My mother often volunteered at Rainbow Grocery in the Mission district, and brought home free bread and vegetables to augment my small salary.[89]

Similarly, the story of Viol de Guzman in the same collection also highlights her privation in choosing to prioritize her activism. But rather than focusing on the hardship she experienced, she constructs her narrative to punctuate her agency, a familiar trope in stories of trauma, where actors portray themselves not only as victims but as "survivors with imagination, energy, and resilience":[90]

> I left my job as an editorial assistant at a publishing firm to work with a radical weekly newspaper, the New York *Guardian*, managed by a cooperative of leftists. The move meant a significant cut in pay, but I was happy to work in that setting with fellow leftists. I managed to survive, eating Puerto Rican and Jewish equivalents of our *turo-turo*[91] fast food joints, sharing a one-bedroom apartment with my sister and two friends, and limiting my wardrobe to three pairs of second-hand Levis, three peace t-shirts, and a winter coat made by my sister's close friend.[92]

As the excerpts show, the frame of courage amid fear, guilt, and uncertainty support anthropologist James Clifford's claim that "constitutive suffering coexists with the skills of survival: strength in adaptive distinction, discrepant cosmopolitanism, and stubborn visions of renewal."[93] In a sense, the discrepant emotions of anguish and fortitude about leaving the homeland followed by the ennui and resolve of settling in a new country become part of a shared language that marks membership in a group. Thus, in the process of (re)telling stories that foreground this frame, whether in memoirs, newsletters, or protests, the boundaries that define a diaspora are consolidated.

In juxtaposition to the frame that stresses courage is one that revolves around the realization that they must leave the Philippines and/or participate in activism, despite or because of the uncertainty of the period. During these moments, the activists grappled with social norms and expectations that had grown to be more salient and restrictive in their day-to-day lives. This is especially the case for many of the female activists, who are compelled to deviate from gender roles in their decision to migrate and/or join the movement. In the process of becoming involved in mobilizations against the Marcos dictatorship, they "found themselves"; as they confronted individual and family conflicts and deliberated on their choices, often based on

STORYTELLERS AND INTERLOCUTORS

145

whether commitment to movement goals should take precedence over personal relationships, they developed and became more aware of their multiple role and social identities—as women, mothers, workers, migrants, Filipinos, Americans, and so on.

In his study of pro-life activists, Ziad Munson states the importance of a turning point in an individual's life as a critical first step in becoming involved in social movements.[94] He defines turning points as "those periods when people are required to make significant changes in their everyday life and, as a result, must also reorient their way of looking at and understanding the world."[95] Throughout a person's life, they go through many turning points that include moving away from home, changing careers, getting married, and so on. In activism, turning points often signal biographical availability,[96] which is often connected to cognitive and emotional openness to new ideas. For the activists in *A Time to Rise* and *Women against Marcos*, a turning point in their life course coincided with or facilitated their involvement in the anti-dictatorship movement. Avila, for example, reflected in *Women against Marcos* on how her activism drove her to move to the US, evading the fulfillment of her expected gender roles:

> Fearing for my safety after my short stint at a prison camp, my parents asked my brother who lived in the U.S., to send me an airplane ticket. My brother pleaded with me to leave. "Why don't you try it out there? If you don't like it, you can always come back." . . .
>
> I faced a difficult dilemma. I felt lost because I hadn't done any political work for months, and my boyfriend, who had already finished school, was hinting at marriage. I was about to turn 19, and deep in my heart I knew I was not yet ready to get married. I couldn't picture myself living as a housewife in my in-laws' home doing domestic chores. Leaving the country became my most viable option, although I still had second thoughts after agreeing to my parents' request.[97]

Second-generation Filipino American Cindy Domingo also shares the constraints she felt due to her gender. Her decision to be away from her parents and live with other activists was a turning point not only for her activism but also for her adulthood; it gave her the autonomy and freedom to explore who she is and who she wants to become. In an excerpt of her story in *Women against Marcos*, she talks about the constraints of parental authority and whiteness to her identity formation:

> As my participation in KDP deepened, the frequent night meetings started creating tension within my family. Every time I went to a meeting, my parents got mad at Silme and questioned him, "Why do you keep bringing your sister

146   CHAPTER FIVE

to meetings?" Then they would turn to me and ask, "Why are you sacrificing your life and career for this?" . . .

In 1975, I decided to move out of my parents' home because the situation had become untenable, and dropping my political work was not an option. I rented a house with three other KDP women members who became lifelong friends. . . .

My newfound independence began to affect my personal life. Growing up in Ballard, the historic home of the Scandinavian population in Seattle, I didn't have the opportunity to socialize with other people of color. My friends were white, and the boys I dated were white. The KDP exposed me to the broader progressive movement, where I met Latino and African-American activists. We relaxed after meetings by socializing at parties or going to bars.[98]

In the stories of Estella Habal and Lourdes Marzan in *A Time to Rise*, they unpack the overwhelming challenges of motherhood and career that often lead female activists to question their place in the revolution and to vacillate in their commitments. But they write about their experiences in a way that constructs them as complex characters with agency of their own in a world that penalizes women for prioritizing themselves. Thus, in their stories, despite facing seemingly insurmountable obstacles, they remained steadfast and confident, because activism has equipped them with the cognitive and emotional tools to transcend these hurdles. In their tales, they are heroines:

> Moving to San Francisco was a turning point, the beginning of my commitment to revolutionary politics and a new life. I had literally run away from a five-year marriage that was the product of two teenage pregnancies and a lot of ignorance. I felt the whole world had opened up to me. Feeling both empowered and scared, with two baby boys to raise on my own, I knew that life would be hard. But my experience as young mother and college student had already somewhat prepared me for the adventures ahead.[99] [Habal]

> And what about my career? I had been brought up to believe that I must aim for the stars and that there was no limit to what I could do. Now I was being asked to give up my career, my vehicle to the stars.
>
> But I had a historical role. I could see the KDP logic. I believed in the cause and its requirements. It was true. New York was, by far, more important than Philadelphia. Philadelphia did not even have a Philippine consulate. I was a rising and promising political leader and community activist. I was just getting good at it. I could really make a difference in New York. I could not possibly fail the movement.[100] [Marzan]

Like the reflections of female ALAB members and anecdotes of mail-order brides such as Jocelyn in chapter 3, the stories of Avila, Domingo, Habal, and

Marzan bespeak the life-changing process and outcome of collective action on the individual level; that is, activism shapes one's self and identity. For these women, regardless of the motivations that initially led them to the anti-dictatorship movement, they went through the same personal growth and empowerment, especially as they began to recognize their ability to adapt to volatile situations and, in the process, subvert rigid gender structures. Focusing on turning points in their narratives where their choices led them to a certain life trajectory, the authors show that while identity formation is an evolving process, it is marked by discontinuities and flows. Filipina labor migrants who do not participate in activism also undergo such transformations, whereby their new sense of personhood derives from their independence and grows with prolonged stay abroad.[101]

Whether fiction or biography, migrant stories include the authors' musings about home, often written in a nostalgic tone that both disguises and reveals displacement and longing. For many activists who came to the US as children or teenagers, the process of adaptation to a new society caused psychological distress, leading to conflict with their parents and uneasiness with their sense of selves. As new migrants, they exalt the homeland as "an implicit standard according to which one makes sense of values, habits and life experiences in the context of immigration."[102] The Philippines becomes synonymous with an earlier life of comfort and modesty compared to the unsettled times associated with migration as seen in the reflection of Romy Garcia in *A Time to Rise*.

> Like many of my Filipino friends, I was confused and felt alienated from my parents who were also struggling to sort out what Filipino traditions and values we should maintain in America and which ones we should eliminate. I was a very angry you man. . . .
>
> On really bad day I would find myself thinking about the Philippines, missing it a lot and wishing somehow that we could go back. The more America hurt, the more I romanticized our life in the Philippines. Our family comes from Santa Rita, Pampanga, not too far from Manila. It seemed to me that everyone in our home barrio was connected to us through family or friendship ties—we truly belonged there, it was our place. . . . It seemed that all my feelings of warmth and protection got tied up with memories of back home— the festive Christmas season, the church gatherings, and Apo Seshia, my great aunt, whom we lived with, who cared for me and spoiled me.[103]

For young Filipino Americans coming of age and recently arrived immigrants from the Philippines, the anti-dictatorship movement offered a physical site where members regularly encountered each other and shared experiences, cultural practices, and values. These interactions were crucial in the activists' exploration and validation of their multiple identities, which were questioned and tested in their conflicts with families and peers. From the excitement of demonstrations and teach-ins in the streets to education forums and meetings in Filipino community centers that both disturb and enlighten, the movement provided spaces to create and sustain collective effervescence and to facilitate mutual learning. Through listening to their Filipino American comrades' stories, and their introduction to the radical history of Filipinos in the US, KDP members who were Filipino nationals gained a deeper understanding and appreciation of immigrant views on the Marcos dictatorship, a framework they would not have fully grasped in the Philippines. Because of this, activists like Esther Hipol Simpson, who was initially interested only in the anti-dictatorship struggle, spearheaded other campaigns, as she recounted in *A Time to Rise*:

> Through discussion groups, I learned about the miseducation of Filipinos and the history of the Philippines and US colonization. I learned that my previous consciousness was a product of these processes. My first political activism was with the NCRCLP, and I was amazed at what I was learning about the symbiotic relationship between the US government and Philippine dictatorship at the expense of the Filipino people's freedom and well-being. This eventually led me to the KDP, which further deepened my new understandings.
>
> As I matured politically, I became involved not only with supporting the struggle in the Philippines but also with organizing around the problems faced by Filipinos as immigrants in America. Our chapter in Chicago, like other KDP chapters, began studying the local Filipino community to prepare for advocating democratic rights in both the Philippines and United States.[104]

Simpson went on to advocate for Filipino nurses, including fighting the case against Filipina Narciso and Leonora Perez, the licensure process for foreign nurse graduates, and the deportation of H-1 visa nurses. Thus, by discovering the histories and experiences that link Filipinos together, activism allowed immigrants to transcend here and there.

Transnational activism also became a way to observe the norms and customs associated with hybridity and syncretism that disturb ideas about cultural distinctiveness and ethnic authenticity.[105] Unlike Filipino hometown associations formed by immigrants from the same place of origin, often at the barrio or provincial level, KDP consisted of both US- and Philippine-born Filipinos from different regions with their own languages and traditions, thus enabling these members to imagine the Filipino nation as culturally diverse. Without the policing of co-ethnics on their performance of Filipinoness or

STORYTELLERS AND INTERLOCUTORS 149

what Karen Pyke and Tran Dang refer to as "intraethnic othering,"[106] activists were able to experiment with their identities and self-presentation. Habal recalls in *A Time to Rise* her interaction with KDP founding member Cynthia Maglaya, who grew up in the Philippines and passed away in the US in 1983, that captures this process:

> Cynthia was always curious and willing to learn about American ways. She'd often ask me about the mannerisms or habits of certain Filipino Americans or other Americans we knew in common. My explanations about what she viewed as our weird and strange ways would sometimes help her and often amuse her. . . . I began to appreciate our cultural differences and how strange Americans can appear to other people. For her part, she also tried to fit. One habit she developed was excessive swearing, both in Tagalog and English. Almost every one of her sentences included some kind of profanity. This had a certain shock value because of her demure appearance.[107]

Finally, alongside a nostalgic representation of activists' past lives in the Philippines is the uneasy engagement with the idea of returning to the homeland. In the memoirs, they recounted their trips to the Philippines to visit relatives, meet with comrades, or connect with other social movements. Some referred to their journey as "going home," since they were born and raised in the Philippines, despite not having plans to stay longer than the itinerary outlined in their airline tickets. A few Filipino Americans were traveling to the archipelago for the first time. In their writings, they justified why they had not gone back and settled permanently in the Philippines; while the goal of homeland return was righteous, as time went by, it grew impractical. For instance, Ka Linda explained in *A Time to Rise,*

> From the inception of our work, certainly in the KDP, we held the position that Philippine nationals would and should repatriate back to the Philippines based on the shifting needs of the revolution. But in fact, over the years only a few of us went back. Without a doubt, life in the United States was more secure and comfortable, but I believe that people stayed mainly because the demands of our international work were so great and relative few of us abroad had the necessary experience to direct that work.[108]

In sum, like in other writings by immigrants and their descendants, using a frame to abstract and convey activists' contradictory emotions and interpretations about home in the memoirs invites readers to see the authors' experience of loneliness, isolation, and desire to have a rightful place as intrinsic in the migration process. While they construct the Philippines as their ideal home, a place where memories of the past are rooted and where visions of the future are moored, they recognize that in their actual day-to-day struggle

150 CHAPTER FIVE

and interactions, they are also making home wherever they are. Thus, in the memoirs, the longing that activists felt are not necessarily negative and demobilizing; rather, it encourages them to find and build spaces to belong.

Shared Memory and History

The construction of diaspora entails a continuous process of delineating and expanding boundaries of membership to incorporate new cohorts of migrants and subsequent generations born abroad. With each migration wave and demographic shift, the range of personal experiences in the community enlarges, some exhibiting similarities while others possessing distinctive features, depending on the sociohistorical environment that shapes individual actions. The collective history that binds together these personal experiences ensures that the diaspora is "constituted as much in *difference and division* as it is in *commonality and solidarity*," as sociologist Floya Anthias argues.[109] The intergenerational transmission of memories rooted in a group's large-scale dispersal, thus, becomes the bridge that connects the then and now as well as the here and there, allowing migrants and their descendants to internalize the unbroken relevance of the homeland.

In this chapter, we saw how the collective memory of the Marcos dictatorship and the transnational movement against it promoted the multigenerational formation of the Filipino diaspora by connecting personal and family histories to community struggles, developing a common language and discourse to make sense of individual experiences, and remembering and sustaining episodes of collective effervescence. Despite its recent growth and relatively modest size and scale compared to the mobilizations against the regime of Marcos and the migrants' rights movement, the memory activism of former dissidents during the dictatorship period confronted the attempts at historical revisionism by the Duterte administration and reminded the migrant communities of the contribution of overseas Filipinos to the downfall of Marcos. In protesting a hero's burial for Marcos, activists once again gathered at the Philippine consulates and embassies, a site where together, in the past, they confronted and experienced the brutality of law enforcement agents, where they appealed to bystanders and passersby who knew little of the oppression Filipinos were going through, and where they found allies with whom they would march through the years—a space that embodied both the tyrannical rule of the dictator and the tenacity of those resisting it. In a way, they have made these state institutions "places of memory" in the host countries.[110]

Through storytelling during official commemorations of the People Power Revolution, the campaign against a hero's burial for the dictator, and in published memoirs, memory activists countered hegemonic narratives and used culturally resonant frames that encouraged the audience to identify with their experiences, permitting the imagination of a sense of shared history and fate among Filipinos abroad.

Conclusion

Since the transnational mobilizations to institute regime change in the Philippines in the 1970s and 1980s, overseas Filipinos, especially those with dual citizenship,[1] have been active in Philippine electoral politics. On October 12, 2015, at the consulate general in Chicago, Walden Bello, one of the leaders of the anti-dictatorship movement in the US, filed his candidacy for Philippine senator in the 2016 presidential elections. News of his "electoral insurgency"[2] spread, and within a month, the Filipino movement communities built during the mobilizations against the Marcos dictatorship in the 1970s and 1980s rallied around Bello, who ran as an independent candidate. As Bello visited migrant communities in Los Angeles, New York, the San Francisco Bay Area, and Seattle, former anti-dictatorship activists of the FFP and KDP organized public forums and fundraising events, which were attended by Filipinos from different migration waves. Second- and third-generation Filipino Americans who did not know Bello used social media to support his campaign by publishing his speeches and accomplishments as chair of the Committee on Overseas Workers' Affairs in the Philippine Congress, articles on neoliberal globalization and democracy, and photos of his participation in demonstrations during the heyday of the global justice movement. Although Bello finished thirty-sixth in the race, his senatorial bid reactivated the networks of the anti-dictatorship movement in the US.

In the same election, OFWs launched a grassroots campaign on online platforms to rally around former Davao City mayor Rodrigo Duterte's bid for the presidency. Dubbed as the "Donald Trump of the Philippines" by mainstream Western media, Duterte's iron fist approach to crime, particularly the proliferation of illegal drugs, appealed to OFWs who believed that he could guarantee the safety of their loved ones while they work abroad.[3] More

CONCLUSION

importantly, they considered him to be "the man who will give dignity and choice to the millions of OFWs around the world"—that is, labor migration will just be an option among many for them to achieve social mobility.[4] An organic network of Diehard Duterte Supporters (DDS) was constituted within the OFW communities in Asia, Europe, and the Middle East as well as among permanent immigrants in North America.[5] DDS members were connected to each other and to their counterparts in the Philippines largely through social media. By January 2016, four months before the elections, around six hundred thousand OFWs whose goal was to use their breadwinner status to influence their families back home to vote for Duterte, had joined 162 DDS chapters.[6] OFW leaders were crucial in maintaining Duterte's stranglehold on the diaspora, as they became "micro-influencers"[7] on Facebook.[8] The 2016 polls had the highest turnout in overseas ballots since overseas absentee voting was introduced in 2004, with 31.65 percent of votes cast.[9] Most Filipinos abroad supported Duterte, who acquired 72 percent of the total overseas votes cast.

Duterte became president thirty years after the overthrow of Marcos in the 1986 People Power Revolution and during the rise to power of populist leaders such as Jair Bolsonaro in Brazil, Narendra Modi in India, and Donald Trump in the US. Through its War on Drugs that includes extrajudicial killings of drug dealers and users, its campaign against the Philippine Left, and its attack on journalists, the Duterte administration has instituted an illiberal democracy, where he claims continued democratic legitimacy based on constitutional rule and high opinion ratings.[10] While elite opposition and social movements have emerged to challenge his administration through elections and protests, they have largely been unsuccessful in gaining popular support. In the US, former anti-dictatorship activists and new groups such as the Malaya Movement and Filipino American Human Rights Alliance were steadfast in their criticism of his rule and mobilized overseas Filipinos on issues such as the War on Drugs, Marcos's burial in Libingan ng mga Bayani, the territorial dispute with China over the West Philippine Sea, the passing of the Anti-Terrorism Act of 2020, media censorship, and the killing of activists on the Left. However, sustained mobilization with strategic goals like the movement against Marcos in the 1970s and 1980s did not materialize.

As Duterte pivoted toward China in his administration's foreign policy, he had rendered his critics in the US—including Filipinos—irrelevant. On his four-day state visit to China on October 18–21, 2016, where he and Xi Jinping signed several trade deals as well as cooperation in cultural, tourism, anti-narcotics, and maritime affairs, Duterte renounced the US twice—first in a meeting with the Filipino community in Beijing and again at the Philippines-China Trade and Investment Forum at the Beijing's Great Hall of the People.[11]

In the former, when he spoke about US colonization of the Philippines, US imperialism in the Middle East, President Barack Obama's criticism of his War on Drugs, and the denial of his application for a US visa, Duterte said to a cheering crowd, "They [Americans] can enter our country visa-free. Why don't we retaliate? He [Obama] might say, 'There are many Filipinos there.' Well, that's nothing. They are all Americans, not Filipinos. In attitudes, habits, customs, food. What about in China, are there no Filipinos? Here and the rest of the mainland, we are 300,000. And yet China is very kind".[12] He reinforced his anti-US message in the latter meeting, starting with, "What is really wrong with an American character and an Oriental gentleman? Many would say that the Filipinos and the Orientals are fundamentally shy. . . . Well, the Americans are a little bit loud, sometimes rowdy, and the voice and the larynx not adjusted to civility."[13] Duterte would reiterate in various forums this message of Filipinos in the US no longer having the character—this Oriental essence—that qualifies them for membership to the nation; thus, their criticism of and opposition to his administration are nullified, for their claims and demands are not anchored to an inherent Filipino essence.

Supporters of Duterte amplified his message. When the video of his speech to Filipinos in Beijing was circulated on Facebook, it generated uproar from permanent immigrants and subsequent generations in North America who asserted "being Filipino in heart and mind" as "members of the Filipino diaspora." Many, however, came to Duterte's defense. For instance, one user posted: "He is referring to those who have taken allegiance to the flag of America . . . if you have renounced (tinalikuran) and abjured (tinalikuran) your Filipino citizenship in favor of another state, then YOU ARE NO LONGER FILIPINO CITIZEN. While we do not . . . condemn such an act[,] for you have your own valid reason of doing so, . . . it is just appropriate that the President addresses primordially the concern of real 'CITIZENS' versus those who have opted to give up their being Filipino citizen[s]. #stopthehate #ListenToUnderstand." The addition of the Tagalog term *tinalikuran*, which means literally to turn one's back on something or someone, after the words "renounce" and "abjure" is an attempt by the user to underscore the disavowal of the nation when Filipino immigrants become American citizens. As OFWs joined forces online to defend Duterte, they distinguished themselves from Filipinos in the US, Canada, or countries of settlement where immigrants can relinquish their Philippine citizenship, constructing a collective identity based on their legal status that binds them to the homeland.

Four years later, another presidential election mobilized Filipinos. On October 4, 2020, Filipino American conservatives and supporters of Donald Trump hosted a caravan rally across California to raise support for Trump

CONCLUSION

and celebrate Filipino American History Month. Gay Deperio is a Filipino immigrant and one of the organizers of the event in West Covina, California. She opened the rally praying for the recovery of the president and First Lady Melania Trump, who tested positive for SARS-CoV-2, but never mentioned the coronavirus or the pandemic. In a post-rally interview, she reflected on why she supports Donald Trump: "Conservative values are aligned with Filipino values." She was unfazed by—and in fact denied—Trump's blatant racism toward people of color.[14] Following the defeat of Trump in the election, a mob of his supporters stormed the US Capitol Building in Washington, DC, on January 6, 2021. In the aftermath of the violence, a photo of a man holding a *walis tambo* (a Philippine whisk broom) inside the Capitol circulated online and went viral among Filipinos in the Philippines and in the diaspora as news of the attack was covered on the Twitter account of the *Philippine Daily Inquirer*. Wearing the American flag as a cape and holding a Captain America shield with emblazoned words that alluded to a coup as solution to electoral fraud and the pandemic, the man was identified as Kene Brian Lazo, a Filipino immigrant living in Norfolk, Virginia. Filipinos were quick to disavow Lazo in their comments on the Twitter post, expressing shame and anger. In their reactions, they likened Lazo to Duterte followers or presumed that, because of his ardent support for Trump, he must also be a fan of Duterte. "If that guy's a Filipino, he is embarrassing. Just because he was able to set foot in U.S. soil, all sorts of things went into his head. He is just like a DDS who got on a plane," said a user who had "#LeniKiko2022" with their name, a hashtag supporting the candidacy of Duterte's major opponents in the 2022 presidential election.

How can we make sense of these current developments? In this book, I argue that diasporas do not automatically form because of migration. Rather, diasporas are created through a conflict-mobilization-collective identity nexus. Social conflicts disrupt the taken-for-granted routines and understandings that constitute everyday life, and individuals turn to their small groups to make sense of and take action on these uncertainties. This opens opportunities for social movements to emerge and mobilize against target authorities. In the process, they question, contest, and reimagine—or validate—ideas and principles that undergird loyalty to and continued belonging to homeland, solidarity with co-nationals/co-ethnics, and shared history. Social movements thus become the main site, means, and actor for this deliberate process of collective identity formation.

I show, through the movement against the dictatorship of Marcos, how in various stages of mobilization activists unpacked and elaborated on the idea of illegitimacy so that being anti-Marcos did not connote being anti-Filipino or against the Philippines. Activists built a constituency among migrants to show that the movement had the legitimacy to challenge the homeland government—that the community had granted these non-state actors the authority to speak for their material and symbolic interests. Through the movement on migrants' rights, I also explain how activists forged solidarity among dispersed overseas Filipinos by using the frame of displacement, marginalization, and empowerment in making sense of their daily struggles in the transnational social fields they inhabit. They interwove diverse, multiple experiences to construct and build a transnational community around a minority worker identity. They deployed these frames and identities during campaigns, serialized them in publications, and publicly enacted them in cultural performances. Finally, by looking at the memory work of former anti-dictatorship activism during a period of historical revisionism, I describe the construction and transmission of collective memories that are crucial to the reproduction of a diaspora across generations. The stories shared during protests and documented in memoirs not only served as a reminder of—and an invitation and a plea not to forget—a dark period in the Philippines that is intentionally being erased by state actors but also served to encourage young overseas Filipinos, especially those born after the overthrow of Marcos, to nurture the zeal to participate in Philippine nation building from afar, as did the anti-dictatorship activists.

Throughout the book, I describe moments of and spaces for diaspora construction, such as at the US Congress, where anti-dictatorship activists used the history of US colonization to hold Americans accountable for the rise of the Marcos regime; at the Permanent Peoples Tribunal on the Philippines held in Belgium, where a migrant domestic worker in Italy delivered a testimony of hardship and empowerment and related it to the struggle of all overseas Filipinos in Asia, Europe, and the Middle East; at community centers in Los Angeles and Seattle, where Filipino residents debated each other and came up with statements in support of migrants' rights; at the National Monument in Amsterdam, where Filipino community organizers memorialized those who disappeared and died during the dictatorship; and at Philippine consulates in New York, San Francisco, and The Hague, where Filipinos in their sixties and seventies recalled and shared their experience of martial law with the younger ones who have no memories of that period. These moments and spaces are not temporally and spatially separate from the institutions that shape the lives of ordinary migrants. They are connected through the social networks and fields that movement actors inhabit and the culture—the tool kit—that they rely on and influence in their activism. Along with identifying structural conditions that enable activists to organize and make claims and demands in

CONCLUSION   157

public, the book also highlights the cultural processes in mobilization to explain why certain discourses become the foundation for collective identities, employing an actor-oriented approach to elaborate on how movement actors and constituents ascribe meaning to their actions and relations, and to their motives and desires. In short, *Insurgent Communities* shows how diaspora formation is intertwined with social movement processes.

But as the events in the last five years show, a diaspora can also be invented beyond contentious, collective claims making. In fact, it appears that at this juncture in Philippine history when Duterte's populism has galvanized OFWs and immigrants to assert their stake in the political development in the country, elections and social media have become the venues for diaspora construction, connecting overseas communities to each other and to the homeland. For those who supported Duterte, they were united by their acceptance of his antielite rhetoric, a sentiment shared by many OFWs who have not benefited from the outcome of the 1986 People Power Revolution and have been disillusioned by the promises of liberal democracy. A Duterte presidency for them means finally fulfilling their goal of ending the cycle of labor migration. On the other hand, for former anti-dictatorship activists, their opposition to Duterte stemmed from their commitment to safeguard what they fought hard and sacrificed for in the past, a continuity of a long struggle for social change.

When elections and social media have been central for the invention of diasporas, as seen not only in the case of the Philippines in 2016, but also in Turkey in 2018, Romania in 2019, and Hungary in 2022, what then is the value of studying diaspora construction through protests? The conflict-mobilization-collective identity nexus has implications for contemporary empirical research. As I have shown throughout the book, social conflict in the homeland or hostland provides an opportunity for individuals to question their normally taken-for-granted identities—whether they are based on their roles as fathers or workers or their membership in groups based on their nationality or gender. These identities may not be relevant in everyday decision making, but in situations where migrants are forced to take sides such as, for instance, Duterte's War on Drugs, they become salient and politicized. Conflict is thus central to diaspora construction, as it exposes the fragility of primordial bonds, the social cleavages that are cloaked by the desire for national loyalty and unity, and the contradictions of belonging, allowing social movements—or in the case of the recent elections in the Philippines, micro-influencers in social media—to instigate or intervene in collective identity formation.

Second and related to the first point, the book foregrounds the role of groups, where day-to-day interactional processes operate. The socialization of political entrepreneurs, the development of claims-making strategies, and the formation and negotiation of collective identities occurred through groups. In both the US and the Netherlands, contention spread through group ties that facilitated the brokerage of actors who presented themselves as living testaments to Marcos's atrocities and thus legitimate political actors. We saw how activists from the Philippines became what Sidney Tarrow refers to as "transnational hinges" that adapted the messages of the movement in the homeland to new sites and situations.[15] As transnational migrants who retained political connections and who continued to identify with their communities of origin, these activists had access to organizational resources and information about the Philippines that strengthened their credibility in the Filipino migrant communities. Through groups, activists engaged in a strategy of redefining and articulating what being Filipino meant, rather than who is Filipino. They focused on interrogating ideas about the nation, particularly whether and to what extent those who had permanently settled outside the Philippines still maintained a relationship with the Philippine state and therefore had the right to criticize it. As they confronted audiences who controlled discursive spaces, they worked within dominant discourses and within familiar cultural norms, codes, and practices, challenging them by changing meanings, categories, and values.

Finally, the book also shows the significance of culture in political mobilization, whether through social movements or through online networks of supporters for elections. In reviewing the cultural impacts of social movements, Edwin Amenta and Francesca Polletta treat culture not as a sphere of social life outside the state and the economy but as "the meaning-making dimension of all policies and practices."[16] Thus, activists can shape ways of thinking and practice through mobilization for regime change or migrants' rights that simultaneously occurs in the political and cultural terrains. After all, they form and articulate claims and demands in performances aimed at audiences that include but are not limited to state targets.[17] We saw in the anti-dictatorship movement how activists invoked the Filipino resistance against Spain in framing their identities. The KDP embraced the historic revolutionary Katipunan name, and both the MFP and the KDP compared their activities to those of the *ilustrados* and the Propaganda Movement from the earlier revolutionary period. By calling to mind the Filipino exiles in Europe in the nineteenth century who fought for the people, they created symbolic connections between past and present, between anticolonialism and anti-dictatorship, and between the struggle against Spain and the resistance against Marcos. Filipino culture—embodied in discourses (e.g., Marcos exploited overseas Filipino labor), artifacts (e.g., published stories), and

CONCLUSION

rituals (e.g., singing of "Bayan Ko")—also linked the anti-dictatorship, migrants' rights, and memory movements across time and space. They shaped collective identity formation in and through protest that in turn altered or stabilized the meanings of the cultural elements that migrants use to create boundaries and imagine belonging to and membership in the Filipino community in interaction with other actors in transnational social fields. While each movement forged a particular collective identity, each was, in some way, engaged in cultivating loyalty, solidarity, and history.

Using national culture or history in mobilization is of course not without its own problems. Movement participants constructed a group narrative that emphasizes national as opposed to ethnolinguistic (e.g., Ilocano), regional, or hometown and village-level loyalties to mobilize migrants to oppose Marcos. References to national heroes such as Rizal and Bonifacio—who belonged to the major ethnic group in the Philippines (Tagalog)—and their resistance to colonialism signified the dominance of a unifying historical narrative in diaspora mobilization. By privileging certain figures, stories, and symbols, homeland-oriented activism can endorse a nationalist elite agenda and legitimize the ruling forces in state and society. Culture can therefore simultaneously enable and constrain people's behaviors, choices, and actions.[18]

Insurgent Communities does more than expand the theory and knowledge in diaspora and social movement scholarship. It joins mainstream, nonacademic conversations on how immigrants are (re)incorporated in their countries of origin and destination. Conservative politicians and mainstream mass media often portray migrants and refugees as unworthy of citizenship in the countries where they settle because of their persistent homeland nationalism, assuming migrants will always be loyal to their countries of origin. These ideologues regard migrants' feelings and activism for their homeland nation as a zero-sum game in which the love of one's country of origin prevents the development of deep affection toward the country of settlement. This book shows that this is not the case. It tells a larger story about the complexity of crossing geographic and symbolic borders, taking unfamiliar routes and surprising detours, touching down and growing roots, and undermining and upholding nationalist narratives. Looking at diasporas as constructions means that migrants' and refugees' allegiance to their homeland is neither natural nor fixed. They make choices based on what they perceive as their continuously evolving position in society.

Acknowledgments

This book is the outcome of more than a decade of research in three countries. It was a challenging but transformative academic and personal journey that would not have been possible without the material, intellectual, and emotional support of many people, organizations, and institutions. They believed in my project since its inception and contributed to the development of my thoughts about diaspora and social movements. My utmost gratitude goes to the activists who shared their time, stories, and personal archives as well as opened their homes and spaces of resistance for me. I am deeply honored for the trust they gave me. They made this book possible. I am particularly indebted to Malu Padilla, Evert de Boer, Carlo and Maya Butalid, Coni Ledesma, Bani and Cecilia Lansang, and Jun and Mitchy Saturay in the Netherlands; Cindy Domingo, Rene Ciria Cruz, Edwin Batongbacal, Abraham Ignacio, Prosy and Enrique dela Cruz, and Pete Fuentecilla in the US; and Rosemary and Byron Bocar in the Philippines who accommodated me from the time I started data collection in 2010 up to the finalization of the manuscript. They gave me boxes of organizational documents to peruse—some containing confidential and privileged information. Through them, I was able to meet and interview their former comrades who were skeptical of researchers that are outsiders to the movement. *Taos-pusong pasasalamat po sa inyong lahat.*

I thank Waverly Duck for motivating and guiding me as I expanded on the findings of my research. Through him, I met Elizabeth Branch Dyson at the University of Chicago Press. Elizabeth's attention to detail and understanding of the broad implications of my work helped me sharpen my arguments. She and Mollie McFee have been patient and encouraging throughout the process. I also appreciate the editorial advice of Jenny Gavacs and the creativity of Vicente Rafael, who suggested the book title. Some sections of chapters 3 and 4 have appeared previously in *Mobilization* and *Journal of Ethnic and Migration Studies*, respectively.

Funding from the American Philosophical Society Franklin Grant, the National Endowment for the Humanities Summer Stipend, the National Science Foundation Doctoral Dissertation Improvement Grant (SES-1434119), several Competitive Grants from the Committee on Support of Faculty Scholarship of Grinnell College, and the University of Pittsburgh Andrew Mellon Predoctoral Fellowship allowed me to enlarge the scope of my project and conduct multisited fieldwork for several months, while a Postdoctoral Research Leave Fellowship from the American Association of University Women and a Harris Fellowship from Grinnell College enabled me to devote a full year to writing this book. As a first-time author, I also benefited from the First Book Subvention Program of the Association for Asian Studies. I am grateful to the administration at Grinnell College, especially Susan Ferrari, Laura Nelson-Lof, and Elaine Marzluff for their assistance in applying to external grants and fellowships, and to my current and former colleagues in the sociology department for reading drafts of my chapters and providing invaluable feedback, writing letters of reference, and bouncing ideas off each other—Ross Haenfler, Karla Erickson, Casey Oberlin, Kesho Scott, Susan Ferguson, Xavi Escandell, Skadi Snook, Chris Hunter, Sara Francisco, Jules Bacon, Lara Janson, Vadricka Etienne, and Roshan Pandian. I am also grateful to the college's academic staff—Cheryl Fleener-Seymour, Laurie Wilcox, Patty Dale, and Marcia Baker—for helping me with administrative matters. Quynh Nguyen and Martha Beliveau provided research assistance for this project.

The seeds for this project were planted during my time at the University of Pittsburgh. Suzanne Staggenborg, my adviser and mentor, acknowledged the importance of studies on diaspora mobilization in theorizing about collective action and encouraged me to push the boundaries of knowledge. She patiently went through countless drafts not only of the manuscript, but also grant proposals, conference papers, and articles. I also owe John Markoff for my interest in global and transnational sociology. My conversations with him about dictatorships, revolutions, and democratization in Eastern Europe, Latin America, and Southeast Asia helped me refine my research questions, methods, and analysis.

As an early career female faculty of color, I benefited from the mentorship of David Cook-Martín and Rhacel Salazar Parreñas who helped me navigate the intricacies of book publishing and the world of academia. David's belief in my abilities has always reassured me of my project's important contribution

ACKNOWLEDGMENTS

to the field of immigration studies. Rhacel has been one of my advocates, promoting my work to other scholars and various audiences, giving me advice with candor and sincerity, and nurturing my passion for sociological analysis. Through her and the community of Filipino sociologists she helped build, elite academic spaces have become less daunting and unwelcoming.

Much of the writing of this book was done while I was a Visiting Postdoctoral Scholar at the Department of Sociology at Vrije Universiteit (VU) Amsterdam in fall 2021 to spring 2022, and I am grateful to Jacquelien van Stekelenburg for facilitating my affiliation. Despite the unfortunate circumstances brought on by the continuing COVID pandemic, I still benefited from an intellectually nurturing environment at VU facilitated by Jacquelien and Bert Klandermans (and his partner Carien Vrij). The feedback I received during my presentation at the Participating in Society research program was indispensable, and I thank Bianca Suanet for organizing my talk. My engagement with the community of scholars at Universiteit van Amsterdam (UvA), especially Floris Vermeulen, Hein de Haas, Saskia Bonjour, Kidjie Saguin, Jessica Soedirgo, and Chei Billedo, allowed me to think more critically about my research and about myself as a scholar of migration. Thank you to the Amsterdam Center for European Studies for inviting me to share the findings of my study. In 2012 and 2014, when I first collected data for my project, the Department of Political Science and Institute for Migration and Ethnic Studies at UvA provided me an institutional base through the assistance of Liza Mügge. And in 2019, with the help of Hung-Wah Lam and Lieke Schreel, I was visiting faculty at the Leiden University College. Various aspects of my project were also enriched by conversations with scholars on migration policies, Philippine Left movements, Netherlands-Philippines relations, and Dutch politics, including Rosanne Rutten, Jun Borras, Alex de Jong, Otto van den Muijzenberg, Marisha Maas, Dovelyn Mendoza, Leo Luccassen, Aniek Smit, and Tycho Walaardt.

Fieldwork in the Philippines would not have been possible without the help of Tesa Tadem, Ed Tadem, Aries Arugay, and my former colleagues at Third World Studies Center—Maria Ela Atienza, Joel Ariate, Verna Dinah Viajar, Caring Francisco, Bienvenida Lacsamana, and Erning Francisco. They made sure I did not lose track of my commitment to advance knowledge on Philippine migration that meaningfully engages with political developments in the Philippines. David Joshua Gines, Glo Shin Hyo Panuelos, Kristi Ana delos Santos, Joy Grace delos Santos, Gregorio Bituin Jr., Mimi Fabe, and Anne Estonilo transcribed all my interviews in a timely manner.

Early drafts of my book chapters have been presented at annual professional meetings of the American Sociological Association, Association for

Asian Studies, Association of Asian American Studies, European Association for Southeast Asian Studies, International Sociological Association, International Studies Association, and Social Science History Association as well as conferences by the University of Notre Dame's Young Scholars in Social Movements, Southeast Asia Research Group, and *Mobilization* and invited talks at Friedrich-Alexander-Universität Erlangen-Nürnberg, Queen's University Belfast (online due to COVID), University of the Philippines Diliman, and L'Université du Québec à Montréal. The constructive feedback I received from David S. Meyer, Kamal Sadiq, Walter Nicholls, Maria Koinova, Gerasimos Tsourapas, Yoni Abramson, Dana Moss, Dan Slater, Amy Liu, Dominique Caouette, Joel Rocamora, Filomeno Aguilar Jr., Caroline Hau, Mark Thompson, Stefaan Walgrave, and Fridus Steijlen helped strengthen my chapter arguments. During these gatherings, I also learned a lot from my conversations with Marco Garrido, Victoria Reyes, Emmanuel David, Maria Hwang, Anthony Ocampo, Ethel Nicdao, Celso Villegas, Pete Simi, Rory McVeigh, Hank Johnston, Rachel Einwohner, Kim Voss, Deana Rohlinger, Lesley Wood, Raúl Pérez, Lisa Martinez, Edelina Burciaga, Minwoo Jung, Dorothy Fujita-Rony, Karen Buenavista Hanna, Robyn Rodriguez, Erik Martinez Kuhonta, Helena Patzer, and Asuncion Fresnoza-Flot. Numerous other scholars have also continued to support my work in various ways, including Patricio Abinales, Walden Bello, Vina Lanzona, Nathan Quimpo, Vince Boudreau, Herbert Docena, Madeline Hsu, Belinda Robnett, Leo Chavez, Nicole Constable, Melanie Hughes, Suzanna Crage, Kelsy Burke, Tarun Banerjee, Beatriz Padilla, Ethel Tungohan, Clement Camposano, Katrin Drasch, Dženeta Karabegović, and Ioana Pop.

My colleagues from other departments in Grinnell College provided a steady source of intellectual stimulation and emotional support, especially during the height of the pandemic when I started conceptualizing the book. I owe a lot to John Garrison, Sarah Purcell, and Dustin Dixon for giving me excellent comments on previous drafts. Their feedback allowed me to think about how my book can be of interest to scholars outside sociology. I am also thankful to John Petrus, Qiaomei Tang, Catherine Chou, Mishita Mehra, Jeremy Chen, Carolyn Lewis, Marion Tricoire, Julie Lascol, Shuchi Kapila, Makeba Lavan, Mina Nikolopolou, Stephanie Jones, Fredo Rivera, Deborah Michaels, Jonathan Larson, Eiren Shea, Elias Gabriel, and Jin Feng for giving me confidence, especially after going through unending revisions. Thank you for the work dates that kept me focused and motivated and for the much-needed respite from the stress of balancing teaching and writing.

My friendships have nourished my spirit and kept things in perspective throughout this journey. Thank you to Mark Villegas, Carolyn Zook, Marie

ACKNOWLEDGMENTS

Skoczylas, Suzanna Eddyono, Anis Nahrawie, Nico Ravanilla, Billy Theiss, Andrew Yeo, and Liza Lansang. I am especially indebted to Anjani Abella and Anne Lunenberg—two of my oldest friends—for their warmth, hospitality, and generosity to make me feel at home in the Netherlands. Each trip was filled with excitement and new adventures because of them.

Finally, I wish to express my heartfelt gratitude to my family. The unconditional love from my parents—Leticia and Rolando—my brother Jeff, my nephew Ivan, and my aunt Esperanza reinvigorates me every time I go back home and reminds me of what is truly important in life. They have given me the courage and fortitude to take on every challenge. I also thank my relatives in the United States, especially Romy and Joice Quinsaat, Luisa and Richard Yee, Binerva and Brandon Garrett, and Sheryl Quinsaat for their enthusiasm about my book and concern for my well-being. And I could not have finished this book without the encouragement, patience, understanding, and joy from my brilliant and talented partner and best friend, Andrew Kaufman. He was a supportive sounding board and reader who helped me think through my ideas more clearly and endured the everyday challenges and frustrations of writing a book. He was my daily source of inspiration to keep going. And, of course, our dog, Olive, brought so much fun and sass through the whole process.

Appendix: Methodology

The research for this book is based on extensive fieldwork I conducted in the Netherlands, the Philippines, and the US from 2013 to 2019 and online from 2020 to 2021, where I immersed myself in the three transnational social movements I studied. I developed a comprehensive understanding of diaspora formation through contention by using data from a wide range of sources. These include archival documents; semi-structured interviews; field notes from ethnographic observations; content analysis of op-eds and commentaries, websites, and memoirs; and published historical accounts. By using multiple methods, I was able to validate data through cross verification from more than two sources. My methodological framework is informed by Max Weber's concept of *verstehen*, or the understanding of social action from the perspective of the agents, in particular, how they make sense of their actions and the world around them.[1]

Archival Research

For the anti-dictatorship and migrants' rights movements from the early 1970s to 1986 and 1980s to 1992, respectively, my primary data sources consist of the following: rare written records from social movement organizations in mostly Dutch, English, and Tagalog (minutes of meetings, position papers, press releases, flyers, official correspondence, internal bulletins, and newsletters); unpublished and published personal accounts of activists (autobiographies, diaries, letters, handwritten meeting notes, and memoirs); government documents (communiqués, official reports, policy papers, transcripts of congressional hearings); and news accounts in ethnic and mainstream press. These were available in the various Philippines collections at the

168 APPENDIX

International Institute for Social History in Amsterdam, the Daniel Boone Schirmer Collection at the University of the Philippines Diliman Main Library in Quezon City, the Suzzallo and Allen Libraries of the University of Washington in Seattle, and the Asian American Studies Center of the University of California, Los Angeles. The International Institute for Social History in Amsterdam houses public documents and writings of cadres of the Communist Party of the Philippines–National Democratic Front (NDF) and their associated organizations who were exiled in the Netherlands, while the Suzzallo and Allen Libraries and Asian American Studies Center hold the organizational documents of *Kalayaan International*, Katipunan ng Demokratikong Pilipino (KDP), the International Association of Filipino Patriots, and the National Committee for the Restoration of Civil Liberties in the Philippines. But the rare internal documents were from the personal archives of activists. When I contacted them to request interviews, they casually mentioned that they still have some documents and invited me to their houses. I spent weeks in their storage rooms and garages going through boxes of unfiled documents, some of which were faded and covered in mold. A key Filipino informant, who is fluent in Dutch, translated several documents from Dutch to English. As a native speaker of Tagalog and Ilocano, I was able to access source materials in those languages with ease.

I used caution and critical reflection in collecting and evaluating historical data, especially with regard to authenticity, credibility, and representativeness. For each organization, I gathered data on the influence of historical circumstances and political environment on the resources, debates, and identities that activists drew upon. I focused on specific events and processes taking place over time within each individual organization to understand how these led to certain outcomes and not others. In assessing the organizational documents, I made sure that I understood the intended audience, since activists framed the messages differently depending on the recipient. For instance, internal bulletins contained details of conflicts and disagreements, while propaganda materials for members of the migrant community used a lot of optimistic language. After constructing a detailed narrative that purports to throw light on how mobilization came about, I converted this chronicle into an analytical explanation couched in explicit theoretical forms.

Content Analysis

For the movement on collective memory, the most recent of the three social movements in the study, I collected data from news coverage of commemora-

APPENDIX 169

tive events in mainstream and community newspapers to construct a historical account of memory-making practices. I also conducted an inductive or qualitative content analysis of op-eds and commentaries written by activists, websites for remembrances of the Marcos dictatorship, and two published memoirs: *Women against Marcos: Stories of Filipino and Filipino American Women Who Fought a Dictator* (by Mila de Guzman, 2016) and *A Time to Rise: Collective Memoirs of the Union of Democratic Filipinos (KDP)* (by Rene Ciria Cruz, Cindy Domingo, and Bruce Occeña, 2017). I did a close and iterative reading of the texts rather than searching for a predetermined list of content items. From this reading, I developed analytic frames in the stories and themes at a higher level of abstraction. My goal was to produce an understanding of the meaning(s) of the content of the texts.

Interviews

To supplement archival data, I conducted eighty-three in-depth key informant and life history interviews with movement participants and their children, constituents, allies, and supporters as well as one focus group interview with six former members of one social movement organization. As I was interested in obtaining descriptive data about the strategies, culture, and internal dynamics of the movements, I identified key informants who have a wealth of knowledge based on their position or role in the organization. These were mostly movement leaders or chairs of specific committees. But retrospective accounts, especially decades after the events had transpired, are often unreliable, with memories influenced by dominant interpretations and discourses as well as intervening historical episodes.[2] Thus, interviews were used as additions to documentary or recorded evidence rather than as the principal source.

Since I was also interested in reconstitution of their individual selves around a collective identity, I utilized life history interviews with all eighty-nine actors. I elicited their own life stories and asked questions concerning family background, school experiences, and peer groups to allow the collection of information on primary and secondary socialization processes. Accounts of these biographical phases are important for understanding the influence of historical events and personal relationships on political choices as adults.[3] The longest section of the interview dealt with periods in the migrant's life more directly connected to political activity, prompting the interviewee to provide detailed information on the whole process of political socialization, from the first encounters with politics to the development of attitudes and beliefs. Thus, through life history interviews, I focused upon the subjectivities of Filipino activists as well as their constituents and adherents and located these within broad sociocultural, economic, and political contexts.

Each tape-recorded interview averaged ninety-five minutes, and nine activists were interviewed more than once. I selected them using snowball sampling, which is typically used for members of a population who have not all been previously identified and are more difficult to locate. This is especially the case for Filipino activists who worked clandestinely in both the Netherlands and the US. Through sampling, I maximized variation in gender, legal status, and migrant generation of the informants. I also ensured that I interview at least two current or former members of the social movement organizations mentioned in the book. I interviewed until I reached a "saturation point," that is, when no new information was being elicited.

I conducted all my interviews in the language that my interviewees preferred. Based on my research experience, Filipinos in both the US and the Netherlands code-switch, often using English to talk about facts and events and Tagalog or Ilocano to express their thoughts and emotions. My project provides a culturally specific and nuanced analysis that stems from the trust and empathy between individuals who share a language. I hired the services of Filipinos who are native fluent in Tagalog for verbatim transcription of the interviews, which I translated to English.

Ethnographic Observation

I also observed and participated in the events of former activists from the KDP, which included discussions of *A Time to Rise* and *Women against Marcos* in San Francisco and Seattle and online meetings of the North America branch of Akbayan Citizens' Action Party, better known as Akbayan, a democratic socialist and progressive political party in the Philippines. I went to informal gatherings that included family celebrations and spontaneous get-togethers in Los Angeles, Manila, San Francisco, and Seattle. In the Netherlands, I frequently visited the office of the NDF in Utrecht, chatting with the people who were there and attending talks, parties, fundraisers, and open meetings. I also spent time with activists formerly associated with NDF, as they invited me to dinners and *vrijmibo* (an informal meet-up with colleagues and friends at the end of the workweek). Finally, I went to parties organized by migrant workers to celebrate their and their children's birthdays and other important social occasions as well as Dutch and Filipino holidays. Most of these gatherings were in Amsterdam, The Hague, and Utrecht. In Manila, I spent time with activists and their families who, like me, were visiting during the Christmas holiday and summer.

APPENDIX   171

Positionality and Reflexivity

Throughout the fieldwork for this project, I was sensitive to how my own positionality informed not only my access to spaces for data collection and my analysis and interpretation but also to what I considered data. I am an immigrant to the US. I left the Philippines for graduate study in 2008. I am the daughter of an overseas Filipino worker (OFW) in Rome, Italy, who was undocumented for four years. I am Ilocano and grew up in a province that was a stronghold of the Marcoses, a place where the dictator was considered a demigod. I was seven years old during the 1986 People Power Revolution, and I have memories of those four days in the last week of February. Finally, I was involved in student activism at the University of the Philippines through an organization that was supportive of the national democratic movement. My multiple identities have shaped the research process, and I exercised reflexivity throughout, being cognizant of my own biases and blind spots while not pretending to achieve neutral scientific objectivity.

The fact that I am a child of an OFW opened doors to migrant organizations and created trust between me and OFWs in the Netherlands, who treated me like their daughter or friend. Being Ilocano also gave me an automatic "in" to groups of co-ethnics, especially since they only speak Ilocano to each other. Interestingly, given the split that occurred in the Philippine Left in the early 1990s and its impact on the Filipino communities in the US and the Netherlands, my immigrant and activist identity, at times, posed as an obstacle in securing access to some second-generation Filipino Americans who were skeptical of my intention and my ability to empathize with the racialized experiences that shaped their politics. In contrast, the same identity allowed me to develop close relationships with both current and former members of the NDF in the Netherlands. This surprised me and made me realize that the effect of some identities and statuses do not work consistently. Moreover, despite my efforts to avoid any discussions of it, I was asked many times about my own politics. I always answered honestly but reassured them that my political views have no bearing on my research.

I did not expect to form and cultivate meaningful friendships with many activists and migrants in seven years of doing this study. I made sure I was always aware of this fact—that it did not detract from my research and "color" my analysis. But sometimes, I think about the stories they shared with me, the food they cooked when I visited their houses, the stacks of photo albums they showed me—things they did because they thought of me as a friend. All of those things gave me insights about social movements and diasporas that I would not have gotten had I been a disinterested researcher. I hope I accurately and fairly portrayed their experiences.

Notes

Preface

1. Abad 2022.

2. See Arugay (2022) and Coronel (2022).

3. Alvarez and Docena 2022.

4. See Bello (2022), de Jong (2022), and Rafael (2022).

5. Throughout the book, I use first names, as commonly practiced in the social sciences. I also use pseudonyms, except in cases where I cite published written works of activists or media coverage of protest events and social movement organizations where I use full names.

6. The au pair program is an internationally recognized cultural exchange program through which young people learn a new language and become acquainted with another society. In the Netherlands, it is regulated by the Immigratie en Naturalisatiedienst (Immigration and Naturalization Service).

7. Kusaka 2020, 426.

8. *Pasaway* is a term used for the "disobedient and hardheaded" who frequently violate rules. It has roots in parenting a difficult or naughty child, whereby *pasaway* included causing younger siblings to cry, interrupting adult conversations by what was perceived to be meaningless or disrespectful chatter, play-fighting with other children or siblings, making noises and disrupting order in the house (Sanapo and Nakamura 2011, 48). The administration of Rodrigo Duterte has deliberately labeled those who violated quarantine regulations during the COVID-19 lockdown in 2020 *pasaway* as a way to scapegoat them for its inability to curb infection rates (Kusaka 2020; Thompson 2022). Thank you to Joel Ariate Jr. for help in defining *pasaway*.

9. Marco Garrido (2021) theorizes primacy given to the value of discipline among the upper and middle class in Metro Manila. Due to their experience with corruption, rule-bending, clientelism, and informal settlement, they associate democracy with disorder. On the other hand, based on his study of poor, rural residents of Leyte province and their embrace of Rodrigo Duterte's "War on Drugs," Wataru Kusaka (2020) argues that the discourse of "discipline" emanates from neoliberal governmentality that shifts the blame for life's misfortunes from the state to individuals.

174   NOTES TO PAGES XIV–5

10. Because actors discuss important issues selectively, often only salient ones and to other actors like them, they experience attitude homogeneity even if they are embedded in networks where the distribution of attitudes is heterogeneous (Baldassari and Bearman 2007).

11. Fine 2012, 3.

Introduction

1. *Gezellig* is a Dutch word that literally means "cozy," "warm," or "pleasant" that is used to describe the atmosphere of a place or situation as well as the feeling when one spends time with friends and loved ones.

2. Valerie Francisco-Menchavez (2018) refers to the type of care in the transnational lives of migrants as "communities of care," characterized by mutual aid within immigrant social networks.

3. In recent years, "diaspora" has appeared in both academic works and journalistic accounts to refer to every group of people that migrate—from Singaporeans to Oaxacans. This is mainly due to its metaphorical usage (Bruneau 2010) to portray the experience of displacement, transition, and belonging among migrants. A tendency to conflate diaspora as a social form—that is, characteristics of an identified group based on relationships, networks, and identities (Vertovec 1997)—and diaspora as a type of consciousness has also led to the term's spread to encompass more and more groups, although Martin Sökefeld (2006) notes the conceptual and empirical difficulty of disentangling the two. Finally, as an interdisciplinary field of inquiry, diaspora has often included in its theoretical elaboration a multiplicity of adjacent phenomena, ideas, and categories such as "exile," "expatriation," "postcoloniality," and "globality" among others (Edwards 2001). Rogers Brubaker (2005, 1–3) characterizes this diffusion of the term and the resultant obfuscation of its meanings as " 'diaspora' diaspora" and warns "the universalization of diaspora, paradoxically, means the disappearance of diaspora." But rather than discard or limit its use to well-known or archetypal cases that scholars have consensually identified, he advocates its treatment as a "category of practice, project, claim and stance" (Brubaker 2005, 13) instead of a presumed destiny for all people who cross borders.

4. The sociological imagination developed by C. Wright Mills (2000) allows us to see the interconnections between our personal experiences and the larger social forces.

5. Wimmer 2013, 9.

6. Dufoix 2003, 56.

7. Butler 2001.

8. In his article entitled "Is the Filipino Diaspora a Diaspora?," Filipino historian Filomeno V. Aguilar Jr. (2005, 457) criticizes the predominance of the experiences of permanent immigrants in the US in the construction of the Filipino diaspora despite the intensity and scale of migration of temporary labor to other countries. He argues that this is due in large part to the influence of Filipino American scholars in "attracting the attention of the broader Anglophone intellectual milieu and influencing discourse in the homeland."

9. Scholars in the field of diaspora studies use "hostland," as opposed to "receiving country," "country of destination," or "host country," which is more common in immigration studies. In this book, I use "hostland" most of the time, although sometimes I also employ the other terms.

10. According to Linda Basch, Nina Glick Schiller, and Cristina Szanton Blanc (1994, 7), through their daily practices, immigrants reconfigure space so that their lives are lived simultaneously within two or more nation-states. They coin the terms "transnational social field" and

NOTES TO PAGES 5–14

"transmigrants" to describe, respectively, this interconnected social experience—a single field of social relations rather than fragmented experiences—and the mobile subjects that create and sustain this field.

11. See Cheyette (2013), Lowe (1996), and Mercer (2016).

12. Marx and Engels 1998, 85.

13. Simmel 1964, 98–99.

14. Coser 1964.

15. Snow et al. (1998) identifies four conditions that are especially likely to disrupt the quotidian and heighten prospects of collective action. These include accidents that throw a community's routines into doubt and/or threaten its existence; actual or threatened intrusion into and/or violation of citizens' sense of privacy, safety, and control; alteration in subsistence routines because of unfavorable ratios of resources to claimants or demand; and dramatic changes in structures of social control. Dana Moss (2022) applies Snow et al.'s theory on quotidian disruption in her analysis of diaspora activism in the Libyan, Syrian, and Yemeni communities in the United Kingdom and the US. She shows how heightened repression in the home country can cross borders and disrupt the norms and routines of migrants, thus encouraging them to mobilize for change.

16. Fine 2012, 30.

17. Tarrow 2011.

18. Swidler 1986, 320.

19. Swidler 1986; Swidler 1995.

20. Swidler 1995, 33.

21. Friedman and McAdam 1992.

22. Swidler 1995, 27.

23. Swidler 1986, 281.

24. Safran 1991.

25. Aguilar (2005, 453–56) questions the intention of return among immigrants who have put down roots in their countries of settlement, especially those in North America and Europe. He states, "for first-generation immigrants, return is not contemplated because they left the homeland precisely to be separated from it; the homeland cannot be idealized so easily, with all its failings that immigrants carry with them in their memories as they settle down in their destination." He adds that because of this, the aspiration of homecoming is not transmitted to their children and the succeeding generations.

26. See Ignacio (2005), Manalansan (2003), Menchavez-Francisco (2018), S. L. Mendoza (2002), Okamura (1998), Velasco (2020), and Villegas (2021).

27. Clifford 1994, 306.

Chapter 1

1. Wright and Zuñiga 2007.

2. Kundnani, Morris, and Hooper 1999.

3. Tseng 2020.

4. Scholars who have used social movement theory in their empirical investigations of diaspora mobilization include Dana Moss (2022) on the Libyan, Syrian, and Yemeni communities in the United Kingdom and the US during the Arab Spring; Amarnath Amarasingam (2015) on the Sri Lankan Tamil refugees and their descendants in Canada during the 2009 protests on the Sri

Lankan Civil War; and Liza Mügge (2010) on the transnational politics of Surinamese, Turkish, and Kurdish migrants and the second generation in the Netherlands. Fiona Adamson (2012) has theorized diasporas as transnational identity networks using framing processes, while Martin Sökefeld (2006), in his argument that the formation of diasporas is based on social mobilization, engages with political process theory and illustrates its dynamics using the Alevi movement in Germany. In an article published in *Sociology Compass*, I explain how political opportunity structures, resource mobilization, and collective identity can be used to analyze migrant mobilization for homeland politics (S. Quinsaat 2013).

5. Cohen 1997; Safran 1991; Tölölyan 1996.

6. Cohen 1997; Safran 1991; Tölölyan 1996.

7. In fact, Yossi Shain (2005, 51–52) describes diaspora as "a people with a common national origin who regard themselves, or are regarded by others, as members or potential members of the national community of their home nation, a status held regardless of their geographical location and their citizenship outside their national soil."

8. Cohen 1997, ix.

9. This belief is central to Safran's (1991) conceptualization of diaspora, such that he did not consider the mass of Polish immigrants who came to the US after the 1880s due to their children's intermarriage with the native born—a canonical measure of assimilation—along with exclusive use of English language in communication and low concern for political developments in the homeland. Safran also considers their goal of settlement and long-term employment as disqualifying them as a diaspora.

10. Anthias 1998; Adamson and Demetriou 2007; Baser and Swain 2010; Bauböck 2010; Butler 2001; Clifford 1994; Cohen 1997; Dufoix 2003; Safran 1991; Schnapper 1999; Sheffer 2003; Tölölyan 1996.

11. Jasper 2018, 105.

12. Safran 1991.

13. Clifford 1994, 306.

14. Clifford 1994, 306.

15. Schnapper 1999, 249–50.

16. Butler 2001.

17. Dufoix 2003, 3.

18. Brubaker 2005, 13.

19. Adamson 2012; Bauböck 2010; Sökefeld 2006.

20. Sökefeld 2006.

21. Bauböck 2010, 299.

22. Abramson 2019, 667.

23. Adamson 2004, 49–50.

24. Lyons and Mandaville 2012.

25. In her study of diasporas and democratization in postcommunist countries in Europe, Maria Koinova (2010) found that "diasporas use the universalist creed of liberalism instrumentally in order to increase their political clout with Western governments while simultaneously pursuing nationalist projects related to their country of origin."

26. Shain 1994/95.

27. Bauböck 2010.

28. Mavroudi 2007a, 474.

29. Mavroudi 2007b.

NOTES TO PAGES 17–21

30. Mavroudi 2007a, 476.

31. Gilroy 1993.

32. Hall 1990, 223–25.

33. To address the theoretical problems derived from the separation of studies concerning strikes, wars, revolutions, social movements, and other forms of political struggle, Doug McAdam, Sidney Tarrow, and Charles Tilly (2001, 5) shifted their focus from stable structures to dynamics mechanisms and processes that occur in what they refer to as contentious politics, or "episodic, public, collective interaction among makers of claims and their objects when (a) at least one government is a claimant, an object of claims, or a party to the claims and (b) the claims would, if realized, affect the interests of at least one of the claimants."

34. Schwalbe and Mason-Schrock 1996, 115.

35. Burke and Stets 2009.

36. Burke and Stets 2009, 124. Identities, even personal, are thus relational.

37. Melucci 1995, 44.

38. Melucci (1995) advocates for a process-based framework to collective identity. But David A. Snow and Catherine Corrigall-Brown (2015) argue that this should not preclude scholars from examining it as a product of collective action. See Fominaya (2019) for a discussion of these approaches.

39. Klandermans 2014, 4.

40. Klandermans and van Stekelenburg 2019.

41. Fominaya 2019; Taylor and Whittier 1992; Zamponi 2018.

42. J. Gamson 1997, 180 (emphasis in the original).

43. Fominaya 2019; W. Gamson 1995; Polletta and Jasper 2001.

44. Friedman and McAdam 1992, 157.

45. Charles Tilly (2006, 35) uses "repertoire" to describe the means by which people protest. Repertoires refer to "claim-making routines that apply to the same claimant-object pairs: bosses and workers, peasants and landlords, rival nationalist factions, and many more." The theatrical metaphor emphasizes "the clustered, learned, yet improvisational character of people's interactions as they make and receive each other's claims."

46. Bosco 2006.

47. Klandermans 2014.

48. Taylor and Whittier 1995.

49. Polletta and Jasper 2001, 284.

50. Polletta and Jasper 2001, 284; Bernstein 1997, 535.

51. Ganz 2000; Jasper 2012; Maney et al. 2012; Meyer and Staggenborg 2012.

52. McAdam, McCarthy, and Zald 1996, 6.

53. W. Gamson 1995; Jasper 1997; Klandermans and Goslinga 1996; Snow et al. 1986; Zald 1996.

54. Polletta 2012.

55. Polletta 1994.

56. Tarrow 2011.

57. Lyons and Mandaville 2012.

58. Ganz 2000; Meyer and Staggenborg 2012; Polletta and Jasper 2001.

59. Jasper 2004.

60. Polletta 2012.

61. Meyer and Staggenborg 2012, 18.

62. V. Taylor 1989, 761.

63. V. Taylor 1989, 761.

64. Despite different terminologies, they all emphasize distance from or absence of authorities and the presence of dense, intimate ties that allow for a movement culture to develop and percolate (Evans and Boyte 1992; Scott 1990; Melucci 1989).

65. Yates 2015; Futrell and Simi 2004; Polletta 1999.

66. Futrell and Simi 2004.

67. Bauböck (2003) further argues that the children of immigrants may consider transnational political membership through the acquisition of dual nationality, but this may eventually fade away over subsequent generations of immigrant descent. Kasinitz et al.'s (2002) research on the second generation of New York City corroborates this. Factors such as distance of the homeland, language preference, membership in ethnic organizations, church attendance, consumption of ethnic media, and interest in New York politics affect the degree of involvement in the politics of their parents' country of origin. But others assert that the reproduction of transnationalism in the second and ensuing generations will endure so long as condition of their lives remain insecure, combined with the continuous flow of migration to the US (Basch, Schiller, and Blanc 1994; Foner 1997; Levitt and Waters 2002).

68. Levitt 2001; R. C. Smith 2006.

69. Landolt 2008; Østergaard-Nielsen 2003.

70. Mavroudi 2018.

71. Asis 2002; Hondagneu-Sotelo 1992; Parreñas 2015; Yeoh and Huang 2000.

72. Yeoh and Huang 2000, 428.

73. Swidler 1986.

74. Swidler 1986, 273.

75. Sewell 1999.

76. For Gramsci (1971), hegemony is a condition where a dominant class has the political, intellectual, and moral leadership within a system. The state embodies "the hegemony of one social group over the whole of society exercised through so-called private organizations, such as the church, trade unions, schools, etc." (Cammett 1967, 204).

77. Johnston and Klandermans 1995.

78. Bourdieu, Wacquant, and Farage 1994, 3–4 (emphasis in the original).

79. Burgess 2020.

80. Burgess 2020, 19.

81. Gamlen 2014, S193.

82. Jasper 2018.

83. Jasper 2018, 103.

84. Jasper 2018, 117.

85. Fantasia 1988.

86. Polletta 2020.

87. Polletta 2020, 23.

88. Hall 1990, 225.

89. Olick 1999.

90. Eyerman 2004; Schwartz 1996.

91. Hashimoto 2015, 21.

92. Daphi and Zamponi 2019; Gongaware 2010; Halbwachs 1992; Jedlowski 2001; Olick 1999.

93. Halbwachs 1992, 22.

NOTES TO PAGES 25–30

94. Zamponi 2018.

95. Cheng and Yuen 2019.

96. Lacroix and Fiddian-Qasmiyeh 2013, 685.

97. Conway 2010.

98. For an evaluation of the body of literature on the cultural outcomes of social movements, see Amenta and Polletta (2019), Earl (2004), and Van Dyke and Taylor (2018).

99. Van Dyke and Taylor 2018, 492.

100. Rochon 2018, 195–96.

Chapter 2

1. In the Philippines, the Philippine Atmospheric, Geophysical and Astronomical Services Administration referred to it as Super Typhoon Yolanda.

2. NDRRMC 2013; Memmott 2013.

3. Gavilan 2016.

4. Hanley, Binas, Murray, and Tribunalo 2014, 17.

5. Montecillo 2014.

6. According to the 2020 World Migration Report, the Philippines ranks ninth in the number of migrants abroad, although the population figure in the report (approximately 5.5 million) is much lower than that of the Commission on Filipinos Overseas. The top five countries of origin of international migrants in 2019 are India, Mexico, China, the Russian Federation, and the Syrian Arab Republic (IOM 2019).

7. CFO 2019.

8. Camroux 2009, 79.

9. Testaverde et al. 2017, 271.

10. Camroux 2009, 52–53.

11. Context of exit constitutes factors in the sending country that impel citizens to migration and thereby influence who leaves, when, why, and how. Context of reception, on the other hand, comprises conditions in the receiving country that shape migrants' settlement experiences and opportunities (Burgess 2020; Portes and Böröcz 1989).

12. Burgess 2020, 17.

13. Sivanandan 2008.

14. Camroux 2009, 62.

15. On October 21, 1995, national, state, and chapter officials of the Filipino American National Historical Society, as well as civic officials of Morro Bay, California, celebrated the first landing of Filipinos in what is now the United States of America, in Morro Bay in 1587 (A. Pido, 1997).

16. Cordova 1983.

17. Okamura 1998.

18. In the context of the Cavite mutiny, Philippine national hero José Rizal stated that *filibustero* means "a dangerous patriot who will soon be hanged, or a presumptuous fellow" (Aguilar 2011).

19. Constantino 2008.

20. For a comprehensive historical account of Filipino exiles in Spain, see Salazar (1999).

21. Baldoz 2011.

22. Abinales and Amoroso 2017.

23. Fujita-Rony 2003.

24. Bonus 2000.

25. Fujita-Rony 2003; Ngai 2004; Posadas and Guyotte 1990.

26. Habal 2007; Cordova 1983.

27. The Ilocos region in the Philippines is in the northwest of Luzon, the biggest and most populous island. It is home to the Ilocanos, the third largest Filipino ethnolinguistic group.

28. Ngai 2004; Okamura 1998.

29. Y. Espiritu 2003; J. Quinsaat 1976.

30. Cordova 1983.

31. Ngai 2004.

32. Fujita-Rony 2003; Ngai 2004; Okamura 1998.

33. Ngai 2004.

34. Baldoz 2011.

35. Daniels 2004.

36. Y. Espiritu 1995.

37. Bonus 2000; A. Pido 1997.

38. Mabalon 2013.

39. Y. Espiritu 1995.

40. Y. Espiritu 2003.

41. Habal 2007.

42. Mabalon 2013.

43. McKay 2007.

44. Habal 2007; Rodriguez 2010.

45. Daniels 2004.

46. Choy 2003.

47. These figures are based on estimates provided by Samahan in its undated document entitled "Filipinos in the Netherlands."

48. Maas 2011.

49. Flores-Valenzuela 2007.

50. Flores and Valenzuela 2007.

51. Overseas employment was supposed to be temporary, lasting only until the country recovered from its economic problems. But both supply and demand factors fueled further migration. As the Philippines under Marcos was unable to achieve sustained growth and development and continued to be plagued by political instability, Filipinos sought work abroad. At the same time, labor shortages in oil-rich countries in the Middle East persisted, and new labor markets opened in East and Southeast Asia (Asis 1992; Guevarra 2010).

52. Bello 2009.

53. Harvey 2007.

54. A structural adjustment is a set of economic—free market—reforms that a country must adhere to in order to secure a loan from the International Monetary Fund (IMF) and/or the World Bank. In 1980, the Philippines received a loan of $200 million from the IMF, as part of its new structural adjustment program (SAP), whereby the country pursued changes in industrial policies. These included lowering of protective tariffs, liberalizing import restrictions, and promoting investment in export-oriented industries among others. For a comprehensive analysis of SAP in the Philippines and its economic and social impact, see Broad (1988).

55. Bello et al. 2005.

NOTES TO PAGES 35-39

56. Ortega 2016.

57. POEA 2017.

58. UNCTAD 2021.

59. Adamson and Tsourapas 2020, 867.

60. Rodriguez 2010.

61. Chee 2020; Guevarra 2010; McKay 2007; Ortiga 2018; Rodriguez 2010; Tyner 2009.

62. Rodriguez 2010.

63. Parreñas 2021, 1044.

64. Misra, Woodring, and Merz 2006.

65. Bridget Anderson 2000; Constable 2007; Hondagneu-Sotelo 2001; Parreñas 2015.

66. Berghaus closed its operation in the Netherlands in 2006 after filing bankruptcy.

67. Flores-Valenzuela 2007; Padilla 2007; Van den Muijzenberg 2001.

68. Van den Muijzenberg 2001.

69. Padilla 2007.

70. Padilla 2007.

71. McKay 2007.

72. A brochure by the Philippine Overseas Employment Agency in the early 1980s read: "What truly makes a Filipino the most dependable shipmate are certain inherent traits. He is adaptable and hard-working. The Filipino's charm and friendliness makes for a harmonious relationship essential to the working situation on board. He is neat and disciplined. Reflective of household breeding, the Filipino is particularly observant of clean surroundings and good grooming. Moreover, he keeps within set rules and regulations" (McKay 2007, 624).

73. Padilla 2007.

74. Van den Muijzenberg 2001.

75. Sampson 2003.

76. Illegal recruitment agencies in the Philippines promised Filipinas jobs in domestic service and hospitality and entertainment industry. But then upon arrival, they ended up in sex trade and prostitution. Often, the trafficker confiscated their passports, restricted their movement, and threatened rape and other forms of violence. In mid-1980s, the case of "Nena," a Filipina who escaped from forced prostitution, hit the Dutch media, attracted public attention, and shaped the political agenda of the Dutch parliament. The life of Nena was depicted in the Dutch-produced film *Cannot Run Away*, which garnered several international awards. The Dutch Foundation against Trafficking of Women was instrumental in taking Nena's case. See Padilla (2007) for a discussion of contemporary migration of Filipino women to the Netherlands.

77. Siruno 2021; Tesorio 2020.

78. Maas 2011, 91.

79. Van den Muijzenberg 2001.

80. Maas 2011. Van den Muijzenberg (2003) argues that even this figure is disputed, since most Filipinas married to Dutch men assumed their husbands' names and dropped their original nationality.

81. Vergara 2009, 6.

82. Okamura 1998.

83. Habal 2007.

84. Bonus 2000; Liu, Ong, and Rosenstein 1991.

85. Y. Espiritu 1995.

86. Portes and Rumbaut 2014.

87. Okamura 1998.

88. Y. Espiritu 1995.

89. Bonus 2000; Y. Espiritu 1995.

90. Unlike Chinatown, Manilatown was not on any map of San Francisco, and most locals were unaware of its existence. During its heyday, Filipinos referred to it as "Filipino town" or simply as "Kearny Street." From the 1940s to the early 1960s, the Kearny Street neighborhood was a bustling community with businesses that served the needs of Filipino workers to domestic servants and culinary workers, from merchant seaman and sailors to war-industry workers and military personnel, and from migrants to retired workers (Habal 2007).

91. Y. Espiritu 2003.

92. Burgess 2020, 134 (emphasis in the original).

93. UNCTAD 2021.

94. Burgess 2020, 139.

95. Kelner 2010, 10.

96. Abramson 2017.

97. The feast commemorates the transfer of the image of the Black Nazarene, which is believed by devotees to be miraculous, from Luneta Park to Quiapo Church in Manila.

98. Blanc 1996, 193.

99. Richter 1980.

100. Koinova 2018, 194.

101. Blanc 1996.

102. Richter 1980, 244.

103. Richter 1980, 245.

104. Richter 1980.

105. Blanc 1996.

106. E. Pido 2017.

107. Congress of the Philippines 1989.

108. Camposano 2012; Fresnoza-Flot 2009; McCallum 2021.

109. CNN Philippines Staff 201.

110. Vergara 2009.

111. Rafael 2000, 2010.

112. Rafael 2000, 211.

113. Guevarra 2010; McKay 2007.

114. See Bagong Bayani Foundation, Inc. at https://www.bbfi.com.ph/.

115. Rodriguez 2010.

116. Encinas-Franco 2013.

117. Aguilar Jr. 2014.

118. McKay 2007, 628.

119. Burgess 2020, 79.

120. Burgess 2020.

121. Parreñas 2021.

122. Parreñas 2022.

123. Parreñas 2022, 54.

124. Caglar 2006; Fitzgerald 2008; Strunk 2014.

125. Hirschman 2004; Menjívar 1999; Min 1992.

126. Bridget Anderson 2010; Hsia 2009; Nicholls and Uitermark 2017.

NOTES TO PAGES 46-54

127. Parreñas 2001.

128. Parreñas 2001, 1151.

129. Benedict Anderson 1991.

130. Manalansan 2003.

131. Manalansan 2003, 47.

132. Manalansan 2003, 60–61.

133. Fresnoza-Flot 2010, 352.

134. Hosoda 2013; Hosoda and Watanabe 2014.

135. Hosoda 2013, 24.

136. Hosoda 2013.

137. Mavroudi 2007a, 475–76.

138. Camroux 2009, 66.

Chapter 3

1. Knight 1977. The university eventually dropped the plan in 1981 because Marcos could not complete payment of the subvention and specialists who were offered the position refused it (Associated Press 1981).

2. "Bayan Ko" is usually translated as "My Country," although the Tagalog word *bayan* can also mean "people" and "nation."

3. The AMLC Seven consisted of Reverend Lloyd Wake (Glide Memorial Church), Sylvia Kimura (American Friends Service Committee), Deborah Kaufman (World Association of Law Students), Steve Wake and Walden Bello (Friends of the Filipino People), Wilma Cadorna (Katipunan ng Demokratikong Pilipino), and Vee Hernandez (AMLC–San Francisco).

4. Anti–Martial Law Coalition, n.d., "Why the San Francisco Consulate Was Occupied," organizational brochure to raise funds.

5. Foa 1983.

6. Brubaker 2005; Redclift 2017.

7. Shain 2005.

8. Jones-Correa 1998.

9. Moss 2016.

10. Polletta and Jasper 2001, 295.

11. In Goffman's dramaturgical approach, all humans are actors performing their carefully constructed roles. He went further to distinguish between the front stage and the backstage. The former is where actors interact with others in public. The latter is the private area where they are their true selves, without managing others' impressions or expectations (Goffman 1959).

12. Bernstein 1997.

13. Taylor and Van Dyke 2004, 270.

14. Ganz 2000; Meyer and Staggenborg 2012; Polletta and Jasper 2001.

15. Jasper 2004.

16. Coy, Woehrle, and Maney 2008, 163.

17. Abinales and Amoroso 2017; Hagimoto 2013.

18. Mojares 2011; Schumacher 1997.

19. Schumacher 1991, 104.

20. Schumacher 1997.

21. Schumacher 1991, 105.

22. Hagimoto 2013.

23. Schumacher 1997, 90.

24. Fanon 2004, 147.

25. *Indio* is the Spanish colonial racial term for the native Austronesian peoples of the Philippines.

26. Mojares 2011, 37.

27. Hagimoto 2013, 6.

28. Overholt 1986.

29. Ang 2010; Lee 2015.

30. Abinales and Amoroso 2017.

31. Broad 1988.

32. Abinales and Amoroso 2017.

33. Bonner 1988, 138–39.

34. Abinales and Amoroso 2017.

35. George M. Taber of *Time Magazine* first used the term "crony capitalism" to refer to the Philippine economy under Marcos in his article "A Case of Crony Capitalism, which was published on April 21, 1980.

36. Bello et al. 2005; Kang 2002.

37. For an analysis of crony capitalism under the Marcos regime, see Bonner (1988), Hawes (1987), Kang (2002), and Manapat (2020).

38. Chebabi and Linz 1998.

39. Abinales and Amoroso 2017.

40. Gaerlan 1999; Pimentel 2012.

41. The Venceremos Brigade is an organization founded in 1969 by members of the Students for a Democratic Society and officials of the Republic of Cuba. It aimed to show solidarity with the Cuban Revolution and to challenge US foreign policy on Cuba.

42. Habal 2007.

43. A. Espíritu 2009, 42.

44. Rene Cruz, "The KDP Story: The First Ten Years," *Ang Katipunan* (Special Supplement) 9, no. 8 (September 1983): 2.

45. "Editorial: An Emerging Alternative," *Kalayaan International*, June 1971, 1.

46. Habal 2007; Mangaoang 1994.

47. Choy 2003; Mangaoang 1994.

48. Habal 2007.

49. Nepstad 2004; Perla 2009; Power 2009; C. Smith 1996.

50. Van den Muijzenberg 2001.

51. Brysk 2009; Hoebnik 1999.

52. According to international law, cofinancing agencies cannot support activities that aim to undermine the political independence of a state or to overthrow a legal government (Van Eldik Thieme 1992).

53. These were the Centrale voor Bemiddeling bij Medefinanciering van Ontwikkelingspro-gramma (Central Agency for Joint Financing of Development Programmes), a Roman Catho-lic foundation; the Interkerkelijke Coordinatie Commissie Ontwikkelingshulp (Inter-Church Organization for Development Cooperation [ICCO]), which has its roots in Dutch-Protestant churches; the Nederlandse Organisatie voor Internationale Bijstand (Netherlands Organization

NOTES TO PAGES 60–68

for International Development Cooperation [NOVIB]), the country's first politically independent and nonreligious development organization; and the Humanistisch Instituut voor Ontwikkelingssamenwerking (Humanist Institute for Cooperation), established in 1968 by the Humanist Association in response to the dominance of religious organizations working in the field of development in the Netherlands (Van Eldik Thieme 1992).

54. Basic Ecclesial Communities (BECs), also referred to as Basic Christian Communities, were part of the concrete realization of the communitarian model of church promoted by the Second Vatican Council. The communities considered the church as part of the grass roots. The earliest BECs emerged in Brazil and the Philippines in the 1960s (Nadeau 1999).

55. Established in 1965 under the Ministry of Foreign Affairs, SNV's mission was to provide technical assistance to developing countries and to understand the cultures of their people.

56. McCarthy and Zald 1977, 1222.

57. Habal 2007.

58. According to a regulation imposed by the Marcos regime in 1973, overseas Filipinos had to pay taxes according to the following schedule: gross income up to $6,000, 1 percent; income $6,000–$20,000, 2 percent; and over $20,000, 3 percent.

59. NCRCLP, "Why Pay Philippine Taxes?" *Kalayaan International* 2, no. 9 (May 1973): 1.

60. "MFP National Convention," *Ang Katipunan* 1, no. 1 (October 1–15, 1973): 5.

61. Manglapus 1986, xix.

62. Fuentecilla 2013, 14.

63. For example, the US Immigration and Naturalization Service denied the application for political asylum of Heherson Alvarez and his wife, Cecile—prominent critics of the Marcos regime in the Philippines—in 1975. The couple used a refugee document given by the UN Commissioner for Refugees during their stay in the US.

64. Gaerlan 1999.

65. Fuentecilla 2013.

66. Fuentecilla 2013, 22.

67. Fuentecilla 2013, 24.

68. Fuentecilla 2013.

69. Conceived in 1971 by the Filipino Youth Activities of Seattle under the leadership of Fred and Dorothy Cordova, the convention provided a space for mostly US-born Filipinos to learn about their history and understand the challenges they face in American society through workshops and cultural performances.

70. "Unity Meeting in New York: Marcos Denounced by Filipino Groups," *Ang Katipunan* 1, no. 5 (January 15, 1974): 5.

71. *Philippine News* published the names of 150 Filipinos in the US accused of being against the government of Marcos.

72. "Consul Baliao Denounces Marcos," *Kalayaan International Special Issue* June 12, 1973, 1.

73. Lachica 1979.

74. Lachica 1979.

75. Vergara 2009, 113.

76. Swidler 1995, 37.

77. Philippine News 1976, 2.

78. Domingo 2010.

79. Vergara 2009, 125.

80. *Ang Katipunan* 1975, cited in Vergara (2009, 125).

81. Philippine National Day Committee, "Fifth Annual Philippine National Day, Barrio Fiesta, a Tribute to Three Waves of Filipino Immigration, ca. 1980," University of Washington Libraries, Cannery Workers & Farm Laborers Union Local 7 Collection, Accession No. 3927-001, Box 32/38, 1980.

82. Miller 2011.

83. Quimpo 2007.

84. Boccagni 2010, 189.

85. Weekley 2001.

86. Dañguilan Vitug and Gloria 2000.

87. Thompson 1995.

88. Furuyama and Meyer 2011, 103.

89. Furuyama and Meyer 2011; McAdam, Tarrow, and Tilly 2001.

90. Keck and Sikkink 1998.

91. DeWind and Segura 2014.

92. Watanabe 1984.

93. Haney and Vanderbush 1999; Shain 1994/95.

94. Karpathakis 1999.

95. Shalom 1990, 20.

96. Jasper 1997.

97. Human Rights in South Korea and the Philippines: Implications for U.S. Policy, Hearings before the Subcommittee on International Organizations of the Committee on International Relations, House of Representatives, Ninety-Fourth Congress, First Session, May 20, 22, June 3, 5, 10, 12, 17, and 24, 1975.

98. Feeney 1984.

99. See Lescaze (1977), Mathews (1976), and *New York Times* (1976, 1977), among others.

100. "Statement on Behalf of the Friends of the Filipino People" presented by James Drew and William Goodfellow for the Subcommittee on Foreign Operations House Appropriations Committee, April 5, 1977.

101. Shain 1994/95; T. Smith 2000.

102. Walaardt 2011.

103. Ghorashi 2005.

104. Staggenborg 1998.

105. The tribunal, which grew out of the Bertrand Russell Tribunal II on Latin America in the early seventies, is a permanent body composed of legal scholars and activists, policy makers and advocates, scientists and medical professionals, and creative artists, from which small groups are selected to hear specific cases. The participation of nonlawyers was intended to weaken the barrier separating law from humanitarian activity and to create a broad human rights constituency (Blaser 1992).

106. Bangsamoro refers to the population of Muslims in the Philippines.

107. The member-jurors were Sergio Mendes Arceo, Archbishop of Cuernavaca, Mexico, and a leading figure in the progressive wing of the Roman Catholic Church; Richard Baumlin, a legal expert and Swiss parliamentarian; Harvey Cox, professor of theology at Harvard University; Richard Falk, professor of international law at Princeton University; Andrea Giardina, professor of international law at the University of Naples; Francois Houtart, professor of sociology at the University of Louvain; Ajit Roy, renowned Indian writer for the *Economic and Political Weekly*;

NOTES TO PAGES 77–89

Makoto Oda, noted Japanese novelist and vice president of the Permanent People's Tribunal; and Ernst Utrecht, fellow at the Transnational Institute in Amsterdam. Nobel Prize–winner George Wald presided over the panel (Komite ng Sambayanang Pilipino 1981).

108. Komite ng Sambayanang Pilipino 1981.

109. Komite ng Sambayanang Pilipino 1981, 25.

110. These included Bank of America, Royal Dutch Shell, Mitsubishi, Dole, Goodyear, Pfizer, General Motors, and Cargill.

111. Four months after the tribunal, the Office of the President of the Philippines issued a ten-page response to the tribunal's verdict. The Philippine Embassy in The Hague circulated the reply to newspapers in the Netherlands.

112. Komite ng Sambayanang Pilipino 1981, 276–77.

113. Komite ng Sambayanang Pilipino 1981.

114. "Postcard Campaign in Solidarity with the International Tribunal of Peoples in Belgium," Memo from the IAFP National Office to All Chapters of the AMLC, FFP, and KDP, October 12, 1980.

115. Komite ng Sambayanang Pilipino 1981.

116. Snow et al. 1986.

117. Komite ng Sambayanang Pilipino 1981.

Chapter 4

1. This is a literal translation. Filipinos usually ask each other this question when they meet each other overseas. According to Filomeno V. Aguilar Jr. (2014, 106), although it is meant to "establish a possible regional or subnational connection," the use of *sa atin* ("our own") means that "belonging to a nation is articulated as a form of possession that one continues to have despite departure from the homeland."

2. This expression can also be translated as "Gosh, as if." The meaning is inferred from the context in which it is used.

3. Aguilar 2014, 111.

4. Clifford 1994, 306.

5. Hall 1990, 227.

6. Liebelt 2008.

7. McAdam 1982, 51.

8. W. Gamson 1992, 56.

9. Nicholls 2013, 14.

10. Martinez 2010.

11. Fantasia 1988.

12. Benedict Anderson 1991.

13. Polletta 2020.

14. Bulosan 1973, 143.

15. Okamura 1998.

16. Fujita-Rony 2003, 170.

17. Cordova 1983; Chew 2012; Okamura 1998; Scharlin and Villanueva 2000.

18. James C. Scott (1985, 1990) introduced the concept of "everyday resistance" to encompass the less dramatic, disguised, and dispersed practices that people engage in, compared to the organized and confrontational ways that we see in social movements, rebellions, revolutions,

and civil wars. Often interchangeably used with "infrapolitics of the powerless," the term encompasses behaviors of subaltern groups that we do not normally associate with resistance (e.g., foot-dragging, pilfering, slander, avoidance, or feigned ignorance).

19. Parreñas 1998.

20. De Vera 1994.

21. DeWitt 1979.

22. San Juan 1994.

23. Y. Espiritu 1996; Mabalon 2013.

24. Bulosan 1973, 98.

25. Friday 1994, 139.

26. Alegado 1991.

27. Fujita-Rony 2003.

28. Mabalon 2013.

29. Fujita-Rony 2003, 97.

30. This is a term that Filipino cannery workers called themselves.

31. Chew 2012; Domingo 2010.

32. The suspension of George Mason Murray, a graduate student in English and part-time instructor in the Educational Opportunity Program who was also the minister of education of the Black Panther Party, triggered the strike.

33. Rojas 2007; Umemoto 2007.

34. Liu and Geron 2008.

35. Filipinos and Filipino Americans refer to every male immigrant of this wave as *manong*, which means "older brother" in the Ilocano language.

36. Habal 2007, 58.

37. Habal 2007.

38. Cordova 1983.

39. Mabalon 2013, 107.

40. Liu and Geron 2008.

41. Habal 2007.

42. Habal 2007, 27.

43. The King County Multipurpose Domed Stadium, or Kingdome for short, was a multipurpose stadium in Seattle, Washington. It was demolished by implosion on March 26, 2000.

44. "Filipino Life Begins, Flows from King Street," in the Fifth Annual Philippine National Day Program (June 12, 1980), Box 32, Folder 38, Cannery Workers and Farm Laborers Union Local 7, Accession No. 3927-001.

45. Scott 1990, 4.

46. Snow and Benford (1992) introduce the concept of "master frames" to describe broad and overarching interpretive schemas, compared to idiosyncratic collective action frames deployed by specific social movement organizations or used within a certain context. An example of a master frame is the civil rights frame, while the latter include "Occupy Wall Street" or "pro-woman, pro-fetus, pro-life."

47. Dufoix 2003, 14.

48. Um 2015.

49. Aguilar 2014, 96–97.

50. San Juan Jr. 1998.

NOTES TO PAGES 96–112

51. Rodriguez 2010.

52. Habal 2007.

53. Nicholls and Uitermark 2017, 61.

54. V. Taylor 1989.

55. National Democratic Front of the Philippines (NDFP), "Orientation Paper on ESMP Building," n.d., 7.

56. NDFP, "General Program of European National Democratic Organization," 3.

57. Fantasia 1988.

58. Valocchi 2008, 81.

59. Gilroy 1993, 19.

60. See Choy (2003) for a detailed historical account of the case.

61. Inday Refi and Rene Cruz, n.d., "Ang Katipunan Special: Filipinos Have a Stake in Jackson's Campaign, *Ang Katipunan Special.*"

62. *Samahan* is Tagalog for "organization."

63. Editorial Board, "Sino ang Manggagawang Pilipino sa Netherlands?," *Samahan*, no. 1 (March 1983): 1–2.

64. Bridget Anderson 2010.

65. Editorial Board, "Sino ang Manggagawang Pilipino sa Netherlands?"

66. National Committee, "ang ating SAMAHAN . . . ," *Samahan*, no. 1 (March 1983): 14.

67. Commission on Filipino Migrant Workers (CFMW) "Initial Recommendations and Comments of the CFMW on the NDF's Proposed European Programme and Structure," n.d., 3.

68. CFMW, "The Truth behind E.O. 857," *Kababayan* 1, no. 1 (November–December 1985): 4.

69. CFMW, "The Truth behind E.O. 857."

70. Rother 2012.

71. Houston and Wright 2003, 22.

72. Boccagni 2010, 189.

73. CFMW, "Editorial: 'Dear Kababayan,'" *Kababayan* 1, no. 1 (November–December 1985): 1.

74. Aguilar 2014, 101.

75. Boyet R., "Langit Nga Ba Ang Holland?," *Samahan*, no. 1 (March 1983): 5.

76. Schiller and Fouron 1999.

77. The play is a musical depiction of the 1948 Declaration of Human Rights that incorporated the literary works of Filipino artists and Chilean poet Pablo Neruda. It dramatizes the human rights situation and US imperialism in the Philippines under the Marcos regime, interspersed with vignettes and traditional dances and songs."

78. Alay ng Bayan, Letter and Proposal for a Concert Tour, July 30, 1984, Tilburg, the Netherlands.

79. Hall 1990, 225.

80. Madge Bello, "Pinoys Try to Build Power Bloc," *Ang Katipunan* 12, no. 11 (October 1986): 10.

81. CFMW, "A Communique to Pres. Aquino," *Kababayan*, January–February 1988, 8.

82. Amado B. Torio, "Tunay Ka Bang Pinoy?," *Kababayan*, February–March 1987, 7.

83. Aguilar 2014, 2.

84. In 1972, Marcos issued Presidential Decree No. 69, amending sections of the National Internal Revenue Code including Section 21, which compelled nonresident Filipino nationals to declare their income and pay taxes to the Philippine government, in addition to paying taxes to their host countries.

190 NOTES TO PAGES 113–123

85. In February 1987, ALAB was one of the guests in a weekly TV program, *Ver van Mijn Bed Show!* (Far from My Bed Show!), where it presented the Maranao dance, *singkil*.

86. Bridget Anderson 2010, 72.

87. Morris and Braine 2001, 21.

88. Takenaka 2009, 1327.

Chapter 5

1. Filippijnenbeweging Amsterdam, Filippijnengroep Nederland, Commission on Filipino Migrant Workers, and Damayang Pilipino sa Nederland, "Silent Commemoration and Protest in Amsterdam," September 21, 1978, 1–2.

2. Alejandro was a prominent activist during the martial law period, who ran for Philippine Congress in 1986, but eventually lost amid reports of electoral fraud. An unidentified gunman shot him on September 19, 1987, just after a failed military coup. No one was arrested for the assassination.

3. Like many universities in the US in the 1960s, Tufts was a hotbed of student activism, and widespread antiwar sentiments on campus ultimately led to the temporary removal of the Cannon, which some viewed as a symbol of imperialism and war (Damokosh 2016).

4. Ferguson 2018.

5. Assman and Shortt 2012, 7.

6. Schuman and Scott 1989.

7. Jansen 2007; Rajevic 2019.

8. Mannheim 1970, 388.

9. Assman and Shortt 2012, 3.

10. Molden 2016; Spillman 1998.

11. Steinberg 1996, 7.

12. Zerubavel 1996.

13. Doerr 2014; Rajevic 2019; Zamponi 2018.

14. Cheng and Yuen 2019, 423.

15. Eyerman 2016.

16. Paul 2000, 28.

17. Um 2012, 834.

18. Zamponi 2018, 15.

19. Gongaware 2003.

20. Gutman 2017, 1–2.

21. Polletta 2006, 9.

22. Cardinoza 2016.

23. Whaley 2016.

24. Chang, Chu, and Park 2007.

25. G. Mendoza 2019.

26. Berdos 2020.

27. Baizas 2019; Pangue 2020.

28. Assman and Shortt 2012, 2.

29. Pinto 2010.

30. Arguelles 2017.

31. Accornero 2019, 449.

NOTES TO PAGES 123–131 191

32. EDSA is the acronym for Epifanio delos Santos Avenue, the longest and the most congested highway in the Metro Manila, where the protests that overthrew Marcos took place from February 22 to 25, 1986. It was named after Epifanio delos Santos, considered one of the best Filipino literary writers in Spanish of his time.

33. Jerne 2020.

34. During the administration of Benigno Aquino III, however, commemoration emphasized the role of civilians as the site of remembrance programs moved from the headquarters of the Armed Forces of the Philippines to the People Power Monument (Arguelles 2017).

35. Durkheim 1995.

36. Polletta 2006; Doerr 2014.

37. Whitlinger 2019, 460.

38. Reyes 2018, 482.

39. Concepcion 2018.

40. These include the Museum of Courage and Resistance—both physical and online—of the nongovernmental organization Task Force Detainees of the Philippines, which has maintained records of human rights violations since 1974; the University Library of the University of the Philippines Diliman; and the Bantayog ng mga Bayani (Monument of the Heroes), a memorial center founded shortly after the People Power uprising to honor the individuals who resisted the Marcos dictatorship (Buenrorstro and Cabbab 2019; Claudio 2010).

41. Rajevic 2019.

42. Sabillo 2016.

43. Halbwachs 1992, 53.

44. Recuber 2012.

45. Recuber 2012, 544.

46. The link to the website is https://remember1081.wordpress.com/.

47. The Martial Law Chronicles Project is a joint project by the Freedom for Media Alternatives and the Martial Law Chronicles Team and endorsed by the Commission on Human Rights. It is available at https://www.martiallawchroniclesproject.com/.

48. On April 23, 2021, he was sworn in as California attorney general, becoming the first Filipino American to occupy the position.

49. "PHL Consulate General, EDSA People Power@30 Committee Celebrates 30th Anniversary of EDSA Revolution," Department of Foreign Affairs, March 2, 2016, https://dfa.gov.ph/dfa -news/news-from-our-foreign-service-postsupdate/8655-phl-consulate-general-edsa-people -power-30-committee-celebrates-30th-anniversary-of-edsa-revolution.

50. "PHL Consulate General, EDSA People Power@30 Committee Celebrates 30th Anniversary of EDSA Revolution."

51. "Recapturing the Spirit of 1986 People Power Revolution . . . ," video uploaded by Edwin Batongbacal on YouTube: https://www.youtube.com/watch?v=bAOji1GtJaE, February 26, 2016.

52. Cantlupe 1987.

53. *Filipino Express* 2008.

54. "The Meaning of EDSA on Its 34th Anniversary, 2020," Statement of Filipinos against Corruption and Tyranny—The Netherlands," posted on the Filipinos against Corruption and Tyranny Facebook page, https://www.facebook.com/FilipinosACTNL/photos/1090482917964791.

55. CNN Philippines Staff 2016.

56. Staggenborg 1993.

57. Amarasingam 2015; Hess and Korf 2014; Koinova and Karabegović 2017.

58. Foucault and Bouchard 1977.

59. Inquirer.net US Bureau 2016.

60. Marcos claimed that he was awarded thirty-two medals including two US Silver Stars and a Distinguished Service Cross (Sharkey 1983).

61. San Francisco Kontra Libing Coalition 2016, A4.

62. San Francisco Kontra Libing Coalition 2016.

63. Ochoa and Rueda 2016.

64. Ochoa and Rueda 2016.

65. Ochoa and Rueda 2016.

66. Lipsitz 1990, 213.

67. Arguelles 2017, 274.

68. Olea 2016.

69. "Anti Marcos Picket (Philippine Embassy, The Hague)," video uploaded by Marlon Lacsamana on YouTube, https://www.youtube.com/watch?v=3pvqHXkJlSo, November 26, 2016.

70. Holland and Cable 2002.

71. Collins 2001.

72. J. Taylor 2008, 722.

73. "UPAD Hosts Philippine Book Launch of 'A Time to Rise: Collective Memoirs of the Union of Democratic Filipinos (KDP)," February 14, 2018, https://cids.up.edu.ph/upad-launches-book-time-rise-collective-memoirs-union-democratic-filipinos/.

74. "UPAD Hosts Philippine Book Launch of 'A Time to Rise: Collective Memoirs of the Union of Democratic Filipinos (KDP).'"

75. Sidonie Smith and Julia Watson (2010, 4) use the term *life writing* to refer to "writing that takes a life, one's own or another's, as its subject. Such writing can be biographical, novelistic, historical, or explicitly self-referential and therefore autobiographical." In this case, both memoir and autobiography are instances of life writing.

76. Smith and Watson 2010, 13.

77. Smith and Watson 2010, 14 (emphasis in the original).

78. Smith and Watson 2010, 33.

79. Fine 1995, 141.

80. Nepstad 2001.

81. Cruz, Domingo, and Occena 2017, 255–57.

82. J. Taylor 2008; Schudson 1992; Doerr 2014.

83. Schiller and Fouron 1998; Shain 2005.

84. Arnone 2008, 330.

85. It was renamed Ninoy Aquino International Airport in 1987 after Senator Benigno "Ninoy" Aquino Jr., who was assassinated at the airport in 1983.

86. Arnone 2008, 326.

87. De Guzman 2016, 25–26.

88. Cruz, Domingo, and Occena 2017, 31–32.

89. De Guzman 2016, 96–97.

90. Smith and Watson 2010, 30.

91. This is the Tagalog term for Filipino street food.

92. De Guzman 2016, 153.

93. Clifford 1994, 312.

NOTES TO PAGES 145–154

94. Munson 2008.

95. Munson 2008, 55.

96. According to Doug McAdam (1986, 70), biographical availability refers to "the absence of personal constraints that may increase the costs and risks of movement participation such as full-time employment, marriage, and family responsibilities."

97. De Guzman 2016, 24.

98. De Guzman 2016, 118–19.

99. Cruz, Domingo, Occena 2017, 53.

100. Cruz, Domingo, Occena 2017, 128.

101. Constable 1999.

102. Boccagni 2010, 188.

103. Cruz, Domingo, Occena 2017, 35.

104. Cruz, Domingo, Occena 2017, 130–31.

105. Gilroy 1993.

106. "Intraethnic othering" refers to othering processes that occur among co-ethnics in subordinated groups (Pyke and Dang 2003).

107. Cruz, Domingo, Occena 2017, 57–58.

108. Cruz, Domingo, Occena 2017, 176.

109. Anthias 1998, 564 (emphasis in the original).

110. Bruneau 2010, 38.

Conclusion

1. Passed on February 13, 2003, the Philippine Overseas Voting Act allowed citizens of the Philippines currently residing or working outside the country to vote in an election.

2. Bello stated on his website (http://www.waldenbello.org/) that he is "running to promote an electoral insurgency against politics-as-usual, injustice, inequality, and corruption."

3. Ranada 2016.

4. *Quartz* (2016).

5. Aranda 2021.

6. Ranada 2016.

7. Micro-influencers are people who create content on social media, and whose opinion is well respected. They typically have between ten thousand and one hundred thousand followers and build online communities around niche audiences.

8. Ong, Tapsell, and Curato 2019.

9. Hegina 2016.

10. Thompson 2021.

11. BBC 2016.

12. Translated from Tagalog. The whole speech is available on the YouTube channel of People's Television Network, the flagship state broadcaster owned by the government of the Philippines: https://www.youtube.com/watch?v=7xTwuEWDOVE.

13. The whole speech is available on the YouTube channel of the Presidential Broadcast Staff Radio Television Malacañang, which is involved in television coverage and documentation as well as news and public affairs syndication of all the activities of the president. The link is https://www.youtube.com/watch?v=8kewxFaNifs&t=37s.

14. Ocampo 2020.
15. Tarrow 2005, 190.
16. Amenta and Polletta 2019, 291.
17. Tilly and Tarrow 2015.
18. Alexander 2003.

Appendix

1. Tucker 1965.
2. Bloom and Martin 2016.
3. Della Porta 2014.

References

Abad, Michelle. 2022. "Marcos, Sara Duterte Win Overseas Filipino Vote." *Rappler*, May 25. Available at https://www.rappler.com/nation/elections/results-presidential-vp-race-overseas-absentee-voting-2022-2/.

Abinales, Patricio N., and Donna J. Amoroso. 2017. *State and Society in the Philippines*. Lanham, MD: Rowman & Littlefield Publishers.

Abramson, Yehonatan. 2017. "Making a Homeland, Constructing a Diaspora: The Case of Taglit-Birthright Israel." *Political Geography* 58:14–23.

Abramson, Yehonatan. 2019. "Securing the Diasporic 'Self' by Travelling Abroad: Taglit-Birthright and Ontological Security." *Journal of Ethnic and Migration Studies* 45 (4): 656–73.

Accornero, Guya. 2019. "'Everything Was Possible': Emotions and Perceptions of the Past among Former Portuguese Antifascist Activists." *Mobilization: An International Quarterly* 24 (4): 439–53.

Adamson, Fiona. 2004. "Displacement, Diaspora Mobilization, and Transnational Cycles of Political Violence." In *The Maze of Fear: Security and Migration after 9/11*, edited by J. Tirman, 45–58. New York: New Press.

Adamson, Fiona B. 2012. "Constructing the Diaspora: Diaspora Identity Politics and Transnational Social Movements." In *Politics from Afar: Transnational Diasporas and Networks*, edited by T. Lyons and P. Mandaville, 25–42. New York: Columbia University Press.

Adamson, Fiona B., and Madeleine Demetriou. 2007. "Remapping the Boundaries of 'State' and 'National Identity': Incorporating Diasporas into IR Theorizing." *European Journal of International Relations* 13 (4): 489–526.

Adamson, Fiona B., and Gerasimos Tsourapas. 2020. "The Migration State in the Global South: Nationalizing, Developmental, and Neoliberal Models of Migration Management." *International Migration Review* 54 (3): 853–82.

Aguilar, Filomeno V., Jr. 2005. "Is the Filipino Diaspora a Diaspora?" *Critical Asian Studies* 47 (3): 440–61.

Aguilar, Filomeno V., Jr. 2011. "'Filibustero,' Rizal, and the Manilamen of the Nineteenth Century." *Philippine Studies* 59 (4): 429–69.

Aguilar, Filomeno V., Jr. 2014. *Migration Revolution: Philippines Nationhood and Class Relations in a Globalized Age*. Singapore: National University of Singapore Press.

Alegado, Dean T. 1991. "The Filipino Community in Hawaii: Development and Change." *Social Process in Hawaii* 33:13–38.

Alexander, Jeffrey C. 2003. *The Meanings of Social Life: A Cultural Sociology*. New York: Oxford University Press.

Alvarez, Maria Khristina, and Herbert Docena. 2022. "Pariah to President." *New Left Review*, May 26. Available at https://newleftreview.org/sidecar/posts/pariah-to-president/.

Amarasingam, Amarnath. 2015. *Pain, Pride, and Politics: Social Movement Activism and the Sri Lankan Tamil Diaspora in Canada*. Athens: University of Georgia Press.

Amenta, Edwin, and Francesca Polletta. 2019. "The Cultural Impacts of Social Movements." *Annual Review of Sociology* 45:279–99.

Anderson, Benedict. 1991. *Imagined Communities: Reflections on the Origin and Spread of Nationalism*. New York: Verso.

Anderson, Bridget. 2000. *Doing the Dirty Work? The Global Politics of Domestic Labour*. London and New York: Zed Books.

Anderson, Bridget. 2010. "Mobilizing Migrants, Making Citizens: Migrant Domestic Workers as Political Agents." *Ethnic and Racial Studies* 33 (1): 60–74.

Ang, Cheng Guan. 2010. *Southeast Asia and the Vietnam War*. London and New York: Routledge.

Anthias, Floya. 1998. "Evaluating 'Diaspora': Beyond Ethnicity." *Sociology* 32 (3): 557–80.

Aranda, Danna. 2021. "'Die-Hard Supporters': Overseas Filipino Workers' Online Grassroots Campaign for Duterte in the 2016 Philippine Elections." *Cornell International Affairs Review* 14 (Spring): 86–118.

Arguelles, Cleve Kevin Robert V. 2017. "Duterte's Other War: The Battle for EDSA People Power's Memory." In *A Duterte Reader: Critical Essays on Rodrigo Duterte's Early Presidency*, edited by N. Curato, 263–82. Ithaca, NY: Cornell University Press.

Arnone, Anna. 2008. "Journeys to Exile: The Constitution of Eritrean Identity through Narratives and Experiences." *Journal of Ethnic and Migration Studies* 34 (2): 325–40.

Arugay, Aries A. 2022. "Foreign Policy and Disinformation Narratives in the 2022 Philippine Election Campaign." *ISEAS Perspective* 59 (June 6): 1–9. Available at https://www.iseas.edu.sg/wp-content/uploads/2022/05/ISEAS_Perspective_2022_59.pdf.

Asis, Maruja B. 1992. "The Overseas Employment Program Policy." In *Philippine Labor Migration: Impact and Policy*, edited by G. Battistella and A. Paganoni, 68–112. Quezon City: Scalabrini Migration Center.

Asis, Maruja B. 2002. "Personal and Family Agendas in Migration." *Asian and Pacific Migration Journal* 11 (1): 67–93.

Assmann, Aleida, and Linda Shortt. 2012. "Memory and Political Change: Introduction." In *Memory and Political Change*, edited by A. Assmann and L. Shortt, 1–14. New York: Palgrave Macmillan.

Associated Press. 1981. "Tufts University Branch Cancels a Marcos Chair." *New York Times*, January 14, A17.

Baizas, Gaby. 2019. "Martial Law 'Peaceful'? Netizens Debate Severity of Marcos Regime." *Rappler*, September 21. Available at https://www.rappler.com/nation/martial-law-2019-social-media-reactions.

Baldassari, Delia, and Peter Bearman. 2007. "Dynamics of Political Polarization." *American Sociological Review* 72 (5): 784–811.

Baldoz, Rick. 2011. *The Third Asiatic Invasion: Empire and Migration in Filipino America, 1898–1946*. New York and London: New York University Press.

REFERENCES

Basch, Linda, Nina Glick Schiller, Christina Szanton Blanc. 1994. *Nations Unbound: Transnational Projects, Postcolonial Predicaments, and Deterritorialized Nation-States*. London and New York: Routledge.

Baser, Baher, and Ashok Swain. 2010. "Stateless Diaspora Groups and Their Repertoires of Nationalist Activism in Host Countries." *Journal of International Relations* 8 (1): 37–60.

Bauböck, Rainer. 2003. "Towards a Political Theory of Migrant Transnationalism." *International Migration Review* 37:700–723.

Bauböck, Rainer. 2010. "Cold Constellations and Hot Identities: Political Theory Questions about Transnationalism and Diaspora." In *Diaspora and Transnationalism: Concepts, Theories and Methods*, edited by R. Bauböck and T. Faist, 295–32. Amsterdam: Amsterdam University Press.

Bello, Walden. 2009. "Neoliberalism as Hegemonic Ideology in the Philippines: Rise, Apogee, and Crisis." *Philippine Sociological Review* 57:9–19.

Bello, Walden. 2022. "Why the Son of a Hated Dictator Won the Philippine Elections." *Foreign Policy in Focus*, May 18. Available at https://fpif.org/why-the-son-of-a-hated-dictator-won -the-philippine-elections/.

Bello, Walden, Herbert Docena, Marissa de Guzman, and Marylou Malig. 2005. *The Anti-Development State: The Political Economy of Permanent Crisis in the Philippines*. London and New York: Zed Books.

Berdos, Enrico. 2020. "Propaganda Web: Pro-Marcos Literature, Sites, and Online Disinformation Linked." *ABS-CBN News*, December 12. Available at https://news.abs-cbn.com/spot light/12/12/20/propaganda-web-pro-marcos-literature-sites-and-online-disinformation -linked?fbclid=IwAR3IEDa8vlK1O3zCksYTvidu6j11VhtZMQAn32GxPF33TJmYNVJ60P nAkkA.

Bernstein, Mary. 1997. "Celebration and Suppression: The Strategic Uses of Identity by the Lesbian and Gay Movement." *American Journal of Sociology* 103 (3): 531–65.

Blanc, Cristina Szanton. 1996. "Balikbayan: A Filipino Extension of the National Imaginary and of State Boundaries." *Philippine Sociological Review* 44 (1/4): 178–93.

Blaser, Arthur W. 1992. "How to Advance Human Rights without Really Trying: An Analysis of Nongovernmental Tribunals." *Human Rights Quarterly* 14 (3): 339–70.

Bloom, Joshua, and Waldo E. Martin Jr. 2016. *Black against Empire: The History and Politics of the Black Panther Party*. Oakland: University of California Press.

Boccagni, Paolo. 2010. "Private, Public or Both? On the Scope and Impact of Transnationalism in Immigrants' Everyday Lives." In *Diaspora and Transnationalism: Concepts, Theories and Methods*, edited by R. Bauböck and T. Faist, 185–203. Amsterdam: Amsterdam University Press.

Bonner, Raymond. 1988. *Waltzing with a Dictator: The Marcoses and the Making of American Policy*. New York: Vintage.

Bonus, Rick. 2000. *Locating Filipino Americans: Ethnicity and the Cultural Politics of Space*. Philadelphia: Temple University Press.

Bosco, Fernando J. 2006. "The Madres de Plaza de Mayo and Three Decades of Human Rights' Activism: Embeddedness, Emotions, and Social Movements." *Annals of the Association of American Geographers* 96 (2): 342–65.

Bourdieu, Pierre, Loic J. D. Wacquant, and Samar Farage. 1994. "Rethinking the State: Genesis and Structure of the Bureaucratic Field." *Sociological Theory* 12 (1): 1–18.

British Broadcasting Corporation (BBC). 2016. "Duterte in China: Xi Lauds 'Milestone' Duterte Visit." *BBC News*, October 20. Available at https://www.bbc.com/news/world-asia-37700409.

Broad, Robin. 1988. *Unequal Alliance: The World Bank, the International Monetary Fund, and the Philippines*. Berkeley, Los Angeles, and London: University of California Press.

Brubaker, Rogers. 2005. "The 'Diaspora' Diaspora." *Ethnic and Racial Studies* 28 (1): 1–19.

Bruneau, Michel. 2010. "Diasporas, Transnational Spaces and Communities." In *Diaspora and Transnationalism: Concepts, Theories and Methods*, edited by R. Bauböck and T. Faist, 35–50. Amsterdam: Amsterdam University Press.

Brysk, Alison. 2009. *Global Good Samaritans: Human Rights as Foreign Policy*. New York: Oxford University Press.

Buenrorstro, Iyra S., and Johann Frederick A. Cabbab. 2019. "Libraries and Their Role in Transitional Justice in the Philippines." *International Federation of Library Associations and Institutions* 45 (1): 5–15.

Bulosan, Carlos. 1973. *America Is in the Heart: A Personal History*. Seattle: University of Washington Press.

Burgess, Katrina. 2020. *Courting Migrants: How States Make Diasporas and Diasporas Make States*. New York: Oxford University Press.

Burke, Peter J., and Jan E. Stets. 2009. *Identity Theory*. New York: Oxford University Press.

Butler, Kim D. 2001. "Defining Diaspora, Refining a Discourse." *Diaspora: A Journal of Transnational Studies* 10 (2): 189–219.

Caglar, Ayse. 2006. "Hometown Associations, the Rescaling of State Spatiality and Migrant Grassroots Transnationalism." *Global Networks* 6 (1): 1–22.

Cammett, John M. 1967. *Antonio Gramsci and the Origins of Italian Communism*. Stanford, CA: Stanford University Press.

Camposano, Clement C. 2012. "Balikbayan Boxes and the Performance of Intimacy by Filipino Migrant Women in Hong Kong." *Asian and Pacific Migration Journal* 21 (1): 83–102.

Camroux, David. 2009. "Nationalizing a 'Transnational' Diaspora? The Philippine State and Filipino Emigration." In *State, Politics and Nationalism Beyond Borders: Changing Dynamics in Filipino Overseas Migration*, edited by J. V. Tigno, 49–105. Quezon City: Philippine Migrant Research Network and the Philippine Social Science Council.

Cantlupe, Joe. 1987. "Filipinos Mark a Year of No Marcos." *San Diego Union Tribune*, February 23, B-1.

Cardinoza, Gabriel. 2016. "Duterte says Marcos Was the Brightest of Them All." *Inquirer.net*, February 10. Available at https://newsinfo.inquirer.net/763290/duterte-says-marcos-was-the-brightest-of-them-all#ixzz70bercm2C.

Cariño, Benjamin V., James T. Fawcett, Robert W. Gardner, and Fred Arnold. 1990. *The New Filipino Immigrants to the United States: Increasing Diversity and Change*. Honolulu: East-West Center.

Chang, Yu-tzung, Yun-han Chu, and Chong-Min Park. 2007. "Authoritarian Nostalgia in Asia." *Journal of Democracy* 18 (3): 66–80.

Chebabi, H. E., and Juan J. Linz. 1998. "A Theory of Sultanism 1: A Type of Nondemocratic Rule." in *Sultanistic Regimes*, edited by H. E. Chebabi and J. J. Linz, 3–25. Baltimore: Johns Hopkins University Press.

Chee, Liberty. 2020. " 'Supermaids': Hyper-resilient Subjects in Neoliberal Migration Governance." *International Political Sociology* 14:366–81.

REFERENCES

Cheng, Edmund W., and Samson Yuen. 2019. "Memory in Movement: Collective Identity and Memory Contestation in Hong Kong's Tiananmen Vigils." *Mobilization: An International Quarterly* 24 (4): 419–37.

Chew, Ron. 2012. *Remembering Silme Domingo and Gene Viernes: The Legacy of Filipino American Labor Activism.* Seattle: Alaskero Foundation and University of Washington Press.

Cheyette, Bryan. 2013. *Diasporas of the Mind: Jewish and Postcolonial Writing and the Nightmare of History.* New Haven, CT, and London: Yale University Press.

Choy, Catherine Ceniza. 2003. *Empire of Care: Nursing and Migration in Filipino American History.* Durham, NC: Duke University Press.

Claudio, Lisandro E. 2010. "Memories of the Anti-Marcos Movement: The Left and the Mnemonic Dynamics of the Post-Authoritarian Philippines." *South East Asia Research* 18 (1): 33–66.

Clifford, James. 1994. "Diasporas." *Cultural Anthropology* 9 (3): 302–38.

CNN Philippines Staff. 2016. "Duterte Confirms Marcos Burial at the Libingan ng mga Bayani." *CNN*, August 7. Available at https://cnnphilippines.com/news/2016/08/07/marcos-libingan -ng-mga-bayani-burial.html.

CNN Philippines Staff. 2018. "Globe, PAL Welcome Returning OFWs with Special Christmas Treats." *CNN*, December 26. Available at https://www.cnnphilippines.com/business /2018/12/25/globe-philippine-airlines-globe-balikbayan-a-wonderful-christmas-reunion .html.

Cohen, Robin. 1997. *Global Diasporas: An Introduction.* Seattle: University of Washington Press.

Collins, Randall. 2001. "Social Movements and the Focus on Emotional Attention." In *Passionate Politics: Emotions and Social Movements*, edited by J. Goodwin, J. M. Jasper, and F. Polletta, 27–44. Chicago: University of Chicago Press.

Concepcion, Mary Grace R. 2018. "Writing the Self and Exigencies of Survival: Autobiography as Catharsis and Commemoration." *Philippine Studies: Historical and Ethnographic Viewpoints* 66 (3): 301–34.

Congress of the Philippines. 1989. Republic Act No. 6768: An Act Instituting a Balikbayan Program. Approved on November 3.

Constable, Nicole. 1999. "At Home but Not at Home: Filipina Narratives of Ambivalent Returns." *Cultural Anthropology* 14 (2): 203–28.

Constable, Nicole. 2007. *Maid to Order in Hong Kong: Stories of Migrant Workers.* Ithaca, NY, and London: Cornell University Press.

Constantino, Renato. 2008. *A History of the Philippines: From the Spanish Colonization to the Second World War.* New York: Monthly Review Press.

Conway, Brian. 2010. "New Directions in the Sociology of Collective Memory and Commemoration." *Sociology Compass* 4 (7): 442–53.

Cordova, Fred. 1983. *Filipinos: Forgotten Asian Americans.* Seattle: Demonstration Project for Asian Americans.

Coronel, Sheila. 2022. "The Triumph of Marcos Dynasty Disinformation Is a Warning to the U.S." *New Yorker*, May 17. Available at https://www.newyorker.com/news/dispatch/the-triumph -of-marcos-dynasty-disinformation-is-a-warning-to-the-us.

Coser, Lewis. 1964. *The Functions of Social Conflict.* Glencoe, IL: Free Press.

Commission on Filipinos Overseas (CFO). 2019. Number of Registered Filipino Emigrants by Major Country of Destination: 1981–2019. Available at https://cfo.gov.ph/wp-content/up loads/2021/07/Emigrant-1981-2019-MajorCountry.xlsx.

Coy, Patrick G., Lynne M. Woehrle, and Gregory M. Maney. 2008. "Discursive Legacies: The U.S. Peace Movement and 'Support the Troops.'" *Social Problems* 55 (2): 161–89.

Cruz, Rene Ciria, Cindy Domingo, and Bruce Occena, eds. 2017. *A Time to Rise: Collective Memoirs of the Union of Democratic Filipinos (KDP)*. Seattle: University of Washington Press.

Damokosh, Emma. 2016. "History on the Hill: The Cannon." *Tufts Daily*, November 28. Available at https://tuftsdaily.com/features/2016/11/28/history-on-the-hill-the-cannon/.

Dañguilan Vitug, Marites, and Glenda M. Gloria. 2000. *Under the Crescent Moon: Rebellion in Mindanao*. Quezon City: Institute for Popular Democracy.

Daniels, Roger. 2004. *Guarding the Golden Door: American Immigration Policy and Immigrants since 1882*. New York: Hill and Wang.

Daphi, Priska, and Lorenzo Zamponi. 2019. "Exploring the Movement-Memory Nexus: Insights and Ways Forward." *Mobilization: An International Quarterly* 24 (4): 399–417.

de Guzman, Mila. 2016. *Women against Marcos: Stories of Filipino and Filipino American Women Who Fought a Dictator*. San Francisco: Carayan Press.

de Jong, Alex. 2022. "Philippines: A Continuity of Violence." *Against the Current*, September/October 2022. Available at https://againstthecurrent.org/atc220/philippines-continuity-of -violence/.

della Porta, Donatella. 2014. "Life Histories." In *Methodological Practices in Social Movement Research*, edited by D. della Porta, 262–88. New York: Oxford University Press.

De Vera, Arleen. 1994. "Without Parallel: The Local 7 Deportation Cases, 1949–1955." *Amerasia Journal* 20 (2): 1–25.

DeWind, Josh, and Renata Segura. 2014. "Diaspora-Government Relations in Forging US Foreign Policies." In *Diaspora Lobbies and the US Government: Convergence and Divergence in Making Foreign Policy*, edited by J. DeWind and R. Segura, 3–28. New York: Social Science Research Council and New York University Press.

DeWitt, Howard A. 1979. "The Watsonville Anti-Filipino Riot of 1930: A Case Study of the Great Depression and Ethnic Conflict in California." *Southern California Quarterly* 61 (3): 291–302.

Doerr, Nicole. 2014. "Memory and Culture in Social Movements." In *Conceptualizing Culture in Social Movement Research*, edited by B. Baumgarthen, P. Daphi, and P. Ulrich. New York: Palgrave Macmillan.

Domingo, Ligaya. 2010. "Building a Movement: Filipino American Union and Community Organizing in Seattle in the 1970s." PhD dissertation, Department of Education, University of California, Berkeley.

Dufoix, Stéphane. 2003. *Diasporas*. Berkeley, Los Angeles, and London: University of California Press.

Durkheim, Émile. 1995. *The Elementary Forms of Religious Life*. New York: Free Press.

Earl, Jennifer. 2004. "The Cultural Consequences of Social Movements." In *The Blackwell Companion to Social Movements*, edited by D. A. Snow, S. A. Soule, and H. Kriesi, 508–30. Malden, MA: Blackwell Publishing.

Edwards, Brent Hayes. 2001. "The Uses of *Diaspora*." *Social Text* 19 (1): 45–73.

Encinas-Franco, Jean. 2013. "The Language of Labor Export in Political Discourse: 'Modern-Day Heroism' and Constructions of Overseas Filipino Workers (OFWs)." *Philippine Political Science Journal* 34 (1): 97–112.

REFERENCES

Espiritu, Augusto. 2009. "Journeys of Discovery and Difference: Transnational Politics and the Union of Democratic Filipinos." In *The Transnational Politics of Asian Americans*, edited by C. Collet and P. Lien, 38–55. Philadelphia: Temple University Press.

Espiritu, Yen Le. 1995. *Filipino American Lives*. Philadelphia: Temple University Press.

Espiritu, Yen Le. 1996. "Colonial Oppression, Labour Importation, and Group Formation: Filipinos in the United States." *Ethnic and Racial Studies* 19 (1): 29–48.

Espiritu, Yen Le. 2003. *Home Bound: Filipino American Lives across Cultures, Communities, and Countries*. Berkeley, Los Angeles, and London: University of California Press.

Evans, Sara M., and Harry C. Boyte. 1992. *Free Spaces: The Sources of Democratic Change in America*. Chicago: University of Chicago Press.

Eyerman, Ron. 2004. "The Past in the Present: Culture and the Transmission of Memory." *Acta Sociologica* 47 (2): 159–69.

Eyerman, Ron. 2016. "Social Movements and Memory." In *Routledge International Handbook of Memory Studies*, edited by A. L. Tota and T. Hagen, 79–83. New York: Routledge.

Fanon, Frantz. 2004. *The Wretched of the Earth*. New York: Grove Press.

Fantasia, Rick. 1988. *Cultures of Solidarity: Consciousness, Action, and Contemporary American Workers*. Berkeley, Los Angeles, and London: University of California Press.

Feeney, William R. 1984. "The United States and the Philippines: The Bases Dilemma." *Asian Affairs* 10 (4): 63–85.

Ferguson, Laura. 2018. "A Tale of Two Protests." *Tufts Now*, October 19. Available at https://now.tufts.edu/articles/tale-two-protests.

Filipino Express. 2008. "FilAms Remember EDSA with Ouster Call." *Filipino Express*, February 29. Available at https://search.proquest.com/docview/212512865?accountid=7379.

Fine, Gary Alan. 1995. "Public Narration and Group Culture." In *Social Movements and Culture*, edited by H. Johnston and B. Klandermans, 127–43. Minneapolis: University of Minnesota Press.

Fine, Gary Alan. 2012. *Tiny Publics: A Theory of Group Action and Culture*. New York: Russell Sage Foundation.

Fitzgerald, David. 2008. "Colonies of the Little Motherland: Membership, Space, and Time in Mexican Migrant Hometown Associations." *Comparative Studies in Society and History* 50 (1): 145–69.

Flores, Eddie, and Orquid Valenzuela. 2007. "The Berghaus Girls." *Munting Nayon News Magazine*, November. Available at http://www.muntingnayon.com/100/100205/.

Flores-Valenzuela, Orquidia. 2007. "History of the Filipino Community in the Netherlands." *Munting Nayon News Magazine*, August 31. Available at http://www.muntingnayon.com/page/100214/.

Foa, Sylvana. 1983. "President Ferdinand Marcos, Shaken by the Worst Anti-Government Rioting . . ." *UPI*, September 22. Available at https://www.upi.com/Archives/1983/09/22/President-Ferdinand-Marcos-shaken-by-the-worst-anti-government-rioting/5576433051200/.

Fominaya, Cristina Flesher. 2019. "Collective Identity in Social Movements: Assessing the Limits of a Theoretical Framework." In *The Wiley Blackwell Companion to Social Movements*, edited by D. A. Snow, S. A. Soule, H. Kriesi, and H. J. McCammon, 429–45. Hoboken, NJ: Wiley Blackwell.

Foner, Nancy. 1997. "What's New about Transnationalism? New York Immigrants Today and at the Turn of the Century." *Diaspora: A Journal of Transnational Studies* 6 (3): 355–75.

Foucault, Michel, and Donald F. Bouchard. 1977. *Language, Counter-Memory, Practice: Selected Essays and Interviews*. Ithaca, NY: Cornell University Press.

Francisco-Menchavez, Valerie. 2018. *The Labor of Care: Filipina Migrants and Transnational Families in the Digital Age*. Urbana, Chicago, and Springfield: University of Illinois Press.

Fresnoza-Flot, Asuncion. 2009. "Migration Status and Transnational Mothering: The Case of Filipino Migrants in France." *Global Networks* 9 (2): 252–70.

Fresnoza-Flot, Asuncion. 2010. "The Catholic Church in the Lives of Irregular Migrant Filipinas in France: Identity Formation, Empowerment and Social Control." *Asia Pacific Journal of Anthropology* 11 (3–4): 345–61.

Friday, Chris. 1994. *Organizing Asian-American Labor: The Pacific Coast Canned-Salmon Industry, 1870–1942*. Philadelphia: Temple University Press.

Friedman, Debra, and Doug McAdam. 1992. "Collective Identity and Activism." In *Frontiers in Social Movement Theory*, edited by A. D. Morris and C. M. Mueller, 156–73. New Haven, CT, and London: Yale University Press.

Fuentecilla, Jose V. 2013. *Fighting from a Distance: How Filipino Exiles Toppled a Dictator*. Urbana, Chicago, and Springfield: University of Illinois Press.

Fujita-Rony, Dorothy B. 2003. *American Workers, Colonial Power: Philippine Seattle and the Transpacific West, 1919–1941*. Berkeley and Los Angeles: University of California Press.

Furuyama, Katie, and David S. Meyer. 2011. "Sources of Certification and Civil Rights Advocacy Organizations: The JACL, the NAACP, and Crises of Legitimacy." *Mobilization: An International Quarterly* 16 (1): 101–16.

Futrell, Robert, and Pete Simi. 2004. "Free Spaces, Collective Identity, and the Persistence of U.S. White Power Activism." *Social Problems* 51 (1): 16–42.

Gaerlan, Barbara S. 1999. "The Movement in the United States to Oppose Martial Law in the Philippines, 1972–1991: An Overview." *Pilipinas* 33:75–98.

Gamlen, Alan. 2014. "Diaspora Institutions and Diaspora Governance." *International Migration Review* 48(S1): S180–S217.

Gamson, Joshua. 1997. "Messages of Exclusion: Gender, Movements, and Symbolic Boundaries." *Gender & Society* 11 (2): 178–99.

Gamson, William A. 1992. "The Social Psychology of Collective Action." In *Frontiers in Social Movement Theory*, edited by A. D. Morris and C. Mueller, 53–76. New Haven, CT: Yale University Press.

Gamson, William A. 1995. "Constructing Social Protest." In *Social Movements and Culture*, edited by H. Johnston and B. Klandermans, 85–106. Minneapolis: University of Minnesota Press.

Ganz, Marshall. 2000. "Resources and Resourcefulness: Strategic Capacity in the Unionization of California Agriculture, 1959–1966." *American Journal of Sociology* 105 (4): 1003–62.

Garrido, Marco 2021. "Democracy as Disorder: Institutionalized Sources of Democratic Ambivalence among the Upper and Middle Class in Manila." *Social Forces* 99 (3): 1036–59.

Gavilan, Jodesz. 2016. "What Typhoon Yolanda Foreign Aid Looks Like without US, EU, and UN." *Rappler*, October 9. Available at https://www.rappler.com/newsbreak/iq/148685-united-nations-european-union-united-states-foreign-aid-philippines-typhoon-yolanda/.

Ghorashi, Halleh. 2005. "Agents of Change or Passive Victims: The Impact of Welfare States (the Case of the Netherlands) on Refugees." *Journal of Refugee Studies* 18 (2): 181–98.

Gilroy, Paul. 1993. *The Black Atlantic: Modernity and Double Consciousness*. New York: Verso.

Goffman, Erving. 1959. *The Presentation of Self in Everyday Life*. New York: Doubleday.

Gongaware, Timothy. 2003. "Collective Memories and Collective Identities: Maintaining Unity in Native American Educational Social Movements." *Journal of Contemporary Ethnography* 32 (5): 483–520.

REFERENCES

Gongaware, Timothy B. 2010. "Collective Memory Anchors: Collective Identity and Continuity in Social Movements." *Sociological Focus* 43 (3): 214–39.

Gramsci, Antonio. 1971. *Selections from the Prison Notebooks*. New York: International Publishers.

Guevarra, Anna Romina. 2010. *Marketing Dreams, Manufacturing Heroes: The Transnational Labor Brokering of Filipino Workers*. New Brunswick, NJ, and London: Rutgers University Press.

Gutman, Yifat. 2017. *Memory Activism: Reimagining the Past for the Future in Israel-Palestine*. Nashville, TN: Vanderbilt University Press.

Habal, Estella. 2007. *San Francisco's International Hotel: Mobilizing the Filipino American Community in the Anti-Eviction Movement*. Philadelphia: Temple University Press.

Hagimoto, Koichi. 2013. *Between Empires: Martí, Rizal, and the Intercolonial Alliance*. New York: Palgrave Macmillan.

Halbwachs, Maurice. 1992. *On Collective Memory*. Chicago: University of Chicago Press.

Hall, Stuart. 1990. "Cultural Identity and Diaspora." In *Identity: Community, Culture, Difference*, edited by J. Rutherford, 222–37. London: Lawrence & Wishart.

Haney, Patrick J., and Walt Vanderbush. 1999. "The Role of Ethnic Interest Groups in U.S. Foreign Policy: The Case of the Cuban American National Foundation." *International Studies Quarterly* 43 (2): 341–61.

Hanley, Teresa, Rusty Binas, Julian Murray, and Baltz Tribunalo. 2014. IASC Inter-Agency Humanitarian Evaluation of the Typhoon Haiyan Response, Prepared on Behalf of the Inter-Agency Humanitarian Evaluation Steering Group, October, UN, New York. Available at https://interagencystandingcommittee.org/system/files/evaluation_report_iahe_haiyan_december_2016.pdf.

Harvey, David. 2007. *A Brief History of Neoliberalism*. New York: Oxford University Press.

Hashimoto, Akiko. 2015. *The Long Defeat: Cultural Trauma, Memory, and Identity in Japan*. New York: Oxford University Press.

Hawes, Gary. 1987. *The Philippines State and the Marcos Regime: The Politics of Export*. Ithaca, NY: Cornell University Press.

Hegina, Aries Joseph. 2016. "Duterte, Marcos Win Overseas Voting." *Philippine Daily Inquirer*, May 15. Available at http://newsinfo.inquirer.net/785664/duterte-marcos-win-overseas-voting.

Hess, Monika, and Benedikt Korf. 2014. "Tamil Diaspora and the Political Spaces of Second-Generation Activism in Switzerland." *Global Networks* 14 (4): 419–37.

Hirschman, Charles. 2004. "The Role of Religion in the Origins and Adaptation of Immigrant Groups in the United States." *International Migration Review* 38 (3): 1206–33.

Hoebnik, Paul. 1999. "The Humanitarianisation of the Foreign Aid Programme in the Netherlands." *European Journal of Development Research* 11 (1): 176–202.

Holland, Laurel L., and Sherry Cable. 2002. "Reconceptualizing Social Movement Abeyance: The Role of Internal Processes and Culture in Cycles of Movement Abeyance and Resurgence." *Sociological Focus* 35 (3): 297–314.

Hondagneu-Sotelo, Pierrette. 1992. "Overcoming Patriarchal Constraints: The Reconstruction of Gender Relations among Mexican Immigrant Women and Men." *Gender & Society* 6 (3): 393–415.

Hondagneu-Sotelo, Pierette. 2001. *Doméstica: Immigrant Workers Cleaning and Caring in the Shadows of Affluence*. Berkeley, Los Angeles, London: University of California Press.

Hosoda, Naomi. 2013. "Kababayan Solidarity? Filipino Communities and Class Relations in United Arab Emirates Cities." *Journal of Arabian Studies* 3 (1): 18–35.

Hosoda, Naomi, and Akiko Watanabe. 2014. "Creating a 'New Home' Away from Home: Religious Conversions of Filipina Domestic Workers in Dubai and Doha." In *Migrant Domestic Workers in the Middle East: The Home and the World*, edited by B. Fernandez and M. de Regt, 118–39. New York: Palgrave Macmillan.

Houston, Serin, and Richard Wright. 2003. "Making and Remaking Tibetan Diasporic Identities." *Social & Cultural Geography* 4 (2): 217–32.

Hsia, Hsiao-Chuan. 2009. "The Making of a Transnational Grassroots Migrant Movement: A Case Study of Hong Kong's Asian Migrants' Coordinating Body." *Critical Asian Studies* 41 (1): 113–41.

Ignacio, Emily Noelle. 2005. *Building Diaspora: Filipino Community Formation on the Internet.* New Brunswick, NJ, and London: Rutgers University Press.

Inquirer.net US Bureau. 2016. "LA Filipino WWII Vets Group Opposes Marcos Burial at Libingan." *Inquirer.net*, August 18. Available at https://globalnation.inquirer.net/142865/la-filipino-wwii-vets-group-opposes-marcos-burial-at-libingan.

International Organization for Migration (IOM). 2019. *World Migration Report 2020.* Geneva: International Organization for Migration.

Jansen, Robert S. 2007. "Resurrection and Appropriation: Reputational Trajectories, Memory Work, and the Political Use of Historical Figure." *American Journal of Sociology* 112 (4): 953–1007.

Jasper, James M. 1997. *The Art of Moral Protest: Culture, Biography, and Creativity in Social Movements.* Chicago: University of Chicago Press.

Jasper, James M. 2004. "A Strategic Approach to Collective Action: Looking for Agency in Social Movement Choices." *Mobilization: An International Journal* 9 (1): 1–16.

Jasper, James M. 2012. "Choice Points, Emotional Batteries, and Other Ways to Find Strategic Agency at the Microlevel." In *Strategies for Social Change*, edited by G. M. Maney, R. V. Kutz-Flamenbaum, D. A. Rohlinger, and J. Goodwin, 23–42. Minneapolis: University of Minnesota Press.

Jasper, James M. 2018. *The Emotions of Protest.* Chicago: University of Chicago Press.

Jedlowski, Paolo. 2001. "Memory and Sociology: Themes and Issues." *Time & Society* 10 (1): 29–44.

Jerne, Christina. 2020. "Event-Making the Past: Commemorations as Social Movement Catalysts." *Memory Studies* 13 (4): 486–501.

Johnston, Hank, and Bert Klandermans. 1995. "The Cultural Analysis of Social Movements." In *Social Movements and Culture*, edited by H. Johnston and B. Klandermans, 3–24. Minneapolis: University of Minnesota Press.

Jones-Correa, Michael. 1998. *Between Two Nations: The Political Predicament of Latinos in New York City.* Ithaca, NY, and London: Cornell University Press.

Kang, David C. 2002. *Crony Capitalism: Corruption and Development in South Korea and the Philippines.* Cambridge: Cambridge University Press.

Karpathakis, Anna. 1999. "Home Society Politics and Immigrant Political Incorporation: The Case of Greek Immigrants in New York City." *International Migration Review* 33 (1): 55–78.

Kasinitz, Philip, Mary C. Waters, John H. Mollenkopf, and Merih Anil. 2002. "Transnationalism and the Children of Immigrants in Contemporary New York." In *The Changing Face of Home: The Transnational Lives of the Second Generation*, edited by P. Levitt and M. C. Waters, 96–122. New York: Russell Sage Foundation.

REFERENCES

Keck, Margaret E., and Kathryn Sikkink. 1998. *Activists beyond Borders: Advocacy Networks in International Politics*. Ithaca, NY, and London: Cornell University Press.

Kelner, Shaul. 2010. *Tours That Bind: Diaspora, Pilgrimage, and Israeli Birthright Tourism*. New York: New York University Press.

Klandermans, Bert, and Sjoerd Goslinga. 1996. "Media Discourse, Movement Publicity, and the Generation of Collective Action Frames: Theoretical and Empirical Exercises in Meaning Construction." In *Comparative Perspectives on Social Movements: Political Opportunities, Mobilizing Structures, and Cultural Framings*, edited by D. McAdam, J. D. McCarthy, and M. N. Zald, 312–37. New York: Cambridge University Press.

Klandermans, Bert, and Jacquelien van Stekelenburg. 2019. "Identity Formation in Street Demonstrations." In *Identities in Everyday Life*, edited by J. E. Stets and R. T. Serpe, 309–27. New York: Oxford University Press.

Klandermans, P. G. 2014. "Identity Politics and Politicized Identities: Identity Processes and the Dynamics of Protest." *Political Psychology* 35 (1): 1–22.

Knight, Michael. 1977. "Marcos Grant Is Protested at Tufts." *New York Times*, December 11, 42.

Koinova, Maria. 2010. "Diasporas and International Politics: Utilising the Universalistic Creed of Liberalism for Particularistic and Nationalist Purposes." In *Diaspora and Transnationalism: Concepts, Theories and Methods*, edited by R. Bauböck and T. Faist, 149–66. Amsterdam: Amsterdam University Press.

Koinova, Maria. 2018. "Sending States and Diaspora Positionality in International Relations." *International Political Sociology* 12:190–210.

Koinova, Maria, and Dženeta Karabegović. 2017. "Diasporas and Transitional Justice: Transnational Activism from Local to Global Levels of Engagement." *Global Networks* 17 (2): 212–33.

Komite ng Sambayanang Pilipino. 1981. *Philippines: Repression and Resistance (Permanent People's Tribunal on the Philippines)*. Kent: Whitstable Litho.

Kundnani, Hans, Chris Morris, and John Hooper. 1999. "Military Action and Three Deaths after Ocalan's Capture." *Guardian*, February 18. Available at https://www.theguardian.com /world/1999/feb/18/kurds.johnhooper.

Kusaka, Wataru. 2020. "Duterte's Disciplinary Quarantine: How a Moral Dichotomy Was Constructed and Undermined." *Philippine Studies: Historical and Ethnographic Viewpoints* 68 (3–4): 423–42.

Lachica, Eduardo. 1979. "Filipino Exiles Keep Opposition Movement Alive in U.S." *Asian Wall Street Journal*, June 27, 1.

Lacroix, Thomas, and Elena Fiddian-Qasmiyeh. 2013. "Refugee and Diaspora Memories: The Politics of Remembering and Forgetting." *Journal of Intercultural Studies* 34 (6): 684–96.

Landolt, Patricia. 2008. "The Transnational Geographies of Immigrant Politics: Insights from a Comparative Study of Migrant Grassroots Organizing." *Sociological Quarterly* 49 (1): 53–77.

Lee, Terence. 2015. *Defect or Defend: Military Responses to Popular Protests in Authoritarian Asia*. Baltimore: Johns Hopkins University Press.

Lescaze, Lee. 1977. "Value of Philippines Air Base Questioned." *Washington Post*, April 10, 2.

Levitt, Peggy. 2001. *The Transnational Villagers*. Berkeley and Los Angeles: University of California Press.

Levitt, Peggy, and Mary C. Waters. 2002. "Introduction." In *The Changing Face of Home: The Transnational Lives of the Second Generation*, edited by P. Levitt and M. C. Waters, 1–30. New York: Russell Sage Foundation.

Liebelt, Claudia. 2008. "'We Are the Jews of Today': Filipino Domestic Workers in Israel and the Language of Diaspora." *HAGAR Studies in Culture, Polity and Identities* 8 (1): 105–28.

Lipsitz, George. 1990. *Time Passages: Collective Memory and American Popular Culture*. Minneapolis: University of Minnesota Press.

Liu, John M., Paul M. Ong, and Carolyn Rosenstein. 1991. "Dual Chain Migration: Post-1965 Filipino Immigration to the United States." *International Migration Review* 25 (3): 487–513.

Liu, Michael, and Kim Geron. 2008. "Changing Neighborhood: Ethnic Enclaves and the Struggle for Social Justice." *Social Justice* 35 (2): 18–35.

Lowe, Lisa. 1996. *Immigrant Acts: On Asian American Cultural Politics*. Durham, NC, and London: Duke University Press.

Lyons, Terrence, and Peter Mandaville. 2012. "Introduction: Politics from Afar; Transnational Diasporas and Networks." In *Politics from Afar: Transnational Diasporas and Networks*, edited by T. Lyons and P. Mandaville, 1–23. New York: Columbia University Press.

Maas, Marisha. 2011. "Filipino Immigrant Entrepreneurship in the Netherlands: Beyond Business." PhD dissertation, Department of Geography, Radboud University, Nijmegen, The Netherlands.

Mabalon, Dawn Bohulano. 2013. *Little Manila Is in the Heart: The Making of the Filipina/o American Community in Stockton, California*. Durham, NC, and London: Duke University Press.

Manalansan, Martin F., IV. 2003. *Global Divas: Filipino Gay Men in the Diaspora*. Durham, NC, and London: Duke University Press.

Manapat, Ricardo. 2020. *Some Are Smarter Than Others: The History of Marcos' Crony Capitalism*. Quezon City: Ateneo de Manila University Press.

Maney, Gregory M., Kenneth T. Andrew, Rachel V. Kutz-Flamenbaum, Deana A. Rohlinger, and Jeff Goodwin. 2012. "An Introduction to Strategies for Social Change." In *Strategies for Social Change*, edited by G. M. Maney, R. V. Kutz-Flamenbaum, D. A. Rohlinger, and J. Goodwin, xi–xxxviii. Minneapolis: University of Minnesota Press.

Mangaoang, Gil. 1994. "From the 1970s to the 1990s: Perspectives of a Gay Filipino American Activist." *Amerasia* 20 (1): 33–44.

Manglapus, Raul S. 1986. *A Pen for Democracy*. Washington, DC: Movement for a Free Philippines.

Mannheim, Karl. 1970. "The Problem of Generations." *Psychoanalytic Review* 57 (3): 378–404.

Martinez, Lisa M. 2010. "Politicizing the Family: How Grassroots Organizations Mobilize Latinos for Political Action in Colorado." *Latino Studies* 8 (4): 463–84.

Marx, Karl, and Friedrich Engels. 1998. *The German Ideology*. Amherst, NY: Prometheus Books.

Mathews, Jay. 1976. "U.S. Bases Adjust to a New Philippine Era." *Washington Post*, July 11, A15.

Mavroudi, Elizabeth. 2007a. "Diaspora as Process: (De)Constructing Boundaries." *Geography Compass* 1 (3): 467–79.

Mavroudi, Elizabeth. 2007b. "Learning to Be Palestinian in Athens: Constructing National Identities in Diaspora." *Global Networks* 7 (4): 392–411.

Mavroudi, Elizabeth. 2018. "Deconstructing Diasporic Mobilisation at a Time of Crisis: Perspectives from the Palestinian and Greek Diasporas." *Journal of Ethnic and Migration Studies* 44 (8): 1309–24.

McAdam, Doug. 1982. *Political Process and the Development of Black Insurgency, 1930–1970*. Chicago: University of Chicago Press.

McAdam, Doug. 1986. "Recruitment to High-Risk Activism: The Case of Freedom Summer." *American Journal of Sociology* 92 (1): 64–90.

McAdam, Doug, John D. McCarthy, and Mayer N. Zald. 1996. "Introduction: Opportunities, Mobilizing Structures, and Framing Processes—Toward a Synthetic, Comparative Perspec-

REFERENCES

tive on Social Movements." In *Comparative Perspectives on Social Movements: Political Opportunities, Mobilizing Structures, and Cultural Framings*, edited by D. McAdam, J. D. McCarthy, and M. N. Zald, 1–22. New York: Cambridge University Press.

McAdam, Doug, Sidney Tarrow, and Charles Tilly. 2001. *Dynamics of Contention*. New York: Cambridge University Press.

McCallum, Derrace Garfield. 2021. "Affectionate Remittances: Materialism and Care in Filipino Transnational Families in Japan." *Current Sociology*, DOI: 10.1177/00113921211034895.

McCarthy, John D., and Mayer N. Zald. 1977. "Resource Mobilization and Social Movements: A Partial Theory." *American Journal of Sociology* 82 (6): 1212–41.

McKay, Steven C. 2007. "Filipino Sea Men: Constructing Masculinities in an Ethnic Labour Niche." *Journal of Ethnic and Migration Studies* 33 (4): 617–33.

Melucci, Alberto. 1989. *Nomads of the Present: Social Movements and Individual Needs in Contemporary Society*. Philadelphia: Temple University Press.

Melucci, Alberto. 1995. "The Process of Collective Identity." In *Social Movements and Culture*, edited by H. Johnston and B. Klandermans, 41–63. Minneapolis: University of Minnesota Press.

Memmott, Mark. 2013. "Estimate of Number Left Homeless by Typhoon Soars." NPR, November 16. Available at https://www.npr.org/sections/thetwo-way/2013/11/16/245584484/shattered-but-not-shuttered-hospital-survived-typhoon-haiyan.

Mendoza, Gemma B. 2019. "Networked Propaganda: False Narratives from the Marcos Arsenal." *Rappler*, November 22. Available at https://www.rappler.com/newsbreak/investigative/networked-propaganda-false-narratives-from-the-marcos-arsenal.

Mendoza, S. Lily. 2002. *Between the Home and the Diaspora: The Politics of Theorizing Filipino and Filipino American Identities*. New York: Routledge.

Menjívar, Cecilia. 1999. "Religious Institutions and Transnationalism: A Case Study of Catholic and Evangelical Salvadoran Immigrants." *International Journal of Politics, Culture, and Society* 12 (4): 589–612.

Mercer, Kobena. 2016. *Travel and See: Black Diaspora Art Practices since the 1980s*. Durham, NC, and London: Duke University Press.

Meyer, David S., and Suzanne Staggenborg. 2012. "Thinking about Strategy." In *Strategies for Social Change*, edited by G. M. Maney, R. V. Kutz-Flamenbaum, D. A. Rohlinger, and J. Goodwin, 3–22. Minneapolis: University of Minnesota Press.

Miller, Arpi. 2011. "'Doing' Transnationalism: The Integrative Impact of Salvadoran Cross-Border Activism." *Journal of Ethnic and Migration Studies* 37 (1): 43–60.

Mills, C. Wright. 2000. *The Sociological Imagination*. New York: Oxford University Press.

Min, Pyong Gap. 1992. "The Structure and Social Functions of Korean Immigrant Churches in the United States." *International Migration Review* 26 (4): 1370–94.

Misra Joya, Jonathan Woodring, and Sabine N. Merz. 2006. "The Globalization of Care Work: Neoliberal Economic Restructuring and Migration Policy." *Globalizations* 3 (3): 317–32.

Mojares, Resil B. 2011. "The Itineraries of Mariano Ponce." In *Traveling Nation-Makers: Transnational Flows and Movements in the Making of Modern Southeast Asia*, 32–63. Singapore and Kyoto: National University of Singapore Press and Kyoto University Press.

Molden, Berthold. 2016. "Resistant Pasts versus Mnemonic Hegemony: On the Power Relations of Collective Memory." *Memory Studies* 9 (2): 125–42.

Montecillo, Paolo G. 2014. "OFW Remittances Rose 5.9% to $1.8B in January—BSP." *Philippine Daily Inquirer*, March 17. Available at https://globalnation.inquirer.net/100539/ofw-remittances-rose-5-9-to-1-8b-in-january-bsp.

Morris, Aldon, and Naomi Braine. 2001. "Social Movements and Oppositional Consciousness." In *Oppositional Consciousness: The Subjective Roots of Social Protest*, edited by J. Mansbridge and A. Morris, 20–37. Chicago: University of Chicago Press.

Moss, Dana M. 2016. "Transnational Repression, Diaspora Mobilization and the Case of the Arab Spring." *Social Problems* 63 (4): 480–98.

Moss, Dana M. 2022. *The Arab Spring Abroad: Diaspora Activism against Authoritarian Regimes*. Cambridge and New York: Cambridge University Press.

Mügge, Liza. 2010. *Beyond Dutch Borders: Transnational Politics among Colonial Migrants, Guest Workers and the Second Generation*. Amsterdam: Amsterdam University Press.

Munson, Ziad W. 2008. *The Making of Pro-Life Activists: How Social Movement Mobilization Works*. Chicago: University of Chicago Press.

Nadeau, Kathy. 1999. "A Basic Ecclesial Community in Cebu." *Philippine Studies* 47 (1): 77–99.

National Disaster and Risk Reduction Management Council (NDRRMC). 2013. Final Report re: Effects of Typhoon "Yolanda" (Haiyan), NDRRMC Update, November 6–9. Available at http://ndrrmc.gov.ph/attachments/article/1329/FINAL_REPORT_re_Effects_of_Typhoon _YOLANDA_HAIYAN_06–09NOV2013.pdf.

Nepstad, Sharon Erickson. 2001. "Creating Transnational Solidarity: The Use of Narrative in the U.S.–Central America Peace Movement." *Mobilization: An International Quarterly* 6 (1): 21–36.

Nepstad, Sharon Erickson. 2004. *Convictions of the Soul: Religion, Culture, and Agency in the Central America Solidarity Movement*. New York: Oxford University Press.

New York Times. 1976. "Bidding of Bases." *New York Times*, December 3, A26.

New York Times. 1977. "Human Rights: Deeds as Well as Words." *New York Times*, February 27, 16.

Ngai, Mae M. 2004. *Impossible Subjects: Illegal Aliens and the Making of Modern America*. Princeton, NJ: Princeton University Press.

Nicholls, Walter J. 2013. *The DREAMers: How the Undocumented Youth Movement Transformed the Immigrant Rights Debate*. Stanford, CA: Stanford University Press.

Nicholls, Walter J., and Justus Uitermark. 2017. *Cities and Social Movements: Immigrant Rights Activism in the United States, France, and the Netherlands, 1970–2015*. West Sussex: Wiley Blackwell.

Ocampo, Anthony C. 2020. "I Went to a 'Filipinos for Trump' Rally. Here's What I Found." *Colorlines*, October 16. Available at https://www.colorlines.com/articles/i-went-filipinos-trump -rally-heres-what-i-found.

Ochoa, Cecile C., and Nimfa Rueda. 2016. "For 'Kontra Libing' Protesters in Los Angeles, It's Personal." *Inquirer.net*, September 9. Available at https://globalnation.inquirer.net/144437 /for-kontra-libing-protesters-in-los-angeles-its-personal.

Okamura, Jonathan Y. 1998. *Imagining the Filipino American Diaspora: Transnational Relations, Identities, and Communities*. New York and London: Routledge.

Olea, Ronalyn V. 2016. "#MarcosNoHero Protests Go Global." *Bulatlat*, November 25. Available at https://www.bulatlat.com/2016/11/25/marcosnohero-protests-go-global/.

Olick, Jeffrey K. 1999. "Collective Memory: The Two Cultures." *Sociological Theory* 17 (3): 333–48.

Ong, Jonathan Corpus, Ross Tapsell, and Nicole Curato. 2019. "Tracking Digital Disinformation in the 2019 Philippine Midterm Election." Report by New Mandala. Available at https:// www.newmandala.org/wp-content/uploads/2019/08/Digital-Disinformation-2019-Mid terms.pdf.

REFERENCES

Ortega, Arnisson Andre. 2016. *Neoliberalizing Spaces in the Philippines: Suburbanization, Transnational Migration, and Dispossession.* Lanham, MD: Lexington Books.

Ortiga, Yasmin Y. 2018. "Learning to Fill the Labor Niche: Filipino Nursing Graduates and the Risk of the Migration Trap." *RSF: The Russell Sage Foundation Journal of the Social Sciences* 4 (1): 172–87.

Østergaard-Nielsen, Eva. 2003. "The Politics of Migrants' Transnational Political Practices." *International Migration Review* 37 (3): 760–86.

Overholt, William H. 1986. "The Rise and Fall of Ferdinand Marcos." *Asian Survey* 26 (11): 1137–63.

Padilla, Malu. 2007. "'In the Service of Our Kababayans'—Bayanihan Philippine Women's Centre." In *In De Olde Worlde: Views of Filipino Migrants in Europe*, edited by F. M. Hoegsholm, 204–24. Quezon City: Philippine Social Science Council.

Pangue, Jene-Anne. 2020. "Disinformation Researchers Unpack the Game of Lies and Its Impact on Democracy." *Rappler*, December 10. Available at https://www.rappler.com/moveph/disinformation-researchers-unpack-lies-social-media-impact-democracy?fbclid=IwAR1q Ch5y3eUHOf8XBFMc96rk2Q-1LlTzjOIJIhyde5lm1cCAyBs7H2Qglak.

Parreñas, Rhacel Salazar. 1998. "'White Trash' Meets the 'Little Brown Monkeys': The Taxi Dance Hall as a Site of Interracial and Gender Alliances between White Working Class Women and Filipino Immigrant Men in the 1920s and 30s." *Amerasia* 24 (4): 115–34.

Parreñas, Rhacel Salazar. 2001. "Transgressing the Nation-State: The Partial Citizenship and 'Imagined (Global) Community' of Migrant Filipina Domestic Workers." *Signs* 26 (4): 1129–54.

Parreñas, Rhacel Salazar. 2015. *Servants of Globalization: Migration and Domestic Work.* Stanford, CA: Stanford University Press.

Parreñas, Rhacel Salazar. 2021. "Discipline and Empower: The State Governance of Migrant Domestic Workers." *American Sociological Review* 86 (6:) 1043–65.

Parreñas, Rhacel Salazar. 2022. *Unfree: Migrant Domestic Workers in Arab States.* Stanford, CA: Stanford University Press.

Paul, Rachel Anderson. 2000. "Grassroots Mobilization and Diaspora Politics: Armenian Interest Groups and the Role of Collective Memory." *Nationalism and Ethnic Politics* 6 (1): 24–47.

Perla, Hector J. 2009. "Heirs of Sandino: The Nicaraguan Revolution and the U.S.-Nicaragua Solidarity Movement." *Latin American Perspectives* 36:80–100.

Philippine News. 1976. "History Repeats Itself." *Philippine News*, March 13–19, 2.

Philippine Overseas Employment Agency (POEA). 2017. Deployed Overseas Filipino Workers by Country/Destination (Total) 2017 vs. 2016. Available at https://www.poea.gov.ph/ofwstat/compendium/2016–2017%20deployment%20by%20country.pdf.

Pido, Antonio J. A. 1997. "Macro/Micro Dimensions of Pilipino Immigration to the United States." In *Filipino Americans: Transformation and Identity*, edited by M. P. P. Root, 21–38. Thousand Oaks, CA, London, and New Delhi: SAGE Publications.

Pido, Eric J. 2017. *Migrant Returns: Manila, Development, and Transnational Connectivity.* Durham, NC, and London: Duke University Press.

Pimentel, Benjamin. 2012. "Defying Marcos, Filipino Americans Emerged as a Force against Tyranny." *Inquirer.net*, September 18. Available at https://globalnation.inquirer.net/50480/defying-marcos-filipino-americans-emerged-as-a-force-against-tyranny.

Pinto, António Costa. 2010. "Coping with the Double Legacy of Authoritarianism and Revolution in Portuguese Democracy." *South European Society and Politics* 15 (3): 395–412.

Polletta, Francesca. 1994. "Strategy and Identity in 1960s Black Protest." *Research in Social Movements, Conflicts and Change* 75:85–114.

Polletta, Francesca. 1999. "'Free Spaces' in Collective Action." *Theory and Society* 28:1–38.

Polletta, Francesca. 2006. *It Was Like a Fever: Storytelling in Protest and Politics.* Chicago: University of Chicago Press.

Polletta, Francesca. 2012. "Three Mechanisms by Which Culture Shapes Movement Strategy: Repertoires, Institutional Norms, and Metonymy." In *Strategies for Social Change*, edited by G. M. Maney, R. V. Kutz-Flamenbaum, D. A. Rohlinger, and J. Goodwin, 43–57. Minneapolis: University of Minnesota Press.

Polletta, Francesca. 2020. *Inventing the Ties That Bind: Imagined Relationships in Moral and Political Life.* Chicago: University of Chicago Press.

Polleta, Francesca, and James M. Jasper. 2001. "Collective Identity and Social Movements." *Annual Review of Sociology* 27:283–305.

Portes, Alejandro, and József Böröcz. 1989. "Contemporary Immigration: Theoretical Perspectives on Its Determinants and Modes of Incorporation." *International Migration Review* 23 (3): 606–30.

Portes, Alejandro, and Rubén Rumbaut. 2014. *Immigrant America: A Portrait.* Oakland and London: University of California Press.

Posadas, Barbara M., and Roland L. Guyotte. 1990. "Unintentional Immigrants: Chicago's Filipino Foreign Students Become Settlers, 1990–1941." *Journal of American Ethnic History* 9 (2): 26–48.

Power, Margaret. 2009. "The U.S. Movement in Solidarity with Chile in the 1970s." *Latin American Perspectives* 36 (6): 46–66.

Pyke, Karen, and Tran Dang. 2003. "'FOB' and 'Whitewashed': Identity and Internalized Racism among Second Generation Asian Americans." *Qualitative Sociology* 26 (2): 147–72.

Quartz. 2016. "Duterte the Hero! Filipinos Working Abroad Say They're Coming Home to a Better Philippines." *Quartz*, November 27. Available at https://qz.com/843446/rodrigo-duterte-the-hero-filipinos-working-abroad-ofws-say-theyre-coming-home-to-a-better-phi lippines/.

Quimpo, Nathan F. 2007. "Barrio Utrecht." In *In De Olde World: Views of Filipino Migrants in Europe*, edited by F. M. Hoegsholm, 340–46. Quezon City: Philippine Migration Network and Philippine Social Science Council.

Quinsaat, Jesse. 1976. "An Exercise on How to Join the Navy and Still Not See the World." In *Letters in Exile: An Introductory Reader on the History of Pilipinos in America*, edited by J. Quinsaat, 96–110. Los Angeles: UCLA Asian American Studies Center.

Quinsaat, Sharon Madriaga. 2013. "Migrant Mobilization for Homeland Politics: A Social Movement Approach." *Sociology Compass* 7 (11): 952–64.

Rafael, Vicente L. 2000. *White Love and Other Events in Filipino History.* Durham, NC: Duke University Press.

Rafael, Vicente L. 2022. "The Return of the Marcoses." *New York Review of Books*, July 21. Available at https://www.nybooks.com/online/2022/07/21/the-return-of-the-marcoses/.

Rajevic, Manuela Badilla. 2019. "The Chilean Student Movement: Challenging Public Memories of Pinochet's Dictatorship." *Mobilization: An International Quarterly* 24 (4): 493–510.

Ranada, Pia. 2016. "Over 600,000 OFWs Mobilizing for Duterte Campaign." *Rappler*, January 30. Available at https://www.rappler.com/nation/elections/120572-overseas-filipino-work ers-support-rodrigo-duterte/.

REFERENCES

Recuber, Timothy. 2012. "The Prosumption of Commemoration: Disasters, Digital Memory Banks, and Online Collective Memory." *American Behavioral Scientist* 56 (4): 531–49.

Redclift, Victoria. 2017. "The Demobilization of Diaspora: History, Memory and 'Latent Identity.'" *Global Networks* 17 (4): 500–517.

Reyes, Portia L. 2018. "Claiming History: Memoirs of the Struggle against Ferdinand Marcos's Martial Law Regime in the Philippines." *SOJOURN: Journal of Social Issues in Southeast Asia* 33 (2): 457–98.

Richter, Linda. 1980. "The Political Use of Tourism: A Philippine Case Study." *Journal of Developing Areas* 14 (2): 237–57.

Rochon, Thomas R. 2018. *Culture Moves: Ideas, Activism, and Changing Values.* Princeton, NJ: Princeton University Press.

Rodriguez, Robyn Magalit. 2010. *Migrants for Export: How the Philippine State Brokers Labor to the World.* Minneapolis: University of Minnesota Press.

Rojas, Fabio. 2007. *From Black Power to Black Studies: How a Radical Social Movement Became an Academic Discipline.* Baltimore, MD: Johns Hopkins University Press.

Rother, Stefan. 2012. "Diffusion in Transnational Political Spaces: Political Activism of Philippine Labor Migrants in Hong Kong." PhD dissertation, Department of Political Science, Albert-Ludwigs-Universität, Freiburg, Germany.

Sabillo, Kristine Angeli. 2016. "WATCH: Clueless Millennials Meet Martial Law Victims." *Inquirer.net*, May 4. Available at https://newsinfo.inquirer.net/783169/watch-clueless-millennials-meet-martial-law-victims.

Safran, William. 1991. "Diasporas in Modern Societies: Myth of Homeland and Return." *Diaspora: A Journal of Transnational Studies* 1 (1): 83–99.

Salazar, Zeus A. 1999. "The Exile in Philippine History." *Asian and Pacific Migration Journal* 8 (1–2): 19–64.

Sampson, Helen. 2003. "Transnational Drifters or Hyperspace Dwellers: An Exploration of the Lives of Filipino Seafarers Aboard and Ashore." *Ethnic and Racial Studies* 26 (2): 253–77.

Sanapo, Margaret, and Yasuhide Nakamura. 2011. "Gender and Physical Punishment: The Filipino Children's Experience." *Child Abuse Review* 20:39–56.

San Francisco Kontra Libing Coalition. 2016. "Statement of the San Francisco Kontra Libing Coalition against a Hero's Burial for Dictator Marcos." *Northern California Asian Journal*, September 2–8, A4.

San Juan, E., Jr. 1994. "Configuring the Filipino Diaspora in the United States." *Diaspora: A Journal of Transnational Studies* 3 (2): 117–33.

San Juan, E., Jr. 1998. *From Exile to Diaspora: Versions of the Filipino Experience in the United States.* Boulder, CO: Westview Press.

Scharlin, Craig, and Lilia V. Villanueva. 2000. *Philip Vera Cruz: A Personal History of Filipino Immigrants and the Farmworkers Movement.* Seattle: University of Washington Press.

Schiller, Nina Glick, and Georges Fouron. 1998. "Transnational Lives and National Identities: The Identity Politics of Haitian Immigrants." In *Transnationalism from Below*, edited by M. P. Smith and L. E. Guarnizo, 130–61. New Brunswick, NJ: Transaction Publishers.

Schiller, Nina Glick, and Georges E. Fouron. 1999. "Terrains of Blood and Nation: Haitian Transnational Social Fields." *Ethnic and Racial Studies* 22 (2): 340–66.

Schnapper, Dominique. 1999. "From the Nation-State to the Transnational World: On the Meaning and Usefulness of Diaspora as a Concept." *Diaspora: A Journal of Transnational Studies* 8 (3): 225–54.

Schudson, Michael. 1992. *Watergate in American Memory: How We Remember, Forget, and Reconstruct the Past.* New York: Basic Books.

Schumacher, John N., SJ 1991. *The Making of a Nation: Essays on Nineteenth-Century Filipino Nationalism.* Quezon City: Ateneo de Manila University Press.

Schumacher, John N., SJ 1997. *The Propaganda Movement, 1880–1895.* Quezon City: Ateneo de Manila University Press.

Schuman, Howard, and Jacqueline Scott. 1989. "Generations and Collective Memories." *American Sociological Review* 54 (3): 359–81.

Schwalbe, Michael L., and Douglas Mason-Schrock. 1996. "Identity Work as Group Process." *Advances in Group Processes* 13:113–47.

Schwartz, Barry. 1996. "Memory as a Cultural System: Abraham Lincoln in World War II." *American Sociological Review* 61:908–27.

Scott, James C. 1985. *Weapons of the Weak: Everyday Forms of Peasant Resistance.* New Haven, CT, and London: Yale University Press.

Scott, James C. 1990. *Domination and the Arts of Resistance: Hidden Transcripts.* New Haven, CT, and London: Yale University Press.

Sewell, William H., Jr. 1999. "The Concept(s) of Culture." In *Beyond the Cultural Turn: New Directions in the Study of Society and Culture,* edited by V. E. Bonnell and L. Hunt, 35–61. Berkeley, Los Angeles, and London: University of California Press.

Shain, Yossi. 1994/95. "Ethnic Diasporas and U.S. Foreign Policy." *Political Science Quarterly* 109 (5): 811–41.

Shain, Yossi. 2005. *The Frontier of Loyalty: Political Exiles in the Age of the Nation State.* Ann Arbor: University of Michigan Press.

Shalom, Stephen R. 1990. "Promoting Ferdinand Marcos." *Bulletin of Concerned Asian Scholars* 22 (4): 20–26.

Sharkey, John. 1983. "The Marcos Mystery: Did the Philippine Leader Really Win the U.S. Medals for Valor? He Exploits Honors He May Not Have Earned." *Washington Post,* December 18. Available at https://www.washingtonpost.com/archive/opinions/1983/12/18/the-mar cos-mystery-did-the-philippine-leader-really-win-the-us-medals-for-valorhe-exploits -honors-he-may-not-have-earned/2af4be05-5b92-4612-a223-d379780991c6/.

Sheffer, Gabriel. 2003. *Diaspora Politics: At Home Abroad.* New York: Cambridge University Press.

Simmel, Georg. 1964. *Conflict and the Web of Group Affiliations.* New York: Free Press.

Siruno, Lalaine. 2021. "In God We Trust: Religious Beliefs and Sensemaking of Filipino Undocumented Migrants in the Netherlands." December 18. Available at https://www.routedmaga zine.com/religious-beliefs-filipinos-netherlands.

Sivanandan, A. 2008. "Catching History on the Wing." Institute of Race Relations, November 6. Available at https://irr.org.uk/article/catching-history-on-the-wing/.

Smith, Christian. 1996. *Resisting Reagan: U.S. Central America Peace Movement.* Chicago: University of Chicago Press.

Smith, Robert Courtney. 2006. *Mexican New York: Transnational Lives of New Immigrants.* Los Angeles and London: University of California Press.

Smith, Sidonie, and Julia Watson. 2010. *Reading Autobiography: A Guide for Interpreting Life Narratives.* Minneapolis and London: University of Minnesota Press.

Smith, Tony. 2000. *Foreign Attachments: The Power of Ethnic Groups in the Making of American Foreign Policy.* Cambridge, MA: Harvard University Press.

REFERENCES

Snow, David A., and Robert D. Benford. 1992. "Master Frames and Cycles of Protest." In *Frontiers in Social Movement Research*, edited by A. D. Morris and C. M. Mueller, 133–55. New Haven, CT, and London: Yale University Press.

Snow, David A., E. Burke Rochford Jr., Steven K. Worden, and Robert D. Benford. 1986. "Frame Alignment Processes, Micromobilization, and Movement Participation." *American Sociological Review* 51 (4): 464–81.

Snow, David A., and Catherine Corrigall-Brown. 2015. "Collective Identity." In *International Encyclopedia of Social and Behavioral Sciences*, edited by J. Wright, 174–79. Oxford: Elsevier.

Snow, David A., Daniel M. Cress, Liam Downey, and Andrew W. Jones. 1998. "Disrupting the 'Quotidian': Reconceptualizing the Relationship between Breakdown and the Emergence of Collective Action." *Mobilization: An International Quarterly* 3 (1): 1–22.

Sökefeld, Martin. 2006. "Mobilizing in Transnational Space: A Social Movement Approach to the Formation of Diaspora." *Global Networks* 6 (3): 265–84.

Spillman, Lyn. 1998. "When Do Collective Memories Last? Founding Moments in the United States and Australia." *Social Science History* 22 (4): 445–77.

Staggenborg, Suzanne. 1993. "Critical Events and the Mobilization of the Pro-Choice Movement." *Research in Political Sociology* 6:319–45.

Staggenborg, Suzanne. 1998. "Social Movement Communities and Cycles of Protest: The Emergence and Maintenance of a Local Women's Movement." *Social Problems* 45 (2): 180–204.

Steinberg, Marc W. 1996. " 'The Labour of the Country Is the Wealth of the Country': Class Identity, Consciousness, and the Role of Discourse in the Making of the English Working Class." *International Labor and Working-Class History* 49:1–25.

Strunk, Christopher. 2014. " 'We Are Always Thinking of Our Community': Bolivian Hometown Associations, Networks of Reciprocity, and Indigeneity in Washington D.C." *Journal of Ethnic and Migration Studies* 40 (1): 1697–1715.

Swidler, Ann. 1986. "Culture in Action: Symbols and Strategies." *American Sociological Review* 51 (2): 273–86.

Swidler, Ann. 1995. "Cultural Power and Social Movements." In *Social Movements and Culture*, edited by H. Johnston and B. Klandermans, 25–40. Minneapolis: University of Minnesota Press.

Takenaka, Ayumi. 2009. "How Diasporic Ties Emerge: Pan-American Nikkei Communities and the Japanese State." *Ethnic and Racial Studies* 32 (8): 1325–45.

Tarrow, Sidney. 2005. *The New Transnational Activism*. New York: Cambridge University Press.

Tarrow, Sidney G. 2011. *Power in Movement: Social Movements and Contentious Politics*. New York: Cambridge University Press.

Taylor, Judith. 2008. "Imperfect Intimacies: The Problem of Women's Sociality in Contemporary North American Feminist Memoir." *Gender & Society* 22 (6): 705–27.

Taylor, Verta. 1989. "Social Movement Continuity: The Women's Movement in Abeyance." *American Sociological Review* 54 (5): 761–75.

Taylor, Verta, and Nella van Dyke. 2004. " 'Get Up, Stand Up': Tactical Repertoires of Social Movements." In *The Blackwell Companion to Social Movements*, edited by D. A. Snow, S. A. Soule, and H. Kriesi, 262–93. Malden, MA: Blackwell Publishing.

Taylor, Verta, and Nancy E. Whittier. 1992. "Collective Identity in Social Movement Communities: Lesbian Feminist Mobilization." In *Frontiers in Social Movement Theory*, edited by A. D. Morris and C. M. Mueller, 104–29. New Haven, CT, and London: Yale University Press.

Taylor, Verta, and Nancy Whittier. 1995. "Analytical Approaches to Social Movement Culture: The Culture of the Women's Movement." In *Social Movements and Culture*, edited by H. Johnston and B. Klandermans, 163–87. Minneapolis: University of Minnesota Press.

Tesorio, Jofelle. 2020. "Undocumented but Not Hiding [COVID-19 Journals]." June 10. Available at https://womenwritingwomen.com/2020/06/10/undocumented-but-not-hiding-covid-19-journals/.

Testaverde, Mauro, Harry Moroz, Claire H. Hollweg, and Achim Schmillen. 2017. *Migrating to Opportunity: Overcoming Barriers to Labor Mobility in Southeast Asia*. Washington, DC: World Bank.

Thompson, Mark R. 1995. *The Anti-Marcos Struggle: Personalistic Rule and Democratic Transition in the Philippines*. New Haven, CT: Yale University Press.

Thompson, Mark R. 2021. "Pushback after Backsliding? Unconstrained Executive Aggrandizement in the Philippines versus Contested Military-Monarchical Rule in Thailand." *Democratization* 28 (1): 124–41.

Thompson, Mark R. 2022. "Brute Force Governance: Public Approval Despite Policy Failure during the COVID-19 Pandemic in the Philippines." *Journal of Current Southeast Asian Affairs* 41 (3): 399–421.

Tilly, Charles. 2006. *Regimes and Repertoires*. Chicago: University of Chicago Press.

Tilly, Charles, and Sidney Tarrow. 2015. *Contentious Politics*. New York: Oxford University Press.

Tseng, Ada. 2020. "Here's Why Armenian Americans in Southern California Are Protesting." *Los Angeles Times*, October 9. Available at https://www.latimes.com/california/story/2020-10-09/why-are-armenian-americans-protesting.

Tölölyan, Khachig. 1996. "Rethinking Diaspora(s): Stateless Power in the Transnational Moment." *Diaspora: A Journal of Transnational Studies* 5 (1): 3–36.

Tucker, William T. 1965. "Max Weber's 'Verstehen.'" *Sociological Quarterly* 6 (2): 157–65.

Tyner, James. 2009. *The Philippines: Mobilities, Identities, Globalization*. London: Routledge.

Um, Khatharya. 2012. "Exiled Memory: History, Identity, and Remembering in Southeast Asia and Southeast Asian Diaspora." *positions* 20 (3): 831–50.

Umemoto, Karen. 2007. "'On Strike!': San Francisco State College Strike, 1968–1969; The Role of Asian American Students." In *Contemporary Asian America: A Multidisciplinary Reader*, edited by M. Zhou and J. V. Gatewood, 25–55. New York and London: New York University Press.

UN Conference on Trade and Development (UNCTAD). 2021. *Review of Maritime Transport 2021*. New York: UN Publications.

Valocchi, Stephen. 2008. "The Importance of Being 'We': Collective Identity and the Mobilizing Work of Progressive Activists in Hartford, Connecticut." *Mobilization: An International Journal* 14 (1): 65–84.

Van den Muijzenberg, Otto. 2001. "Philippine-Dutch Social Relations." In *The Philippines: Historical and Social Studies*, edited by G. A. Persoon, 471–509. Leiden: KITLV/Royal Netherlands Institute of Southeast Asian and Caribbean Studies.

Van den Muijzenberg, Otto. 2003. "A Short History of Social Connections between the Philippines and the Netherlands." *Philippine Studies* 51 (1): 339–74.

Van Dyke, Nella, and Verta Taylor. 2018. "The Cultural Outcomes of Social Movements." In *The Wiley Blackwell Companion to Social Movements*, edited by D. A. Snow, S. A. Soule, H. Kriesi, and H. J. McCammon, 482–98. Hoboken, NJ: John Wiley & Sons.

REFERENCES

Van Eldik Thieme, Hanneke. 1992. "Dutch Development Assistance to the Philippines." In *European Official Development Assistance to the Philippines*, edited by J. Rocamora, H. van Eldik Thieme, and E. M. Hilario, 1–37. Manila: Transnational Institute and Council for People's Development.

Velasco, Gina K. 2020. *Queering the Global Filipina Body: Contested Nationalisms in the Filipina/o Diaspora*. Urbana, Chicago, and Springfield: University of Illinois Press.

Vergara, Benito M., Jr. 2009. *Pinoy Capital: The Filipino Nation in Daly City*. Philadelphia: Temple University Press.

Vertovec, Steven. 1997. "Three Meanings of 'Diaspora,' Exemplified among South Asian Religions." *Diaspora: A Journal of Transnational Studies* 6 (3): 277–99.

Villegas, Mark R. 2021. *Manifest Technique: Hip Hop, Empire, and Visionary Filipino American Culture*. Urbana, Chicago, and Springfield: University of Illinois Press.

Walaardt, Tycho. 2011. "'The Good Old Days of the Cold War': Arguments Used to Admit or Reject Asylum Seekers in the Netherlands, 1957–1967." *Continuity and Change* 26 (2): 271–99.

Watanabe, Paul Y. 1984. *Ethnic Groups, Congress, and American Foreign Policy: The Politics of the Turkish Arms Embargo*. Santa Barbara, CA: Greenwood Press.

Weekley, Kathleen. 2001. *The Communist Party of the Philippines, 1968–1993: A Story of Its Theory and Practice*. Quezon City: University of the Philippines Press.

Whaley, Floyd. 2016. "30 Years after Revolution, Some Filipinos Yearn for 'Golden Age' of Marcos." *New York Times*, February 3, A8.

Whitlinger, Claire. 2019. "The Transformative Capacity of Commemoration: Comparing Mnemonic Activism in Philadelphia, Mississippi." *Mobilization: An International Quarterly* 24 (4): 455–74.

Wimmer, Andreas. 2013. *Ethnic Boundary Making: Institutions, Power, Networks*. New York: Oxford University Press.

Wright, Thomas C., and Rody Oñate Zuñiga. 2007. "Chilean Political Exile." *Latin American Perspectives* 34 (4): 31–49.

Yates, Luke. 2015. "Everyday Politics, Social Practices and Movement Networks: Daily Life in Barcelona's Social Centres." *British Journal of Sociology* 66 (2): 236–58.

Yeoh, Brenda S. A., and Shirlena Huang. 2000. "'Home' and 'Away': Foreign Domestic Workers and Negotiations of Diasporic Identity in Singapore." *Women's Studies International Forum* 23 (4): 413–29.

Zald, Mayer N. 1996. "Culture, Ideology, and Strategic Framing." In *Comparative Perspectives on Social Movements: Political Opportunities, Mobilizing Structures, and Cultural Framings*, edited by D. McAdam, J. D. McCarthy, and M. N. Zald, 261–74. New York: Cambridge University Press.

Zamponi, Lorenzo. 2018. *Social Movements, Memory and Media: Narrative in Action in the Italian and Spanish Student Movements*. London: Palgrave Macmillan.

Zerubavel, Eviatar. 1996. "Social Memories: Steps to a Sociology of the Past." *Qualitative Sociology* 19 (3): 283–99.

Index

Page numbers in italics refer to illustrations.

abeyance, 21, 99, 138

Abramson, Yehonatan, 16

activism, 8–9, 21, 49; anti-eviction movement, 93; and changes in culture, 25–26; and collective identity, 10, 52; and diasporas, 7, 81; discursive strategy of, 86; and fictive kinship, 87; Filipino, 3, 58–59, 61–62, 64, 70, 81–82, 92–93; and framing, 20; "identity deployment," 52; in Netherlands, 5, 128, 131, 170; as political entrepreneurship, 87; protest repertoire for, 134–35; and "Serve the People" rallying cry, 93; solidarity, 60–61, 99; transnational, 4; transnational anti-dictatorship movement, 52; "transnational hinges" of, 158; in US, 5, 50–51, 63, 92, 126, 128, 131, 170; US military bases in Philippines, targeting of, 75

Adamson, Fiona B., 16, 36, 176n4

agency, 17, 41, 110, 124, 133, 137, 144, 146; collective, 51; and identity, 63; limited, 14; of migrants, xii–xiv, 11, 63, 80–81, 96, 104, 113, 115; political, 86; and structure, 20

Agnew, Spiro, 56, 97

Agricultural Workers Organizing Committee, 89

Aguilar, Filomeno V., Jr., 9–10, 44, 95, 108, 112, 174n8, 175n25, 187n1

Akbayan Citizens' Action Party, 170

Alaska, 31, 90, 94

Alaskeros, 90

Alay sa Bayan (Gift to the People) (ALAB), 146–47, 112–14, 116; *Oratoryo ng Bayan* (The nation's oratorio), staging of, 109

Alejandro, Leandro, 117

Alforque, Armin, 138–39

Aliens Law (1965), 76

Amarasingam, Amarnath, 175n4

Amenta, Edwin, 158

American dream, 143

American Empire, 34

American Israel Public Affairs Committee, 18, 73

Amnesty International, 122

Amsterdam (Netherlands), xii, 33–34, 38, 83, 103, 106, 114, 117, 134–35, 170; National Monument in, 156

Anderson, Benedict, "imagined communities," 86–87

Anderson, Bridget, 106

Ann Arbor Veterans Affairs Hospital, 104

Anthias, Floya, 150

anti-dictatorship movement, 11, 53–54, 61, 65–67, 70–71, 88, 96–102, 104, 114–15, 120, 128, 135, 138, 143, 145, 147–48, 152, 155, 157–59, 167; certification and decertification, strategies of, 72; and Filipino diaspora formation, 82; memoirs, of activists, 124; "memory entrepreneurs" of, 12; memory work of, 156

anti-imperialism, 58

Anti–Martial Law Coalition (AMLC), 51, 68–69, 138–39; AMLC Seven, 50, 183n3; National Conference, 79

Anti-Terrorism Act (2020), 153

antiwar movement, 91

Apeldoorn (Netherlands), 33

Apostol, Rebecca, 141

Aquino, Benigno, III, 191n34

Aquino, Benigno "Nonoy" S., Jr., 51, 53, 110, 114, 116; assassination of, 81, 100, 134, 192n85

Aquino, Corazon, 35, 42–43, 51, 82, 117, 123

Arab Gulf States, 48

218   INDEX

Arab Spring, 175n4
Armenians, 9; and Armenian genocide, 119
Arroyo, Gloria Macapagal, 129
Asia, 5–6, 10–11, 34, 49, 54–56, 74–75, 79, 106–7,
    122, 180n51; Filipinos in, 35, 37, 40, 96, 153, 156;
    national liberation struggles, 91; US racist im-
    perialism in, 59
Asian American Political Alliance, 91
Asian Americans, 94, 138
Assman, Aleida, 118
asylum, 63, 99, 112, 185n63
au pair program, xii, 1, 173n6
Avila, Geline, 53, 142–47

Bagong Alyansang Makabayan (New Patriotic
    Alliance) USA, 129
bagong bayani (new hero), 43–44, 46
Bagong Lipunan (New Society) ideology, 42
balikbayan, 42–44
Balikbayan Program: institutionalized as Republic
    Act 6768, 42–43; launching of, 41
Bangsa Moro Army, 72
Bangsamoro people, 77–78, 186n106
Bantayog ng mga Bayani (Monument of the
    Heroes), 191n40
Barangay sa Holland (Village in Holland), 114
Basch, Linda, 174n10 (intro)
Basic Ecclesial Communities (BECs), 60, 185n54
Bauböck, Rainier, 16, 178n67
"Bayan Ko" (song), 109, 117, 129, 136–37, 158–59,
    183n2
BBM-Sara Netherlands (Facebook group),
    xiii–xiv
Beatrix, Princess, 33
Bello, Walden, 50–51, 152, 183n3
belonging, 15, 18, 24, 87; alternative forms of, 47;
    and attachment, 16; contradictions of, 157; gen-
    erational, 125; to homeland, xv, 4, 17, 26, 42, 48,
    62, 81–82, 108, 141, 155; among migrants, 174n3;
    national, 47–49, 51, 66, 111, 187n1; in other
    communities, 103; racial, 105, 115; recogniz-
    ing boundaries of, 115; transnational, 64–65,
    67, 71, 159
Benford, Robert D., 188n46
Berghaus textile factories, 33, 37; "Berghaus girls," 34
Bernstein, Mary, 52
Black Panther Party, 8, 58, 93, 188n32
Black Student Union, 91
Blanc, Cristina Szanton, 42, 174n10 (intro)
Boccagni, Paolo, 71
Bonifacio, Andrés, 59, 91–92, 159
Bulosan, Carlos, 90, 96; America Is in the Heart,
    88–89
Burgess, Katrina: Courting Migrants, 23; on
    diaspora-making, as political project, 28–29
Bussum (Netherlands), 33

Butler, Kim D., 5, 15
bystander publics, 7

California, 2, 39, 49, 63, 97, 105, 154–55; Delano, 92,
    102; Salinas Valley, 31, 89; San Diego, 32, 88, 91;
    San Francisco, 31, 40, 50, 91–93, 98, 110, 126–27,
    132, 152, 156, 170, 182n90; San Joaquin Valley, 89;
    Southern California, 13, 40; Stockton, 93; Uni-
    versity of California, 91; Watsonville, 89
Campaign against the Return of the Marcoses to
    Malacañang, 125
Camroux, David, 49
Canada, 27, 33, 37, 42, 77, 135, 154, 175n4
Cannery Workers' and Farm Laborers' Union
    (CWFLU), 89–90
Carter, Jimmy, 75–76
Catholic Church, 69; Social Action Centers, 60
Cavite mutiny (1872), 29–30, 179n18
Central America Resource Center, 98
Chinatowns, 32, 93
Citizenship Retention and Reacquisition Act, 45
civil rights movement, 91
Clark Air Base, 56, 58, 75
Clifford, James, 15, 85, 144
Coalition against the Marcos Dictatorship
    (CAMD), 53, 132, 134
co-ethnics/co-nationals, 4, 84, 90, 96, 131, 134–35,
    148–49, 155, 171; solidarity with, 87–88
cognitive liberation, 86, 93, 96
Cohen, Robin, 14–15
Cold War, 33, 75
collective action, 175n15; and framing, 20
collective identity, 7, 12, 14–15, 48, 51–52, 112, 156–
    57, 169, 177n38; through activism, 10, 52; and
    acts of remembering, 25; and agency, 17; and
    co-ethnics/co-nationals, solidarity with, 121;
    cognitive element of, 19; and collective mem-
    ory, 25, 120; as defined, 19; and diasporas, 11, 17;
    and displacement, common experience of, 49;
    emotive element of, 19; and ethnic/national
    solidarity, based on, 45–46; of Filipinos, 115;
    fluidity of, 17; and framing, 20; as group char-
    acteristic, 20; homeland-oriented, 56; hybridity
    of, 17, 20; interactive and communicative ele-
    ment of, 19; and loyalty, to homeland, 24, 121;
    and Marcos dictatorship, memories of, 138; of
    migrants, 3, 49, 100; of migrant workers, 80–81;
    vis-à-vis "other," 19; personal transformative ef-
    fects of, 114; as politicized, 19; as public good, 8;
    and sense of self, 19–20; and shared language,
    47; and solidarity, 86–87; and storytelling, 124;
    and unions, role of, 90
collective identity formation, 4–6, 21, 26, 95, 115;
    and diaspora formation, 22; and memoirs, 138;
    and social movements, 155, 157; and storytell-
    ing, 124

INDEX

collective memory, xv, 10, 168–69; and collective identity, 25, 120; and diaspora, 118, 156; and identity formation, 24–25; of Marcos dictatorship, 12, 120, 131, 150; of Marcos's burial, 138; regulatory function of, 120; of trauma, 119. *See also* memory

Collins, Randall, 138

colonialism, 28, 40, 75, 95, 159; and immigration, 29; and political entrepreneurs, 28

colonization, 5, 10–11, 14, 32–34, 48, 54, 59, 76

Commission on Filipino Migrant Workers (CFMW), 106–8, 110–11, 116; Schengen Agreement, opposition to, 112

Commission on Filipinos Overseas (CFO), 27, 44, 179n6

Commission on Human Rights, 191n47

Committee on Overseas Workers' Affairs, 152

Communist Party of the Philippines (CPP), 56–57, 91–92, 103; and Consuelo Ledesma, 76

Communist Party of the Philippines–National Democratic Front (CPP-NDF), 59, 61–62, 70, 76–79, 81, 96, 103–4; Filipino migrant communities, organizing, 129

conflict, 13, 17–18, 61, 72, 80, 99, 103, 120, 127, 147, 157; centrality of, 6; collective, as necessary for, 6; contradictions, exposing, 7; Filipino diaspora, as central to, xv; in group relations, 6; and meaning making, 21–22; during power relations, 8; through social movements, 23; in social systems, 6; and solidarity, 87; between "us" and "them," 51

conflict-mobilization-collective identity, 7, 14, 155, 157

Constantino, Renato, 91–92

Contemplacion, Flor, 44–45

Cordova, Dorothy, 185n69

Cordova, Fred, 185n69

coronavirus, 155, 173n8

Coser, Lewis A., 6

Cuban Revolution, 92

culture, xiv, 3–4, 17, 44, 47–49, 51, 54, 69, 106, 125, 127–28, 169; and action-constructing entities, 7–9, 22; and activism, 25–26, 156; common, 85, 95; and diaspora, 5; dominant, 23; ethnic, 101; Filipino, 109, 158–59; in host societies, adjusting to, 46, 80, 108; national, 55, 159; oppositional, 21, 92; political, 62, 73, 99; in political mobilization, 158; preserving of, 15; shared, 83; as sphere of social life, 158; as strategic, 20; as symbolic vehicles of meaning, 22–23

Damayan (Mutal Aid), 114

Declaration of Human Rights (1948), 189n77

de Guzman, Mila, 144; *Women against Marcos*, 139–43, 145, 170

dela Cruz, Enrique, 133

del Pilar, Marcelo, 54, 67

diaspora, 10, 13, 176n7, 176n9, 176n25; activism, created from, 7, 81; and belonging, sense of, 15, 17; characteristics of, 15; and collective memory, 118, 156; as commonality and solidarity, 150; as construction, 150, 156, 159; culture, hybridity and heterogeneity in, 5; definition of, 15; as difference and division, 150; as discursive, 28; endurance of, 12; and forced dislocation, 14; hybridity in, 95; Jewish, as "ideal type," 15; metaphorical usage, 174n3; and migrants, 46; as multigenerational, 118; and nation, imagined community of, 9; and oppositional collective identity, 82; and political entrepreneurs, 26; and protests, 157; separate identity, and migrants' loyalty, 15; as shared history and memory, 121; as social form, 174n3; and social relationships, 85; and solidarity, 114–15; and state, influence of, 46; sustaining of, 17; as term, 3, 5, 174n3; transnational activism, creation through, 4; as transnational identity network, 176n4; transnational mobilization, as product of, 16, 22, 26; and trauma, collective memory of, 119; as type of consciousness, 174n3

diaspora formation, xv, 3–6, 8, 10, 12, 18, 25, 41, 82, 85, 118, 167; agency in, 17; and collective identity, 22, 45–46, 110; fluidity in, 17; and homeland, loyalty to, 23; and human agency, 110; hybridity in, 17; and memoirs, 140–41; migrants' engagement in, 49; political entrepreneurs, reliance on, 16, 28–29; and religion, 47; and shared language, 47; social mobilization, based on, 176n4; and social movement processes, 157; state, role of in, 45–46

diaspora studies, 10, 174n9

Diehard Duterte Supporters (DDS), 153, 155

discipline, xiii–xiv, 122, 173n9

"discursive legacies," 54

disinformation, xi–xii, xiv, 66, 122

displacement frame, 12, 17, 85, 94–95, 103, 107, 110, 113, 116, 156, 174n3

dispossession, and trauma, 17

Domingo, Cindy, 138, 145–47

Domingo, Silme, 94, 145–46

Dubai (United Arab Emirates), 47; *kababayan* street community in, 48

Dufoix, Stéphane, 95

Durkheim, Émile, 20; "collective effervescence," 123

Dutch Foundation against Trafficking of Women, 181n76

Dutch-Philippine Association, 69

Dutch-Philippine Club, 69

Dutch-Pilipino Association, 114

Duterte, Rodrigo, xi–xii, 2–3, 12, 118, 121, 124, 126, 130–32, 150, 155, 173n8; China, pivot toward, 153;

Duterte, Rodrigo (*cont.*)
Filipino critics of in US, as irrelevant, 153–54; illiberal democracy of, 153; iron fist approach to crime, 152; Marcos, admiration for, 120; US, renouncement of, 153–54; visit to China, 153–54; War on Drugs, 129, 153–54, 157, 173n9

EDSA (Epifanio delos Santos Avenue), 123, 127, 130, 191n32
EDSA People Power@30 Committee, 132
Educational Opportunity Program, 91
Eindhoven (Netherlands), 33
El Salvador, 18; *El Dia del Salvadoreño* (festival), 68–69; Salvadoran American National Association (SANA), 68–69
empowerment frame, 11–12, 87, 110, 113, 116, 147, 156; pastoral, 45
Engels, Friedrich, 6
England, 63, 77. *See also* United Kingdom
Eritrean People's Liberation Front, 99
Espiritu, Augusto, 58
Europe, 5–6, 11, 13, 30, 34, 73, 109, 175n25, 176n25; Filipinos in, 10, 35, 37, 40, 43, 53–55, 70, 76, 79–80, 85, 96, 103, 106–7, 110, 153, 156, 158; "Fortress Europe," 112
European Community, 112
Exchange Visitor Program (EVP), 33
exiles, 20, 141; Filipino, 55, 64, 72, 88, 138–39, 158; political, 13

Facebook, xii–xiv
Fanon, Frantz, *The Wretched of the Earth*, 55
Fantasia, Rick, 24, 86
Far West Convention, 65, 67
fictive kinship, 1; of activists, 87; as relationship schema, 88, 94–95
filibusteros, 29–30
Filiippijnse Arbeiders Vereniging Nederland (Philippine Workers Association of the Netherlands) (Samahan), 105–6
Filipino Advocates for Justice, 104
Filipino American Community of Los Angeles (FACLA), 98, 104
Filipino American History Month, 154–55
Filipino American Human Rights Alliance, 153
Filipino American National Historical Society, 179n15
Filipino Americans, 32, 58, 102, 131, 149, 155, 188n35; and anti-dictatorship movement, 62, 147–48; and anti-eviction movement, 93; Cannon replica protests, 117–18; class consciousness, developing of, 93; collective identity of, 91; cultural struggle of, 127–28; diaspora consciousness of, 9; discrimination, fight against, 138; displacement of, 94–95; and EDSA, 127; KDP, membership in, 67; Marcos's suppres-

sion of, 66; marginalization of, 94–95; national imaginary, as part of, 133; oppositional consciousness among, 91–92; political socialization of, 91; privilege of, 68; second-generation, 59, 94, 129, 140–41, 152, 171; third-generation, 128, 152; union organizing of, 90; uprising against Marcos, role in, 133; and US aid to Marcos, 73. *See also* Filipino diaspora; Filipino immigrants
Filipino American Unity Conference, 110
Filipino Community of Seattle, 104
Filipino diaspora, 3, 12, 48, 112; among biggest in world, 27–28; global population of, 49; heterogeneity of, 49, 61. *See also* diaspora
Filipino farmworkers, 105; immigrant, 102
Filipino Federation of Labor, 89
Filipino gay men, swardspeak of, 47
Filipino *ilustrados* (erudite or enlightened ones), 30, 54, 158
Filipino immigrants, 6, 8, 11, 14, 22, 26, 61, 70, 73, 99, 105–6, 116, 120–21, 135–36, 154; agency among, 41, 80–81, 96, 115; and anti-dictatorship movement, 96, 110; and anti–martial law work, 98; and antimiscegenation laws, 89; assimilation of, 62, 67; associational life of, 47–48; and au pair program, 37; autonomous spaces, reclaiming of, 94; as *bagong bayani*, 44; as *balikbayans*, 42, 54; betrayal of homeland, 51; class cleavages among, 40; class diversity among, 39; class identity of, 100–101; collective identity of, 87; collective memory of, 12; and colonialism, 95; demographic characteristics of, 28; diaspora formation, engagement in, 29, 49; exiles, 55, 64, 72, 88, 138–39, 158; export of, 36; first wave of, 39, 89–94; and friendship associations, 69; global dispersion of, 41; "good behavior," reward for, 31–32; health-care workers, 39; heterogeneity of, 85; homeland ties, 13; and KDP, 110; kinship among, 95; loneliness of, 48; marginalization of, 12, 48; and national belonging, 111; and national consciousness, 32; in Netherlands, 55–56, 71; and nonpolitical groups, 114; nurses, 39, 102, 104; and out-migration, 9; overseas workers, sociodemographic composition of, 34–35; patriotism, reconstruction of, 53; professionals, 39; publications of, 46–47; quota of, 31; as racialized, 67, 88; racism toward, 3, 64, 89, 92, 100; and religion, 47; and resistance, forms of, 89; rights of, 96–97, 110, 112; second wave of, 32, 39, 90–91, 94; and segregation, 89; social movements of, xv; solidarity among, 5, 95; state, struggles against, 54; strikes, support of, 103–4; third wave of, 40; as traitors, 43; and transnational belonging, 65–66; in transnational movement, 49, 64–65; undocumented, 38; unionization of, 89; in US, 2, 31, 43, 55–56, 67, 71, 90, 93–94; in US Armed Forces, 31; as

"US nationals," 31; white male resentment toward, 89; women, dominance of, 39; workplace discrimination against, 102
Filipino Labor Union, 89
Filipino Reporter (newspaper), 66
Filipinos against Corruption and Tyranny (FACT), 129, 130, 132, 136
Filipinos for Affirmative Action, 104
Filipinos in the Netherlands against the Marcoses and Their Return to Power (FLAME), 136–37
Filipino Youth Activities of Seattle, 185n69
Filippijnen Bulletin (Philippine Bulletin), 69
Filippijnengroep Nederland (Philippine Group Netherlands) (FGN), 69, 71, 77; education campaigns, 70
Fine, Gary A., xiv, 140; "tiny publics," 7
Ford, Gerald M., 75
Foreign Assistance Act, 76
Foucault, Michel: biopower, 36; "countermemory," 131
framing, 20, 51, 65, 176n4; frame bridging, 79; master frames, 188n46
Francisco-Menchavez, Valerie, 174n2
Fraser, Donald, 73–74
free spaces, 21
Friends of Akbayan USA, 132
Friends of the Filipino People (FFP), 62, 65, 74–75, 79, 152
Fuentecilla, Jose, 64
Fujita-Rony, Dorothy B., 89
Furuyama, Katie, 72

GABRIELA (General Assembly Binding Women for Reform, Integrity, Equality, Leadership and Action), 132
Garcia, Romy, 147
Garrido, Marco, 173n9
Gasthuis, Wilhelmina, 33
Gendringen (Netherlands), 33
genocide, 78, 95; Armenian, 119; cultural, 119
Gentlemen's Agreement (1908), 31
gentrification, 3, 92
German Ideology, The (Marx and Engels), 6
Gilroy, Paul, *The Black Atlantic*, 17, 104
Global Day of Protest, 132; and Filipino transnational communities, 138
Goffman, Erving, dramaturgy, 52, 183n11
Goodfellow, William, 75
Gramsci, Antonio, hegemony, 23, 178n76

Habal, Estella, 92–93, 146–47, 149
Hague, The (Netherlands), xiv, 38, 136–37, *137*, 156, 170
Halbwachs, Maurice, 25, 125
Hall, Stuart, 17, 109; "Cultural Identity and Diaspora," 24

Hart-Celler Act (1965), 39
Hawai'i, 31, 39, 97, 105, 133
Hawai'i Sugar Planters Association, 31
hearings, 73–74; congressional, 21, 75, 167
Heerenveen (Netherlands), 33
hegemony, 23, 82, 118, 178n76; cultural, 44
heterogeneity, of transnational Filipino community, 11
homeland, 22, 62, 64, 71, 73, 80, 85, 88, 97, 100, 108, 115, 147, 159, 174n8; belonging to, 26, 48, 81–82, 141, 155; intention of return to, 175n25; and kinship, 118; loyalty to, 23–25, 27, 49, 51, 53, 61, 81, 120; migrants' maintaining links with, 46; and newspapers, 90; returning to, 149; solidarity with, 65; tourism, 41; and transnational communities, 46
Hong Kong (China), 35, 46, 48, 77, 135
Hosoda, Naomi, 48
Houston, Serin, 107
Hurston, Zora Neale, 84

Ibañez, Florante, 133
identity, 2, 11, 15–17, 22; and agency, 63; construction, 23, 49, 52, 90–91, 131; deployment, 52; fluidity of, 66; framing of, 52; movements, 67, 142; persecution, rooted in, 64; personal, 19, 86; quest for, 67; role, 19–20; social, 19, 45
identity formation, 11, 86, 145; and collective memory, 24–25; as evolving process, 147; trauma as foundation for, 119
identity making, 22–23
identity work, 18–19
ilustrados (erudite or enlightened ones), 30, 54, 158
immigrant farmworkers, 102
Immigration and Nationality Act (1952), 63
Immigration and Nationality Act (1965), 37, 97
Immigration Reform and Control Act (1986), 110
imperialism, 190n3; critique of, 59; in Third World, 90, 99; US, 2, 59, 90, 129, 154, 189n77
International Association of Filipino Patriots (IAFP), 79
International Hotel (I-Hotel), 40, 92–94, 102, 139
International Longshoremen's and Warehousemen's Union (ILWU), 89–90, 110
International Monetary Fund (IMF), 35, 56, 58, 78, 180n54
Iranian revolution, 75–76
Israel, 16, 73; Filipino domestic workers in, victimhood of, 86
Italy, xiv, 46, 48, 77–78, 135
Itliong, Larry, 127

Jackson, Jesse, 104
Jaena, Graciano Lopez, 67
Jalandoni, Luis, 76, *78*
Jasper, James, 23, 52

Johnson, Lyndon B., 39, 56
Justice for Filipino American Veterans (JFAV), 131; and political entrepreneurship, 132

Kabataang Makabayan (Nationalist Youth) (KM), 56–58, 138
Kalayaan collective, 64; *Kalayaan International (Freedom International)* (newspaper), 59, 107–11
Katipunan, 59; and Andrés Bonifacio, 59, 91–92, 159
Katipunan ng Demokratikong Pilipino (Union of Democratic Filipinos) (KDP), 53, 62–63, 66–67, 73, 79, 96, 101–2, 110, 129, 132, 142, 152, 158; *Ang Katipunan* (newspaper), 65, 68, 97, 104; against capitalism in US, 64; against Marcos dictatorship, 64; socialism in US, advocacy for, 64; *A Time to Rise*, 138–41, 143, 145–49, 170; US-born Filipinos, membership of, 97
Kelner, Shaul, 41
King County Multipurpose Domed Stadium (Kingdome), 93–94, 188n43
kinship: among Filipinos in US, 95, 115; and homeland, 118
Kissinger, Henry, 57
Klandermans, Bert, 19–20
Koinova, Maria, 42, 176n25
Kontra Libing (Anti-Burial) Coalition, 132, *134*; memory repertoire of, 133
Kusaka, Wataru, 173n9
kuskos at kudkod (scrub and scrape), 1

labor migrants, 9, 100, 107; Filipino, 43, 101, 103, 106–7, 143, 147
La Solidaridad (The Solidarity) (newspaper), 30, 55, 72
Lazam, Jeanette Gandionco, 143
Ledesma, Consuelo, 76
Leiden (Netherlands), 33, 69
Lelio Basso Foundation's Permanent People's Tribunal, 77, *78*
Levitt, Peggy, 22
Libingan ng mga Bayani (National Heroes Cemetery): Marcos's burial at, 130–31, 137; mobilizations against Marcos's burial at, 2, 12, 131, 134, 136–37, *137*, 150–51, 153
Liebelt, Claudia, 86
life writing, 192n75
Line of March, 110
lobbying, 18, 75–76, 97; and Foreign Assistance Act, 73; foreign policy, 11, 72, 73, 81, 98–99
Los Angeles (California), 13, 31, 68–69, 98, 133–34, 152, 156, 170
loyalty, 51, 77, 157; and common past, 24; to homeland, 23–25, 27, 49, 53, 61, 81, 120, 155
Luce-Celler Bill, 32

Maas, Marisha, 38
Madres de Plaza de Mayo (Mothers of Plaza de May), 19; as "mothers of the disappeared," 20
Maglaya, Cynthia, 149
mail-order brides, 113–14
Malaya Movement, 153
Manalansan, Martin F., IV, 47
Maney, Gregory M., 54
Manglapus, Raul S., 53, 62–63, 67, 74
Manila (Philippines), 29, 33, 35, 43, 50, 56, 58, 72–73, 81, 83, 97, 101, 170, 191n32; discipline among upper and middle class in, 173n9
Manila–Acapulco galleon trade, 29
Mannheim, Karl, 118
manongs (older brothers), 92–93, 102, 127, 188n35
Marcos, Ferdinand, xiii–xv, 34, 52, 77, 113, 117, 121, 144, 169, 180n51, 183n1, 184n35, 185n63; anti-dictatorship movement against, 11–12, 53–54, 61, 65–67, 70–72, 82, 88, 96–102, 104, 114–15, 120, 124, 128, 135, 138, 143, 145, 147–48, 152, 155–59, 167; *Bagong Lipunan* (New Society) ideology, 42; *Balikbayan* Program, 41–42, 66; blacklisting of anti-Marcos Filipinos in US, 66; burial of, at Libingan ng mga Bayani, 130–37, *137*, 150–51, 153; decertification strategy against, 72, 81; delegitimization of, 79–80, 98; dictatorship of, 10, 12, 150; and disinformation campaign, xi–xii; Dutch citizens against, 60–61; fall of, 126; Filipino Americans, suppression of, 66; and "First Quarter Storm," 56; first term of, 56; and Global Day of Protest, 132; human rights violations, 76, 78, 80, 96, 123, 189n77; image-enhancing tactics of, 50; and income taxes on overseas Filipinos, 185n58, 189n84; indirect repression and disinformation, 66; labor export program, 84, 95, 110, 135–36, 158–59; martial law, declaring of, 41, 57, 61, 65–66; martial law, lifting of, 81; Masagana 99 agricultural program, 122; military aid to, 75; naming and shaming of, 73, 81; NGOs, banning of, 60; opposition to, 50, 54, 56–65, 67, 71, 112, 158–59; overthrowing of, 35, 49, 81, 97, 110, 123, 129, 156; "Philippines Will Be Great Again" mantra, 57; Presidential Decree No. 69, 189n84; protests against, 2–3, 50, 56, 81; rule of, as sultanistic, 57; second term of, 57; "steak commandos," 66–67; tourism, fostering of, 66; transnational movement against, 55, 58, 150; as tyrant, 57; underground movement against, 103; US accountable for dictatorship of, 74, 156
Marcos, Ferdinand "Bongbong," Jr. (BBM), 123–25, 130, 139
Marcos, Imelda, 50, 117–18
marginalization frame, 16, 68, 87, 94, 105, 110, 113, 116, 156; in host societies, 1, 9, 11–12, 48, 80, 95, 107–8

INDEX

martial law, xiii, 58, 62–63, 72, 100, 122, 125–27, 129, 139, 143, 156; declaring of, 41, 57, 61, 65–66; lifting of, 81
Martial Law Chronicles Project, 191n47
Marx, Karl, 6
Marzan, Lourdes, 146–47
Mavroudi, Elizabeth, 17
McAdam, Doug, 177n33
McCarran-Walter Act (1952), 63
Melucci, Alberto, 19, 177n38
memoirs, 150, 169; and collective identity formation, 138; and diaspora formation, 140–41
memory, 118; activism, 28, 120–21, 126, 129, 132, 137–38, 142, 150; entrepreneurs, 12, 128; narrative frame of, 25; processes, 137; regime, 119; repertoire, 126, 128, 133; and shared history, 121; sociology of, 25; work, 119, 122, 139, 156. *See also* collective memory
Meyer, David S., 21, 72
microblogging, 125
micro-influencers, 193n7
Middle East, 5, 10–11, 34–35, 37, 40, 43, 49, 96, 106–7, 153–54, 156, 180n51
Migrante International, 135–36
migrants, 73, 109, 118, 131, 159, 175n15; agency of, 104; collective identity of, 95; rights of, 95; stories, 147. *See also* Filipino immigrants; migrant workers
migrants' rights movement, xv, 1, 10–11, 28, 138, 150, 156, 158–59, 167
migrant workers, 28, 45, 80, 87, 170; collective identity of, 106; Filipino, 1, 107, 110; poems and stories of, 111
Migrant Workers and Overseas Filipinos Act (1995), 45
Military Bases Agreement (1947), 32
Mills, C. Wright, 174n4; "sociological imagination," 3
mnemonic agents, 119, 123
Moro National Liberation Front (MNLF), 77–79, 81
Moro people, 79
Moro separatist movement, 72
Morris, Aldon, 114
Morro Bay (California), 29, 179n15
Moss, Dana, 175n15 (intro), 175n4 (chap. 1)
Movement for a Free Philippines (MFP), 53, 62–67, 72–74, 134, 158
Mügge, Liza, 176n4
Munson, Ziad, 145
Museum of Courage and Resistance, 191n40

naming and shaming, 73, 77, 81
Narciso, Filipina, 104, *105*, 148
National Alliance for Filipino Concerns, 129
National Association for the Advancement of Colored People (NAACP), 110

National Association of Filipinos in the US, 65
National Committee for the Restoration of Civil Liberties in the Philippines (NCRCLP), 65–66, 148; migrant agency frame, advancing of, 63; Philippine income tax, fight against, 62–63
National Democratic Front (NDF), 103, 132, 170–71
nationalism, 11, 20, 34, 46–47, 54–55, 100, 103, 159; Filipino, 32, 43, 59, 62, 92, 94
nation-state, 174n11; and collective identification, 103
neoliberalism, 35–37, 40–41, 152; and discipline, discourse of, 173n9; and political entrepreneurs, 28
Netherlands, xii, xiv, 1, 36, 71–73, 81, 101–2, 105, 110, 112, 114, 120, 132, 135–36, *137*, 142, 158, 167, 176n4; activists in, 130; *allochtoon* (foreigners) in, 2; anti-dictatorship activists in, 12, 96, 98–99; asylum policy, 76–77; au pair program, 37, 83, 173n6; Filipino activism in, 5, 128, 131, 170; Filipino factory workers in, 33–34; Filipino seafarers in, 37–38; Filipinos in, 4, 11–12, 28, 37–38, 55–56, 69–70, 84, 87, 100, 103–4, 106, 117, 131, 171; Filipino women in, trafficking of through marriage migration, 113; memory activists in, 137–38; National Monument in, 117; Netherlands Fellowship Program, 38; and Philippines, relations between, 60–61; political refugees in, 129
New People's Army (NPA), 56–57, 61
New York City, 39, 47, 65, 98, 152, 156; as Little Manila, 129; Mexicans in, 22
Nicaraguan revolution, 75–76
Nicholls, Walter, 86
Ninoy Aquino International Airport, 192n85
Ninoy Aquino Movement, 129
Noli Me Tangere (Rizal), 55
nongovernmental organizations (NGOs), 77; banning of, 60
North America, 35, 42, 49, 79, 153–54, 170, 175n25

Obama, Barack, 154
Occeña, Bruce, 58
Ojeda-Kimbrough, Carol, 133
Olick, Jeffrey K., 24–25
oppositional consciousness, 114
Overseas Absentee Voting Act, 45
overseas Filipinos, 109, 115, 121, 151; associational life of, 47–48; political influence of, in homeland, 63; and salary remittances, 106–7; and transnational anti-dictatorship movement, 52
overseas Filipino workers (OFWs), 35, 41, 83, 88, 96, 101, 103, 108, 110, 114, 116, 134, 143, 157, 171; ALAB's popularity among, 112–13; as *bagong bayani* (new hero), 43–44; collective identity of, 1, 45, 112; Duterte, grassroots campaign for, 152–54; films about, 44; homeland, loyalty to,

Overseas Filipino workers (OFWs) (*cont.*)
49; *Kababayan* (newsletter), distribution of to, 111; and *kuskos at kudkod* (scrub and scrape), 1; marginalization of, 1; as micro-influencers, 153; as modern-day heroes, 9, 43, 135; and pastoral empowerment, 45; salary remittances, 106–7; suffering of, 79–80
Overseas Workers Welfare Administration, 44

Pahlavi dynasty, 57, 75–76
Paras, Melinda, 57–58, *134*
Parreñas, Rhacel Salazar, 36, 45–46
pasaway (disobedient and hardheaded), 173n8
Pensionado Act (1903), 30
People Power Monument, 191n34
People Power Revolution, xi–xii, 2–3, 35, 122–23, 139, 141, 151, 153, 157, 171, 191n40; anniversaries of, 124–26, 130; and California farmworkers' movement, parallels between, 127; commemoration of, 126–29
Perez, Leonora, 104, *105*, 148
Permanent Peoples Tribunal, 156
Philippine Independence Day, 68–69
Philippine Left, xi–xii, 58, 153, 171
Philippine National Day, 68
Philippine Nautical School, 33
Philippine News (newspaper), 64, 66–67
Philippine Overseas Employment Agency (POEA), 35, 181n72; Bagong Bayani Awards, 44
Philippine Overseas Voting Act (2003), 193n1
Philippines, xi–xv, 2–3, 10, 37–38, 67–68, 73, 78, 81–85, 87, 92, 94, 97–98, 101, 103, 108–12, 116, 120–21, 126, 131–33, 136, 139, 142, 144, 147–50, 152–53, 155–59, 167, 170–71, 184n25, 185n54; American colonization of, 11, 32–34, 76, 154; annexation of, 29; anti-dictatorship movement, 128; anti-Marcos movement, 127; au pair program, 1; authoritarianism in, 79; biopower, exercising of, 36; Christmas tradition in, 41–43; colonialism in, 40; colonization of, 54, 59; communist movement in, 63, 72, 99; "crony capitalism" in, 57, 184n35; diaspora formation, political project of, 41; and displacement, 95; dual citizenship law, 12; Dutch volunteers against, 60–61; Executive Order (EO) 857, 106–7; as homeland, 64–65; hometown associations, 114; human rights violations, 69, 74, 117, 123, 191n40; Ilocos region, 180n27; income tax, 62–63; independence of, 31–32; as labor broker, 96; and labor migrants, remittance of salary, 106–7; and labor migration, 9; loyalty to, 51; martial law in, 58, 62, 72, 100, 127, 129, 143; as migrant-sending nation, 29; migration, and nation-building, 48; and migration, as official policy, 35–36; Moro separatist movement, 72; national culture, creation of, 55; National Day of Sorrow, 51; national lan-

guage of, 90; national liberation movements, 77; nation-building project, 51; neoliberalism in, 35–36, 41, 48–49; and Netherlands, relations between, 60–61; and number of migrants, 179n6; and out-migration, 43; and overseas employment, 180n51; and peripatetic workers, 32–33; protests against, 51, 117–18; revolutionary movement, 59, 79; role of in managing overseas citizens, 28–29, 49; and sex trade, 181n76; Spain, opposition to, 55; structural adjustment program (SAP), 180n54; Tagalogs in, 102; traitors to, 43; and transitional justice, 122–23; transnational network of communist movement in, 71; transnational political community, building of, 45, 49; and Typhoon Haiyan, 27; US, ceded to, 30; US annexation of, 63; US colonization of, 11, 32–34, 76, 154; US interests in, 74; US military bases in, 56, 75. *See also* Marcos, Ferdinand
Philippine Seafarers' Assistance Program (PSAP), 106
Philippine Times (newspaper), 66
Pilipino American Collegiate Endeavor (PACE), 91, 93
Pilipino Workers Center, 133–34
Pinoys for Good Governance, 134
Pinto, Antònio Costa, "double legacy," 122
political entrepreneurs, 5, 14, 16, 18, 25–26, 28, 34, 71, 87, 132; socialization of, 157–58
Polletta, Francesca, 52, 121, 158; *Inventing the Ties That Bind*, 24; relationship schemas, 87
Ponce, Mariano, 54
pool halls, 89
prefigurative politics, 21, 26
Presidential Commission on Good Government, 123
Presidential Decree 442, creating Labor Code of 1974, 34
Propaganda Movement, 30, 54–55, 63, 67, 71, 88, 91–92, 158
public sphere, 21, 66, 118; occupation of, 47–48

Quezon, Manuel Luis, 30
Quimpo, Nathan Gilbert, 124
Quimpo, Susan F., 124
"quotidian disruption," 6–7, 175n15

Rafael, Vicente, 44
Reagan, Ronald, 51
Recuber, Timothy, "prosumption of commemoration," 125
Red Guard Party, 93
refugees, chain migration of, 76
remembrance, 117, 123, 125, 129; and memory activism, 124; programs, 191n34
Remembrance of the Dead, 117
Republic Act 6768, 42–43

INDEX

Rizal, José, 44, 54–55, 67, 91–92, 137, 159, 179n18
Robredo, Maria Leonor "Leni" Gerona, xi, xiii–xiv
Rochon, Thomas R., 25–26
Rome (Italy), 79, 106, 171
Rotterdam (Netherlands), 33, 37–38, 103, 106, 115

Safran, William, 176n9
sakadas, 31
Samahang Demokratiko ng Kabataan (Association of Democratic Youth), 138
Samahan ng Manggagawang Pilipino (Association of Filipino Laborers), 47
Samahan sa Netherlands, 114
San Francisco (California), 31, 50, 92, 98, 110, 126–27, 132, 152, 156, 170; Chinatown, 93, 182n90; Manilatown, 40, 91, 182n90; "Red Block," 91
San Francisco State College, 91
San Francisco State University, PACE of, 132
San Juan, E., Jr., 95
Saudi Arabia, 27, 35, 111, 135; Riyadh, 49
Schengen Agreement, 112, 116
Schiller, Nina Glick, 174n10 (intro)
Schumacher, John N., 54
Scott, James C., "everyday resistance," 187n18
Second Propaganda Movement, 59
Service Employees International Union (SEIU), 110
Severn, Joshua, 127–28, 141
sex trafficking, 38, 101, 112–13, 181n76
Shain, Yossi, 176n7
Shalom, Stephen R., 73
Shortt, Linda, 118
Simmel, Georg, 6
Simpson, Esther Hipol, 148
Singapore, 27, 35, 44–45, 48
Sison, José María, 91–92
Sivanandan, A., 29
slavery, 14, 119
Snow, David A., 177n38, 188n46; "quotidian disruption," 6–7, 175n15
social boundary making, 4
social media, xi, xiii, 2, 25, 122, 132, 152–53; diaspora construction, as venues for, 157; micro-influencers in, 157, 193n7
social movements, xv, 9, 18, 20, 51–52, 86, 119, 126, 138, 159, 168; and collective identity formation, 22, 155, 157; constituents and adherents of, 7, 19, 21, 49, 79, 96, 132, 157, 169–70; and culture, 158; and diaspora formation, 157; as dynamic, 26; and meaning making, 22; among migrants, 8, 23, 25; social movement organization (SMO), 61; social movement studies, 14; social movement theory, 175n4
Sökefeld, Martin, 16, 174n3, 176n4
solidarity, 95, 99–100, 110–11, 115, 117, 156; activism, 60–61, 99; building of, across borders, 85; with co-ethnics/co-nationals, 25–26, 120–21; and

collective identity, 86–87; and common past, 24; cultures of, 24; and homeland, 65; imagined communities, based on, 86–87; and migrants' rights, 87–88; and mutual association, 24; and shared history, 25–26, 83; working-class, 94
Soliman, Celia, 79–80
Somoza dynasty, 57, 75–76
Southern California, 40; Little Armenia, 13
South Korea, 73–74, 135
Spain, 29–30, 44, 53–55, 59, 63, 72, 158
Spanish-American War, 30
Spanish Empire, 30, 54–55
spatial proximity, 77; and transnational social movements, 5, 29
Staggenborg, Suzanne, 21
storytelling, 121, 142, 151; American dream in, 143; and collective memory formation, 124; as dialogic performance, 125; as memory repertoire, 123–25; microblogging, 125–26
Subcommittee on International Organizations of the House of Representatives Committee on International Relations, 73–74
Subic Bay Naval Base, 56, 58, 75
Sweden, 77
Swidler, Ann, 7–8, 67; on culture, 22–23

Taber, George M., "crony capitalism," 184n35
Taft, William Howard, 30
Takenaka, Ayumi, 114–15
Tarrow, Sidney, 158, 177n33
Task Force Detainees of the Philippines, 191n40
taxi dance halls, 89
Taylor, Verta, 25
Third World, 59, 88, 90, 98–99
Third World liberation, 94
Third World Liberation Front (TWLF), 58; strikes, 91–92
Tilly, Charles, 177n33; "repertoire," 177n45
tinalikuran (to turn one's back on something or someone), 154
Tinig Filipino (magazine), 46–47
transnational advocacy network (TAN), 77, 80
transnational anti-dictatorship movement, 52, 54; Propagandists, adoption of strategies from, 55
transnational belonging, among US-born Filipinos, 67
transnationalism, 178n67
transnational mobilization, 28
transnational networks, 13
Tropwind Trading, 103
Trump, Donald, 12, 152–55
Tsourapas, Gerasimos, 36
Tufts University, 117–18, 120, 190n3; Fletcher School of Law and Diplomacy, 50
Tydings-McDuffie Act (1934), 31
Typhoon Haiyan, 27

Ulft (Netherlands), 33–34
Um, Khatharya, 95, 119
United Arab Emirates, 27, 35, 135
United Filipino-Dutch Association, 114
United Kingdom, 27, 33, 135, 175n15 (intro), 175n4 (chap. 1). *See also* England
United Nations (UN), 42, 112, 122; Inter-Agency Standing Committee, 27
United States, 13, 18, 34, 36, 42–43, 45, 48, 64, 68–69, 71–78, 80–81, 94, 110, 112, 115, 119–20, 132, 139, 147, 149, 158, 167, 175n15 (intro), 175n4 (chap. 1), 178n67; activists in, 130; annexation of Philippines, 63; anti-dictatorship activists in, 3, 12, 88, 99, 143, 152; and "benevolent assimilation," 30; blacklisting of anti-Marcos Filipinos in, 66; class consciousness among workers in, 86; colonization of Philippines, 154, 156; Filipino activism in, 5, 50–51, 92, 96, 126, 128, 131, 170; Filipino nurses in, 33; Filipino quota of, 32; Filipinos in, 2, 4, 9–12, 27–29, 31–33, 39–41, 55–56, 61–63, 65–67, 84, 87–90, 93, 95, 97–98, 101, 104, 126–27, 131, 133, 148, 153–54, 171; Filipino tourists in, 83; H-2A and H-2B programs, 37; imperialism, 2; memory activists in, 137–38; Philippines, policy toward, 57
Universal Declaration of the Rights of Peoples (1976), 77
University of the Philippines, 138, 171, 191n40
US-Philippines Military Bases Agreement, 75–76
US v. Narciso and Perez, 104
Utrecht (Netherlands), 1, 33, 69, 77, 170; Filipino activists in, 98

Valocchi, Stephen, 104
Van den Muijzenberg, Otto, 181n80
Van Dyke, Nella, 25
Veloria, Velma, 110
Venceremos Brigade, 58
Vera Cruz, Philip, 127
Vietnam War, 2, 56–57, 67, 75, 91–92; anti-Vietnam War movement, 58, 90; US racist imperialism in, 59

Wald, George, 186n107
War Brides Act (1946), 32
Washington (DC), 39, 134
Washington (state): Chinatown–International District (CID), 93–94; Seattle, 31, 90–91, 96, 98, 115, 152, 156, 170, 185n69, 188n43; University of Washington, 91; Yakima, 93; Yakima Valley, 31
Watsonville anti-Filipino riot, 89
Weber, Max, *verstehen*, 167
Wehl (Netherlands), 33
Wimmer, Andreas, 4
World Bank, 28, 35, 42, 56, 78, 180n54
World War II, 32–33, 90, 93, 115, 117, 131; brides, 61–62
Wright, Richard, 107

Xi Jinping, 153

YouTube, xiii

Zamponi, Lorenzo, 120

Printed and bound by CPI Group (UK) Ltd, Croydon, CR0 4YY
02/02/2025

14636546-0001